MW01136071

SHOULD THE WORLD FEAR CHINA?

ZHOU BO

Should the World Fear China?

HURST & COMPANY, LONDON

First published in the United Kingdom in 2025 by
C. Hurst & Co. (Publishers) Ltd.,
New Wing, Somerset House, Strand, London, WC2R 1LA

Distributed in the United States, Canada and Latin America by
Oxford University Press, 198 Madison Avenue, New York, NY 10016,
United States of America.

The articles in this book were first published by The Ambassador
Partnership, *The Australian, China Daily,* China-US Focus, *Die Zeit,
The Economist, Financial Times, Foreign Affairs, Foreign Policy, The New
York Times, South China Morning Post, The Straits Times, The Wall Street
Journal,* and UK National Committee on China.

A Cataloguing-in-Publication data record for this book
is available from the British Library.

ISBN: 9781805263456

www.hurstpublishers.com

Printed and bound in Great Britain by Bell & Bain Ltd, Glasgow

CONTENTS

INTRODUCTION

The title of the book *Should the World Fear China?* was not my idea. It's the first question I was asked in an interview with the German newspaper *Die Zeit* in 2023. I have been unable to forget this question since. For me, it best represents the uncertainty of the West towards China, which has brought twitches of anxiety and even fear.

Today, China wears many hats; it is the largest trading nation; the largest exporter; the largest industrial nation; and the largest economy by purchasing power parity. However, China describes itself as a developing country. This is certainly right in terms of China's per capita income. But it is also baffling: can a developing country be the largest economy in the world at the same time? And if so, what is the point of making a distinction between developed countries and developing countries?

China's image depends on where its beholders are standing. For the United States, it is a strategic competitor and "pacing threat"—"the only country with both the intent to reshape the international order and, increasingly, the economic, diplomatic, military, and technological power to do it." For Europe, it is a "partner for cooperation, an economic competitor and a systemic rival," a conclusion that seems to tell us more about Europe's confusion about China than what China really is. For NATO, China is a "decisive enabler" of Russia's war against Ukraine. But China has a different yet far more positive image in the Global South in which China considers itself a "natural member." It is not rare to hear people describing China already as a superpower. Some China-centred organisations like the Shanghai Cooperation Organization (SCO) and BRICS are thriving with expansion.

* * *

That is why I have put together 102 of my essays and opinion pieces, written between 2013 and 2024, trying to answer some of the most important questions about China that I believe are still relevant today.

First and foremost, does China really want to reshape the international order, as the US claims? Washington regards the international order after World War II as the "liberal international order." There is no such order. In my opinion piece, "Why the International Order is Not Falling Apart," I argued that this is but a Eurocentric view with an apparent air of Western triumphalism. It simplistically takes rules, regimes and institutions such as the IMF, the World Bank and GATT/WTO that are indeed made by the West in the economic field as the international order itself, but these are just parts of the whole. The international order is far more complicated. It should also include different but coexisting religions, cultures, customs, national identities and social systems and above all, civilisations.

If there is no liberal international order, then there is no "democracy vs autocracy," which is but an American strategy to rally around alliances at a time when American primacy looks shaky. According to Freedom House, liberal democracy has been in steady decline since 2006, and it risks continuing to decline. Today, the BRICS economies are already larger than those of the G7 countries. In a report on the 2020 Munich Security

Conference, titled "Westlessness," one of the conclusions is that not only is the world becoming less Western, but more importantly, the West itself is becoming less Western too.

Then comes China's position in the international order. China isn't a "revisionist power" as the US describes. In the last four decades, no other country than China has benefited more from globalisation, which is rooted in an international system characterised by an open and market-driven world economy. Therefore, it is in China's own interests to become further integrated with the rest of the world. Of course, China's growing strength will bring global changes. However, these changes shouldn't be taken as an erosion of the international order, rather, they could change the world for the better. Take China's Belt & Road Initiative for example. As it sprawls across continents, it most certainly will spread China's influence and generate geopolitical implications. Yet it is essentially an economic project that aims at improving the underdeveloped infrastructure across the world.

* * *

Much has been said about whether we have entered a new cold war. In my article written for *The Ambassador Partnership*, I hold that it is too early to tell. We shall only be able to conclude that we have entered a cold war when the prospect of an all-out war has disappeared. This is exactly what happened before—the Soviet Union collapsed without a war, so we know what took place was but a cold war. But the future is not ours to see.

It is not unusual to hear the Chinese talking about the US trying to contain China. My answer is, even if the US wants to contain China, it can't. The United States is tired of policing the world. Therefore, it is refocusing on the new centre of gravity, which is obviously the Indo-Pacific, where the US sees endless opportunities but also a fierce strategic competitor—China.

But America's global retrenchment will be a gradual process, in part because the US allies will hold it back. Europe's strategic autonomy won't take shape in the next ten years, if at all. Israel's confidence in being able to stabilise the Middle East in its own favour has crumbled thanks to the war in Gaza.

Two developments in the Indo-Pacific, that is, the Quadrilateral Security Dialogue (Quad) among the US, Japan, Australia and India, and the security partnership among Australia, the United Kingdom and the United States, known as AUKUS, reflect what America intends to do in the region. Simply put, Quad is in place because of China, and AUKUS is against China. But Quad won't evolve into a military alliance because of India's position. Unless China and India have a full-blown conflict, India is unlikely to become an American ally. As a rising power and a founder of the Non-Aligned Movement, India is too proud to be dependent on any major power.

AUKUS could grow further militarily to include other American allies in the region, yet it won't become a mini-NATO, as some Chinese have asserted. Although America has over 60 allies and partners around the globe, when it comes to a war with China, those that are helpful to the US won't be more than a handful, as I wrote for the *South China Morning Post*. For example, Japan has treaty obligations to provide logistical support to the American military in a conflict, but public opinion in Japan is generally against getting ensnared in a Taiwan Strait conflict. Having fought in every major US war since World War II, Australia looks like the most reliable ally, but the Australian government has made it clear that it has not promised the US that it will take part in any conflict over Taiwan in exchange for American nuclear-powered submarines.

Another reason that it is premature to talk about a new cold war is because there is no evidence that the China–Russia partnership has turned the relationship into the most feared alliance in the West. Twenty days before Russia invaded Ukraine in February 2022, China and Russia signed a statement proclaiming there were "no limits to Sino-Russian cooperation ... no forbidden zones". I couldn't understand why such an expression of goodwill for bilateral ties was hyped in the West. As I asked in my op-ed in the *Financial Times*, if two countries vow to develop their friendship, then how could they place limits on it? Russia is China's largest neighbour and vice versa. For peaceful coexistence, this relationship must be amicable.

China has almost never voted against or vetoed any of the UN resolutions condemning Russia, but rather only abstained. While the US-led NATO has provided full military support to Ukraine, Beijing has provided no military aid or weapons to Moscow. True, China's trade with Russia has helped it to skirt Western sanctions, but the trade went on before the war and none of the trading violates international rules or regimes.

Perhaps the best way to describe the relationship is to say they are like two lines in parallel, that is, however close they are, they won't meet to become an alliance. It is not only that non-alliance allows flexibility, but also because China and Russia's world views are subtly different even if both talk about a multipolar world order. China is the largest beneficiary of globalisation, which relies on the existing international order; Russia resents that order and considers itself a victim of it. Beijing has at least maintained a plausible relationship with Europe; this appears to be impossible for Moscow now.

With the centre of global power shifting from West to East, the Asian Century that Chinese leader Deng Xiaoping described to Indian Prime Minister Rajiv Gandhi in 1988 appears to be dawning. Can the dragon and the elephant coexist? The Chinese and Indian militaries had a deadly brawl in the border areas in 2020 resulting in the death of four Chinese soldiers and twenty Indian soldiers—the first case with casualties in over 40 years.

Despite regular meetings between front-line senior military officers; efforts to deconflict in the most dangerous areas along the Line of Actual Control; and even record-breaking bilateral trade, the relationship is still chilly. India places the border issue almost as a precondition for improving bilateral ties. This doesn't look like a wise policy. India doesn't only have territorial disputes with China. If Pakistan says to India that their relationship won't improve unless they agree to resolve the Kashmir issue, what will India do?

China–India relations are about more than the border issue now. India frets about China's increased economic and military presence in the Indian Ocean while China is wary of India drawing closer to the US. With China–US competition intensifying, Washington naturally needs New Delhi, just as it needed Beijing during the Cold War to counterbalance Moscow.

People often read in the media that China and India are jostling for leadership of the Global South. This is incorrect. China's economy is five times larger than India's. Even if India could sustain an average annual growth of about 5 per cent, its gross domestic product will still only be where China's is today in around 2050. So it is impossible for India to become the Global South leader if China remains a member of the Global South. In my op-ed for the *South China Morning Post*, I expressed my hope that China and India will become Global South anchors, not power competitors.

* * *

Are China and the US destined for war? This should be one of the overriding questions for the twenty-first century. There are two scenarios that might trigger a conflict between the PLA and the US military—the South China Sea and the Taiwan Strait. Contrary to what most people think, I believe the South China Sea is far more dangerous than the Taiwan Strait. In "War in the Taiwan Strait? It's the South China Sea, stupid", I pointed out that a war in the Taiwan Strait between China and the US is very unlikely to be triggered by an accident like we saw in the South China Sea. The Taiwan issue is so flammable, every word from Beijing and Washington would be scrutinised. However, there is no easy way to deconflict in the South China Sea. American military aircraft regularly conduct close surveillance and reconnaissance in China's exclusive economic zones. US naval vessels sail through waters off the islands and rocks in the South China Sea over which China claims sovereignty. But an ever-stronger PLA can only become more determined in checking what it believes to be American provocations. Since neither wishes to back down, I assume—and I hope I am wrong—that it is only a matter of time before another deadly collision like the one in 2001 between a Chinese jet fighter and an American spy plane reoccurs.

Although the South China Sea is more dangerous, it is hard to say that a collision at sea or in the air, even deadly, will surely trigger a conflict. The only issue that could drag China and the US into a full-blown conflict is over Taiwan. How likely is that? US Secretary of Defense Lloyd Austin said at the Shangri-La Dialogue in 2023 and again in 2024 that a conflict with China was neither imminent nor inevitable. Such an assessment is a welcoming denial of the irresponsible remarks made by some American generals and admirals when they predicted when and how mainland China might attack Taiwan.

The conflict in Ukraine also gives people food for thought. If Nato, an alliance of 32 states, hesitates to take on Russia, then what gives the US absolute confidence to fight China far away from its shores with a few half-hearted allies on China's doorstep? China's economy is ten times larger than Russia's while its defence budget is three times bigger. The 2 million-strong PLA is the largest military in the world and the PLA Navy outnumbers the US Navy in ships. The only obvious advantage Russia has over China is its store of nuclear warheads, the biggest in the world. Should China decide to increase its nuclear arsenal, it is only a matter of political decision.

How can war be avoided in the Taiwan Strait? My answer is simple: let China believe peaceful reunification with the island is still possible. So far there is no indication that Beijing has lost confidence or patience. China has never announced a timetable for reunification. It is still talking about peaceful development of cross-strait relations. But provocations from either Taipei or Washington will be checked with more robust responses from the PLA. They will lead to a new, irreversible status quo that favours the mainland. For example, after former US House Speaker Nancy Pelosi's Taiwan visit, the PLA conducted four days of live-fire exercises around the island. Now the median line in the Taiwan Strait that was tacitly observed by both sides no longer exists. Chinese fighter jets regularly fly to the other side of the line in different sorties.

For peace to prevail in the Taiwan Strait, as I have written in *Foreign Affairs*, the United States should reassure China that it has no intention of straying from its professed commitment to the "One China" policy. US leaders have refused to enter into direct conflict with Russia over Ukraine despite the extent of Russian transgression. Equally, they should consider war with China a red line that cannot be crossed.

* * *

Once at an international seminar, I heard what I thought was the most intriguing question: what is the most ideal world for the Chinese people, in which most of the Chinese are happy, but foreigners can also survive? I don't think there is such a world. Although the twenty-first century might indeed be an Asian century, unlike Pax Britannia in the nineteenth century and Pax Americana in the twentieth, the twenty-first century won't be Pax Sinica. Instead, this Asian century will be characterised by the collective rise of nations, including China, India and Indonesia, etc, and regional organisations like ASEAN and BRICS.

However, this question does raise an issue of how China might live with others. Thanks to China's seemingly inexorable rise, nowadays everything that doesn't seem to have anything to do with China eventually ends up having something to do with China. This is particularly the case with the war in Ukraine—a faraway conflict that China is not involved in. China was nevertheless asked which side it would take; whether it would become a mediator between Russia and the West; and whether it might seize the opportunity to launch an attack on Taiwan. Is this unfair to China? As I wrote in the *Financial Times*, this is the price to pay for being a global power.

For China to fulfil its international responsibilities, it should start at home. First and foremost, it needs to overcome its lingering victimhood. Admittedly, victimhood is not confined to the Chinese. In 2016 and 2024, Donald Trump succeeded in making the majority of American voters believe the strongest nation on earth was in "carnage" and he was the man to "Make America Great Again."

For China, its victimhood over the "century of humiliation" stems from the Opium War in 1840. But the century of humiliation should have ended with the founding of the People's Republic of China in 1949 when Chairman Mao Zedong declared that "the Chinese people have stood up." I wrote for the *South China Morning Post* that, rather than a victim, China today is the envy of the world. China must leave its past behind and embrace its strength. Victimhood is not the foundation for patriotism. It leads to nationalism, populism, and isolationism. This is the last thing China wants.

A global power has two things that are not found in a small country—huge overseas interests and greater international responsibilities. In "The future of the PLA," in *Foreign Policy*, I argue that in spite of China's territorial disputes with some countries, a major power like China should look beyond its borders into the horizon to protect China's overseas interests and shoulder more international obligations.

The need to protect China's overseas interests is easy to understand, but what exactly are China's international responsibilities? China's success in restoring diplomatic ties between Iran and Saudi Arabia is a turning point in Chinese diplomacy. It indicates not only China's willingness but also capabilities in shouldering its international obligations. The signing of the Beijing Declaration by 14 Palestinian factions is another good example of how China can play a role as an honest broker in a most volatile region. In my interview with *Time* magazine, I said that when China started to reform and open up, it was trying to "cross the river by feeling the stones on the riverbed," as Deng Xiaoping said, but now China is entering the ocean. You can't feel the seabed. These are uncharted waters, but there is no turning back.

As for the PLA, I hope its international responsibilities will be confined exclusively to humanitarian operations. So far, all the military operations of the Chinese military overseas, be it peacekeeping, counter-piracy or disaster relief, are invariably humanitarian in nature. This is not accidental; it is a careful choice. These military operations other than war will help war-stricken nations, reduce casualties to a minimum level, but won't turn China into a warring party.

China's peacekeeping is the best example. China is the largest troop-contributing country among the five permanent members of the UN Security Council and the second-largest financial contributor to peacekeeping. In "How China can improve UN peacekeeping" in *Foreign Affairs*, I mentioned that China has good reason to beef up its peacekeeping commitments because it serves China's image as a responsible nation on a peaceful rise. And two of peacekeeping's guiding principles—impartiality and the "non-use of force except in self-defense and defense of mandate"—resonate with China's foreign policy and military ethos.

* * *

In the last four and half decades, China has changed a few defence policies, such as not stationing troops abroad, not establishing military bases overseas and not conducting joint exercises with foreign armed forces. However, some still remain, and I hope they will continue to be upheld in the years to come.

1. Caution in use of force. After the founding of the People's Republic of China in 1949, China was involved in wars and conflict virtually every decade until the late 1970s when China started to reform and open up. China's rise in the last four decades is a miracle in human history in that few, if any, major powers have risen so peacefully. It is made possible thanks in no small way to Beijing's restraint in use of force in spite of serious challenges such as bombs hitting the Chinese embassy in Belgrade, when NATO was bombing Yugoslavia, and the collision of Chinese and American military planes in the South China Sea.

   The China–India clash in the Galwan Valley in 2020 is most unfortunate, yet there are still positives. In this deadly brawl with stones, wooden clubs and fists, neither side attempted to shoot at the other. This shows the confidence-building measures made in a litany of agreements have worked to a certain extent. Some people may point out that the Chinese coast guard used water cannons against Filipino ships in 2024. But that is not exactly use of force. It is an effort to deter the Filipinos from violating their promise by carrying building materials to fortify a rusted Filipino war ship into a permanent base in the disputed Ren Ai Jiao/Second Thomas Shoal.

For over four decades, China's military expenditure has been lower than 2% of its GDP, a NATO standard for its member states. Most probably it will remain at this level short of a war. At a time when NATO members are being pushed by the US to spend 2% of their GDP on defence, and some of China's neighbours like Japan and India have drastically increased their defence budgets, China's sustainable and predictable defence budget says a lot about China's self-control and self-confidence. This is important for the stability of the region.

2. Don't seek spheres of influence. Many people confuse two things—influence and spheres of influence. I have argued that precisely because China's influence, especially in the economic field, is already ubiquitous around the world, it doesn't need spheres of influence that are costly and difficult to maintain.

If China doesn't seek spheres of influence, then it doesn't need to build many military bases overseas. Twenty years ago, some international analysts assumed China would adopt a "string of pearls" strategy of building bases stretching from the Middle East to southern China. This is proven wrong. So far, the only Chinese military base overseas is a logistic base in Djibouti [*Ed - In 2024, China reportedly has outposts in Cambodia and Tajikistan. The Chinese government has not publicly acknowledged the existence of these bases.*] Even if China might need to have a few more bases abroad, so long as Chinese military operations overseas remain humanitarian in nature, the PLA doesn't need to have many bases.

3. Don't seek military alliances. If a group of small nations comes into alliance to resist major powers, the rationale is understandable. But if, say, the US, the strongest nation on earth, would ally itself with other countries, apparently it is not for self-defence. NATO is not only a military organisation, it is also a political one. It is a stick of the West to defend and spread its values. It needs "threats" to survive and thrive. The fact that Finland and Sweden joined NATO might prove its popularity, but as I wrote at the invitation of *The Economist*, the more popular NATO becomes, the more insecure Europe will be. Europe's security is essentially how NATO and Russia might coexist. French President Macron once said NATO is braindead. I said to *Die Zeit* and Bloomberg that it is a zombie that is still walking.

4. Adhere to no-first-use of nuclear weapons. Of the five nuclear states that have signed the Treaty on the Nonproliferation of Nuclear Weapons (NPT), China is the only country that has declared not to be the first to use nuclear weapons and not to use or threaten to use nuclear weapons against non-nuclear states or nuclear-weapon-free zones. In *Foreign Policy*, I argue that all nuclear powers could afford to adopt a formal no-first-use policy—taking the moral high ground without reducing their capabilities for retaliation.

In Europe, NATO can start with a unilateral no-first-use pledge against Russia as a gesture of goodwill. Even if such an offer isn't immediately reciprocated by Russia, it might begin to thaw tensions. As a second step, NATO could pledge to halt any further expansion of its alliance in exchange for Moscow adopting a no-first-use policy. In Asia, China and the United States could reach a similar agreement, thus de-escalating potential conflicts involving

US allies as well as the dangers that could be provoked through accidental collisions at sea or in the air.

* * *

The essays and opinion pieces in this book are selected from what I have written in the last eleven years. My life is not one of a scholar. Before I retired from the Chinese military as a senior colonel in 2020 and started to work as a senior fellow at the Center for International Security and Strategy Tsinghua University, I had already worked for 41 years in the Chinese military. For the last 27 years, I worked in different posts in the Ministry of National Defense of China on foreign affairs. I was desk officer and then desk chief for South Asia, Deputy Director General of West Asia and Africa Bureau and then Deputy Director General of General Planning Bureau of the Foreign Affairs Office of the Ministry of National Defense, Chinese Defense Attaché to the Republic of Namibia and Director of the Centre for Security Cooperation in the Office for International Military Cooperation, Ministry of National Defense.

These experiences helped me tremendously when I started writing in 2013 as a hobby in my spare time. Gradually, my articles started to draw attention, in part because they were written in English and most of them were published overseas, and in part because Chinese voices were rare in the international media. When I was invited to King's College London in 2018 to give a talk, the organiser told me how they lamented that over the years, most people talking about China were foreigners, so they decided to invite Chinese people to come and talk about China! I then made a speech on the role of the PLA in safeguarding China's overseas interests and shouldering its international obligations. I eventually turned my remarks into an essay and had it published in *Foreign Policy* magazine, titled "The Future of the PLA".

INTRODUCTION

Half of the articles collected in this book were published by *South China Morning Post* where I am a SCMP expert. And some were published in mainstream international media outlets such as *Foreign Affairs*, *Foreign Policy*, *The New York Times*, *The Wall Street Journal*, *Financial Times*, *The Economist*, *The Australian* and *Die Zeit*. My two essays in *The New York Times* were published on the front pages of the newspaper. The second one "In Afghanistan, China is ready to step into the void" was highlighted by the Deputy International Editor, Yara Bayoumy, who kindly wrote that I have a unique vantage point to clarify how Beijing is positioning itself in Afghanistan. This was a great honour for me. It also reflected how eager the world is to hear Chinese views in world affairs.

Some of these articles have made waves globally. *China Daily* informed me that my op-ed, "China's subs in Indian Ocean no worry to India," was cited by over one hundred international media outlets within four days. I think this has something to do with the fact that this was the first time that Chinese submarines in the Indian Ocean had been mentioned in a leading state-run Chinese newspaper.

My essay in *The Economist,* "Senior Colonel Zhou Bo says the war in Ukraine will accelerate the geopolitical shift from West to East," was among the earliest Chinese views expressed in the international arena on the Russo-Ukrainian war. In my essay, I started by asking: If the enemy of my enemy is my friend, is the enemy of my friend also my enemy? My answer is: not necessarily. On the one hand, China is Russia's strategic partner. On the other, China is the largest trading partner of Ukraine. Beijing therefore tries painstakingly to strike a balance in its response to the war between two of its friends.

Three years have passed, and some of my assessments have proven tenable. For instance, I argued that this looks like a protracted war; Putin will fight until he can declare some sort of "victory" that involves Ukraine's acceptance that Crimea is part of Russia, its promise not to join NATO and the independence of the two "republics" of Donetsk and Luhansk.

My most influential op-ed is on how "China can use its leverage with Russia to prevent a nuclear war," published in the *Financial Times* in October 2022. At the end of my article, I said in the most straightforward manner that if Putin now opens a nuclear Pandora's box that was kept closed even during the Cold War, it would be a moment of infinite stupidity. I further argued that China can help the world by simply telling Putin: don't use nuclear weapons, Mr President. I am happy that not using nuclear weapons in Europe is now a crystal-clear Chinese policy towards the war in Ukraine.

If China's rise is already a given, then can a Global China help to make the world safer, if not better? This is the ultimate question. As I have expressed in this book, my best hope for my country in the twenty-first century, is that it will maintain some pleasant features of the Tang Dynasty. Tang China was prosperous, multiethnic, cosmopolitan and inclusive. It was home to "foreign" religions ranging from Buddhism, Nestorianism, Zoroastrianism and Islam to Manichaeism. It shows that a great power that is next to none can be confident but humble, and loved rather than feared.

1

MANAGING CHINA–US RELATIONS

AMERICA, CHINA, AND THE TRAP OF FATALISM

According to the National Security Strategy that the Biden administration issued in 2022, the United States faces a "decisive decade" in its rivalry with China. Chinese officials have come to believe the same thing. As Washington has grown ever more voluble in its desire to compete with Beijing, the Chinese government has turned from surprise to protest to an avowed determination to fight back. In Beijing's view, the United States fears losing its primacy and forces this struggle on China. In turn, China has no choice but must "dare to fight," as the report of the 20th National Congress of the Chinese Communist Party insisted.

Such intensifying confrontation is lamentable but not inevitable. Beltway analysts have greatly exaggerated China's supposed threat to Western democratic systems and international order. In recent years, U.S. leaders have cast China as a revisionist power and invoked the specter of a global clash between democracy and autocracy. But democracy's troubles in the twenty-first century have little to do with China. According to a 2023 report from Freedom House, liberal democracy around the world has been in steady decline for 17 years. That is not China's doing. China has not promoted its socialist values abroad. It has not been directly involved in any war since 1979. Despite its partnership with Russia, it has not supplied lethal aid to the Russian war effort in Ukraine.

Indeed, far from being a revisionist power seeking to upend the world, China upholds the status quo. It has joined almost all the international regimes and institutions established by the U.S.-led West after World War II. As the world's top trader and the largest beneficiary of globalization, China is deeply embedded in the existing international order and wishes to safeguard that system. Despite disagreements, tensions, and even disputes, China maintains robust ties with the West; neither side could countenance the kind of severing of relations that has occurred between the West and Russia since the invasion of Ukraine.

China has advanced new institutions such as the Shanghai Cooperation Organization, the multilateral BRICS grouping, and the Belt and Road Initiative to build global infrastructure, all of which could change the international political and economic landscape. But these shifts would serve to reform, rather than replace, the international order, making it more equitable and elevating the interests of many less prosperous countries.

And yet if one listens to the policymaking establishments in the West, one can hear the sound of lines being drawn. A refrain one hears often today suggests that the world has entered a new cold war. It is still too early to judge whether the rivalry between China and the United States really resembles the one between the Soviet Union and the United States—and, indeed, if it will continue to remain cold. But the analogy fails to capture a critical distinction: unlike the Cold War, this rivalry is between two individual titans rather than two confrontational camps. Washington cannot rally an implacably anti-Chinese alliance, just as Beijing cannot lead a bloc that is uniformly hostile to the United States. Most U.S. allies have China as their largest trading partner. Like all other countries in an increasingly multipolar world, they will pick and choose positions on specific issues, not blindly take the United States' side. Washington has enjoyed modest success in rallying allies and partners in arrangements meant to contain China, such as the Indo-Pacific security partnership known as the Quad and the military partnership between Australia, the United Kingdom, and the United States known as AUKUS. But these groupings do not amount to much: they look like a few tiny islands in a vast ocean. In many parts of the world, especially in Africa, the United States has already lost to China, which helps local economies without delivering moralizing bromides about governance and values.

But those ties do not represent the formation of an anti-Western, pro-Chinese camp. Relations between China and the United States cannot simply be defined by "extreme competition," as U.S. President Joe Biden once declared. Instead, they combine competition and cooperation in an ever-shifting balance. At a time when Washington is focused on competition with Beijing, it is useless for Beijing to insist on cooperation when such calls fall on deaf ears. What both sides can agree on is a fundamental red line—not letting their competition slide into outright confrontation. To that end, China and the United States must remain willing to talk to help avoid misunderstandings and miscalculations—and to reassure an anxious world.

Trust But Talk

Unfortunately, Beijing and Washington have talked to each other much less in recent years than the two superpowers did during the latter half of the Cold War. Back then, both sides remained committed to dialogue even if they were wary of each other. When U.S. President Ronald Reagan used a famous Russian proverb—"trust but verify"—after signing the Intermediate-Range Nuclear Forces Treaty with Soviet leader Mikhail Gorbachev in December 1987, he was politely suggesting that he did not, in fact, trust the Soviets, but that that would not stop him from entering into negotiations and agreements with them. The same logic still applies: trust is not necessarily a precondition for dialogue or interaction. In the absence of trust, the Soviet Union and the United States still managed to cooperate in a number of areas, including arms control, the eradication of smallpox, and the joint exploration of space for peaceful purposes.

If "trust but verify" characterized the later years of the Cold War, a modified version of the proverb is the right paradigm for China and the United States today: "trust but talk." The relative bonhomie of the Obama administration, when the countries held wide-ranging talks on bilateral, regional, and global issues, is unlikely to return any time soon. The hard-line policies of the Trump administration, the COVID-19 pandemic, and U.S. House Speaker Nancy Pelosi's visit to Taiwan in 2022 put a definitive end to that era. Biden has retained many of Trump's positions on China, and a bipartisan consensus has emerged in Washington that the United States must get tougher on its closest geopolitical peer.

Talks, however, have now haltingly resumed, notably including the military-to-military communications that were severed after Pelosi's Taiwan visit. They have included phone calls between high-level officials, the U.S.-Chinese Defense Policy Coordination Talks between defense officials, discussions relating to the U.S.-Chinese Military Maritime Consultative Agreement about maritime and aviation disputes, and a new channel of communication between Chinese and American theater commanders. Such talks represent a good start, but they are only a start. Senior military officers should visit with one another more regularly, both sides should use the hotline that was established in 2008 for crisis management more often, and they should encourage direct communications between pilots and sailors to help avoid dangerous close encounters in the air and at sea.

Accidents and Guardrails

Few in Beijing and Washington disagree about the need to establish guardrails or confidence-building measures to make conflict less likely. One area that produces considerable friction and tension are the waters and airspace in the South China Sea, where China's territorial claims are seldom respected. U.S. aircraft regularly conduct close surveillance and reconnaissance in China's exclusive economic zones. U.S. naval vessels sail through waters off the islands and rocks in the South China Sea over which China claims sovereignty. In the Pentagon's latest report on China's military, the United States documented over 180 instances of Chinese aircraft conducting "coercive and risky" intercepts of U.S. aircraft in the region between the fall of 2021 and the fall of 2023, a measure of growing tensions.

This dynamic will likely persist, as neither side is willing to back down. The Americans want to have technical discussions in the hope of making accidents and potential skirmishes less likely. The Chinese, for their part, find such conversations a bit odd. They are focused more broadly on their security, interpreting the U.S. Navy's operations in China's exclusive economic zones and maneuvers in the South China Sea as reckless provocations. Put another way, the Americans may want to ask Chinese ships that are monitoring U.S. ships to maintain a particular distance; the

Chinese would respond by saying that the Americans would be safest if they weren't there at all.

China in principle agrees to guardrails proposed by the United States, but Beijing fears that such guardrails are meant to freeze in place a status quo that favors Washington. Obviously, the overall military strength of the PLA lags behind that of the U.S. military. But in China's vicinity, the gap between the PLA and the U.S. military is closing, as Chinese military capacities have grown by leaps and bounds in recent decades. The United States fears that China wants to drive it out of the western Pacific. As a result, Washington is investing more militarily in the region and calling on its allies and partners to gang up on China. This in turn irks Beijing and makes the situation more volatile.

Neither Beijing nor Washington wants an accident, let alone a confrontation. In 2020, the Chinese Ministry of National Defense and the U.S. Department of Defense convened the first Crisis Communication Working Group, meeting by video teleconference to discuss how to prevent a crisis. Such a working group represents a step in the right direction. Were an accident in the South China Sea to occur, it might spur nationalist outrage in both countries, but it is hard to believe that it would trigger a full-blown war. The deadly collision between a Chinese fighter and an American spy plane in 2001 didn't prove to be the end of the world; the crisis produced by the fatal incident was resolved in 11 days. Skillful diplomacy prevailed and both sides saved face.

Dire Strait

The only issue that could drag China and the United States into a full-blown conflict is the dispute over Taiwan. Currently, a dangerous cycle is unfolding. The United States fears a potential attack from the mainland and is speeding up arms sales and expanding training and personnel exchanges to boost Taiwan's defense and turn the island into a "porcupine." An angry but increasingly confident China has responded by sending more warplanes to routinely fly over the median line in the Taiwan Strait, which previously acted as a buffer between the sides.

Many Western observers suggest that Taiwan will be the next Ukraine. And yet U.S. Secretary of Defense Lloyd Austin said at the Shangri-La Dialogue in 2023 that a conflict with China was neither imminent nor inevitable. A war over Taiwan will not come to pass as long as Beijing believes peaceful reunification with the island is still possible. If it suspects that the prospect of peaceful reunification is exhausted forever, then its calculus will change. But there is no indication that Beijing has drawn such a conclusion even after Taiwan elected William Lai of the Democratic Progressive Party as the Taiwanese leader in January 2024. (Lai has in the past described himself as a "political worker for Taiwanese independence.") In a meeting with former Taiwanese leader Ma Ying-jeou in April, Xi Jinping said it was imperative to promote the peaceful development of cross-strait relations, adhering to the one-China principle, the notion that China and Taiwan remain formally one country.

China has never announced a timetable for reunification. As a proportion of GDP, China's defense budget remains low—below two percent, where it has been for decades. That figure speaks volumes about China's confidence and about Beijing's assessment of its relationship with Washington. China is exercising restraint. Pelosi's visit to the island triggered Chinese military exercises around Taiwan that involved firing live ammunition and missiles. But Taiwanese leader Tsai Ing-wen met with Pelosi's successor, Kevin McCarthy, in California in April 2023, and China's subsequent exercises were much more subdued.

Beijing is also trying its best to win the hearts and minds of the Taiwanese people. Before the COVID-19 pandemic, around 1.5 million Taiwanese worked and lived on the mainland—a figure that equals around six percent of the Taiwanese population. It seems that they did not mind living in a totally different political system as long as it provided them with better economic opportunities than they had in Taiwan. In September 2023, China unveiled a plan in which Beijing would make it easier for Taiwanese people to live and work in Fujian Province (across the strait from the island), including by allowing them to buy property, promising equal treatment for Taiwanese students enrolled in public schools, and linking the Chinese port city of Xiamen with the Taiwanese island of Kinmen, which are just a few miles apart, via a bridge and gas and electricity connections.

Taiwan's status remains a very sensitive issue for Beijing, something that Washington should never take lightly. For peace to prevail in the Taiwan Strait, the United States should reassure China that it has no intention of straying from its professed commitment to the "one China" policy. U.S. leaders have refused to enter into direct conflict with Russia over Ukraine despite the gravity of the Russian transgression. Equally, they should consider war with China a red line that cannot be crossed.

Not Friends, But Not Enemies

Beyond these areas of friction, there remains plenty of room for collaboration. Three areas are particularly noteworthy: cyberspace, outer space, and artificial intelligence. As the strongest countries on earth, China and the United States should take the lead in crafting rules and regulations in these domains. In cyberwarfare, countries should refrain from striking critical information networks, such as military command-and-control systems. Beijing and Washington should exchange a list of sensitive targets that should be considered out of bounds and should not be attacked in any circumstances. To avoid an arms race in outer space, they should agree to negotiate a binding treaty that would commit countries to not placing weapons in outer space and encourage deliberations on rules and responsible behavior. At their meeting in California in November 2023, Biden and Xi agreed to establish an intergovernmental dialogue on AI. Even if it is not possible to prevent AI from being used for military purposes, China and the United States should at least lead in reducing risks related to AI-enabled military systems. In this regard, nothing is more important than ensuring absolute human control over nuclear command-and-control systems.

Another important area for cooperation, much as it was during the Cold War, is in limiting the risks posed by nuclear weapons. But discussions about nuclear disarmament between China and the United States won't happen in the foreseeable future. China's nuclear inferiority to the United States makes Beijing reluctant to join bilateral or multilateral talks on nuclear disarmament. Currently, there are no high-level talks in the nuclear field planned between the two sides.

But China and the United States have cooperated in this field in the past. After India and Pakistan successfully tested nuclear bombs in 1998, China and the United States jointly condemned the tests and reached an agreement on "nontargeting" of nuclear weapons; that is, they pledged not to target nuclear weapons at each other. In 2000, the five major nuclear powers (China, France, Russia, the United Kingdom, and the United States) all agreed to do so. The logical next step would be to issue mutual "no first use" pledges, promising never to initiate a nuclear attack. China already maintains such a policy, but the United States does not, although the current policy, as described by the Biden administration, comes awfully close: the United States will only "consider the use of nuclear weapons in extreme circumstances to defend the vital interests of the United States or its allies and partners." Committing to no first use does not exclude nuclear retaliation, so it would not neutralize the deterrent power of nuclear weapons.

The narrowing power gap between China and the United States may intensify their competition, but it also means they have more reason to confront shared challenges. For example, in the Middle East, Beijing and Washington now have a similar stance on two major issues: finding a two-state solution to resolve the Israeli-Palestinian conflict and preventing Iran from developing a nuclear bomb. As the Israeli war in Gaza continues, the two-state solution may look like a fanciful dream. But the war has led more people to realize that the status quo is unsustainable. No war will last forever. Beijing and Washington should work together in making the two-state solution the paramount principle guiding any future road maps that sketch the way to peaceful coexistence between Israelis and Palestinians.

Beijing and Washington must also work together to prevent Iran from developing nuclear weapons. On this issue, China has a major role to play: it enjoys Iran's trust. China has given Iran an economic lifeline in the face of U.S. sanctions by buying the country's oil. Beijing should make it clear to Tehran that although it is entitled to develop nuclear power for peaceful uses, it must not develop nuclear weapons. Doing so would very likely spur a preemptive strike by Israel or even a joint strike by Israel and the United States. Going nuclear will also surely invite severe UN sanctions on Iran—and China, despite being Iran's largest trading partner, would have to abide by them.

As great powers, China and the United States may never become great friends. But they can resist becoming enemies. Level heads and cautious optimism will help maintain the stability of the world's most important relationship. Fatalism and recklessness will only drive the countries toward a conflict that neither wants.

CHINA AND AMERICA CAN COMPETE
AND COEXIST

First published in *The New York Times*, 3 February 2020

BEIJING—Forget the trade war. If the gravest challenge of the 21st century is finding ways that China and the United States can coexist competitively, the real danger is that an unexpected incident might trigger a conflict that neither side has anticipated or could possibly control. The likeliest potential flash point is the South China Sea.

China believes, and has said as much in a 2014 position paper, that it has "indisputable sovereignty" over the South China Sea islands and the adjacent waters. This claim is solidly grounded in history and law, the government argues, because "China was the first country to discover, name, explore and exploit the resources of the South China Sea islands and the first to continuously exercise sovereign powers over them."

Some coastal states in the region disagree—most notably perhaps the Philippines, but also Vietnam, Brunei, Malaysia and more recently, Indonesia. They defend other, sometimes competing, territorial claims, based on their own accounts of history and geography.

29

The United States, for its part, has historically vowed not to take sides in these disputes over sovereignty, arguing that it only wants to protect free navigation in the region's waters.

But China has denounced America's professed commitment to neutrality as hypocritical in several ways. And as academics like M. Taylor Fravel have argued, there seems to be something of an inherent contradiction in the United States' policy: between its claim to want to stay out of local disputes and the resurgence of its operations in the region, particularly since it identified one country—China—as "the primary source of increased tensions" there.

What's more, whenever an American vessel sails close to islands or rocks controlled by China, in waters patrolled by Chinese ships, the risk of a dangerous encounter rises.

In 2001, a Chinese fighter jet collided with a United States Navy surveillance plane, killing the Chinese pilot. A tense diplomatic standoff over the detained American pilot and crew was resolved after Washington said, twice, that it was "very sorry"—without officially accepting responsibility for the accident and death. Since then, there have been quite a few close encounters between American and Chinese military vessels and aircraft, again in 2001, and then in 2009, 2013, 2014, 2015 and 2018.

Under the Trump administration, the United States Navy has increased its freedom-of-navigation operations, including in waters that China claims as its own, and those maneuvers increase the risk of an incident. The American destroyer *Decatur* and the Chinese destroyer *Lanzhou* narrowly avoided a collision, by just 45 yards, in September 2018—the hairiest encounter in years.

Should another collision occur today, it won't be resolved as easily as the one in 2001 was. An ever-rising China can only be more determined to safeguard what it sees as its sovereign rights, especially when Washington has deliberately intensified its competition with Beijing, and rather aggressively. Thucydides identified three motivations—fear, honor and interest—as the main causes of a war, and the South China Sea features them all.

Partly because China has ramped up its military arsenal and fleet in recent years, as well as built up outposts in the South China Sea, the Trump administration has called it a "strategic competitor," including in the 2017 National Security Strategy paper and the 2018 National Defense Strategy. Washington has also said that Beijing is a "revisionist power."

China, in turn, released a defense white paper last summer that described the United States as having "adopted unilateral policies" and "provoked and intensified competition among major countries."

With the temperature seeming to rise on both sides, how can a conflict, or something like a new cold war, between China and the United States be avoided? Precisely by looking at the actual Cold War.

In the early years of that protracted standoff, American and Soviet aircraft didn't hesitate to fire at one another. There were three crises over the status of divided Berlin, in 1948, 1958 and 1961. The Cuban missile crisis brought the two superpowers to the brink of nuclear war in October 1962. And yet outright conflict was averted, thanks to a few modest agreements and well-established hotlines for emergency communication. Even bitter enemies can build trust, and with imperfect tools, when they measure the stakes of a full-on clash.

In 1972, Washington and Moscow signed the Agreement on the Prevention of Incidents on and Over the High Seas—vowing, among other things, to use clear communication signals, avoid "embarrassing or endangering" even ships under their surveillance and exercise "the greatest caution and prudence in approaching" vessels on the high seas. The accord didn't prevent two Soviet ships from bumping into two American ships in Soviet territorial waters in February 1988, but that was an outlier incident, and the agreement does seem to have drastically reduced the overall risk of dangerous encounters. Within two years of its entry into force, according to a 2012 paper by Raul (Pete) Pedrozo, then a law professor at the United States Naval War College, the number of incidents per year had dropped from 100 to 40.

If the Soviet Union and the United States managed to avoid a major conflict during the Cold War, then some degree of confidence seems in order today about the far less confrontational relations between China and the United States.

Unlike the military rivalry between the United States and the Soviet Union, which was global, any military competition between the United States and China is confined to the western Pacific. America thinks that China wants to drive it out of the region; China believes America wants to block its legitimate ambition to develop a blue-water navy and hopes instead to confine China's influence to the eastern coast of continental Asia.

Yet even though China has built up its military capacity at an awesome speed, it has shown no appetite to replace the United States as world policeman. China's operations far from its shores, such as in the Gulf of Aden or on the African continent, are limited to addressing threats such as piracy or participating in peacekeeping and disaster relief. The United States Navy, on the other hand, regularly sends ships to the Asia-Pacific region in a deliberate effort to "challenge"—its own term—the "excessive maritime claims" of some coastal states.

Still, even the wariest of observers have yet to describe China and the United States as actual enemies. At the last Xiangshan Forum in October—the Chinese government's version of the Shangri-La Dialogue—Wei Fenghe, the defense minister, said, "The China-United States military relationship is generally stable, but we are confronted with many difficulties and challenges."

The confidence-building measures that exist today between China and the United States are rudimentary compared to those between the Soviet Union and the United States during the Cold War. In a way, this may be a comforting fact: a suggestion that relations haven't become so hostile as to require many such measures. Yet more of them will be necessary in the long run.

In 1998, China and the United States, acting in "the spirit of mutual respect," signed the Military Maritime Consultative Agreement to "establish a stable channel for consultations between their respective maritime and air forces." In 2014 came the nonbinding Code for Unplanned Encounters at Sea and the Memorandum of Understanding regarding the Rules of Behavior for Safety of Air and Maritime Encounters.

Chinese and American aircraft nonetheless collided after the 1998 agreement, and there have been dangerously close calls even since the two later sets of guidelines. In other words, confidence-building measures alone can neither prevent incidents nor overcome strategic distrust—today no more than in the past. And yet they remain essential to preventing any mishap from escalating and to developing working relations between China and America despite their divergent interests.

As China's military strength continues to grow and it closes the gap with the United States, both sides will almost certainly need to put more rules in place, not only in areas like antipiracy or disaster relief—where the two countries already have been cooperating—but also regarding space exploration, cyberspace and artificial intelligence.

For Chinese people, who traditionally believe in yin and yang, the notion that rivals can cooperate isn't a contradiction in terms. It seems to be a problem for America, however. Officials in Washington and other Western capitals have expressed dismay that China hasn't become more like the United States, or at least more democratic. But did China ever pledge to become like the United States? And so what if it hasn't become that? Competitive coexistence is still possible.

WHY CHINA MUST BEWARE A LESS CONFIDENT US, POLITICALLY DIVIDED AND PESSIMISTIC ABOUT ITS FUTURE

First published in *South China Morning Post*, 27 July 2020

Has China's foreign policy restraint ended? This is the question raised recently by Kurt M. Campbell and Mira Rapp-Hooper in their essay "China is done biding its time" in *Foreign Affairs*. They argue that since the pandemic first engulfed the world, China's government has engaged in an unprecedented diplomatic offensive taking advantage of the chaos of the pandemic and the global power vacuum left by a no-show US administration. Likewise, in a recent opinion in *Financial Times*, Michele Flournoy, a former US Under Secretary of Defense for Policy concludes that China's border clash with India is another sign of the county's growing assertiveness.

Such views, preponderant in western media, need serious examination. China's "assertiveness", be it in the South China Sea or in Galwan Valley, is invariably a response to the challenges she perceives to her sovereignty. But China doesn't need to make use of the "chance" provided by the pandemic since China is certainly stronger than these countries militarily.

In Hong Kong where "one country, two systems" is applied, obviously one country comes first and two systems doesn't mean the central government should tolerate riot and unrest that plagued the city, crippled the economy and hijacked the local authority in the last couple of years. The sweeping national security law is an "enough is enough" response that has finally arrived.

As a victim of the pandemic, China could only empathize with those countries that are also suffering. This explains why China has provided the largest external assistance to over 150 countries since the founding of the People's Republic, pledged $2 billion to assist developing countries and suspended debt payments for 77 developing countries. If such assistance promotes China's image, China cannot choose to do things that tarnish its own image at the same time.

Whether the US has declined has been a debate in which most people agree at least the US has declined relatively amid the rise of other nations such as the new emerging economies. But no declinists look bigger than Donald Trump. His tactical sketch of "American carnage" and then champion of "America first" helped him strategically in winning the presidential election in 2016. Both Joe Biden and John Bolton called Trump "an aberration", but he is surely not if he is reelected in November. This president engaged in aberrant behavior on a daily basis would then look more like the culmination of long-standing trends in a country that is politically divided and broadly pessimistic about the future of America.

Even if the US is in retrenchment, Beijing has more serious business to do than to confront Washington. Nothing down the road is more important than the "great rejuvenation of the Chinese nation" by mid-century. A good example is that even if the Chinese government has decided not to set a 2020 GDP target as a result of the pandemic, it hasn't relented on its commitment to eliminate extreme poverty by the end of this year.

It is particularly ludicrous to hear Washington describing Beijing as "assertive" or "coercive". In a telephone conversation with President Trump in 2019, former US President Jimmy Carter referred to the US as "the most warlike nation in the history of the world" and said the US has been at peace for only 16 of its 242 years as a nation. Professor Michael Lind pointed out in *The National Interest* in 2019, "The US is now engaged in more simultaneous small wars on more fronts than at any point in its history". In comparison, China has had no wars since 1979. The deadly brawl in Galwan Valley is most unfortunate; still, soldiers from both sides had a tacit understanding of not shooting at each other.

Over many years American policies towards China are based on narcissism—"we rebuilt China in the last forty years" as remarked by Vice President Mike Pence; and hallucination—China's development and engagement with the world would lead to "convergence with the citizen-centric, free and open order as the United States had hoped", as was described by the White House in its "Strategic Approach" to China. But Beijing should have never misled Washington in this regard. China has always made clear that the stability in its political system and society is her core interest.

An over-confident US after the Cold War has proven dangerous. America's war in Afghanistan alone killed tens of thousands of people including more than 2,300 American troops. But a less confident US is probably more dangerous. For Beijing, Washington has finally dropped its mask and is making all instruments available to maintain its primacy and suppress China.

This is seen in its bills one after another on Taiwan and increased arms sale thereto, its change of policy of not taking sides on the South China Sea issue and overt call on allies and partners to stand together with Washington against Beijing.

America's whole of government efforts around the world against Chinese telecom company Huawei is not really because Huawei's 5G network is a "trojan horse" of Chinese intelligence as secretary of state Mike Pompeo asserted, but that if Huawei's 5G is widely adopted, America might lose its technological supremacy in communication to China.

How could China continue to develop peacefully facing headwinds? The narrative that "the world is experiencing profound changes unprecedented in a century" reflects China's concern. But China is also confident that she is currently "in the best time for development since modern times". Even if the world is experiencing profound changes unprecedented in a century, the most profound change is China getting ever stronger.

In Asia-Pacific, the fear of China's neighbors is that either China or the U.S. pushes them to take sides. During an Asian tour in August 2019, the U.S. Secretary of Defense Mark T. Esper suggested that the Pentagon would like to deploy intermediate-range American missiles in Asia within months. It fell on deaf ears. Some ASEAN countries might wish the U.S. could balance China, but never at a cost of turning the South China Sea into a battlefield on their doorsteps.

It is fair to say neither Beijing nor Washington wants a conflict. But should a conflict occur between the two, it will only occur in the Western Pacific rather than in the waters off Hawaii or the continental USA. In China's periphery, the PLA at least enjoys convenience of geography. There is no guarantee that the U.S. military will prevail. The war games of the Rand Corporation showed that if a war broke out, the U.S. could very well lose.

At the 74th session of the UN General Assembly last year, UN Secretary-General Antonio Guterres talked about his fear of a Great Fracture—the world splitting in two with the two largest economies on earth creating two separate and competing worlds. Sadly, this looks more real than ever.

CHINESE AND US NAVIES MUST BRING DOWN TENSIONS

First published in *Financial Times*, 30 May 2019

As Asia's premier security forum, commonly known as the Shangri-La Dialogue, starts this week, a central question looms over the gathering: how will the US Navy deal with its strengthening Chinese counterpart.

Between 2014 and 2018, China built more submarines, warships, amphibious vessels and auxiliaries than the combined active navies of Germany, India, Spain and the UK, says the International Institute for Strategic Studies. China's navy has the means to develop into a formidable sea power: sustained investment, a self-sufficient defence industry and a government committed to building the People's Liberation Army into a world-class military.

Less combat-tested than the army or air force, China's navy has come into focus as its sense of vulnerability at sea has grown. The US Navy regularly sends warships through the South China Sea in Freedom of Navigation Operations that challenge what China sees as its sovereign territory and the US considers militarisation. China, as the largest trading and exporting nation, is also growing more concerned about the security of international sea lanes. At least five Chinese merchant vessels were hijacked in the Gulf of Aden and the Gulf of Guinea between 2009 and 2013.

Beginning in 2008, counter-piracy efforts gave the PLA Navy its first chance to conduct "military operations other than war" beyond Chinese waters. Since then its ships have spread far and wide, and China set up a naval logistic supply station in Djibouti in 2017.

China aspires to be admired rather than feared by the outside world. Since 2010, the Chinese naval hospital ship *Peace Ark* has visited 43 developing countries to provide free medical services. More than half of the 6,631 ships escorted by Chinese task forces in the Gulf of Aden are foreign-owned. When violence spread in Libya and Yemen, the PLA Navy evacuated foreigners along with Chinese citizens.

I predict that the Chinese navy will not seek to dominate maritime "choke points" and fears that it is creating a "string of pearls" system of military bases for power projection in the Indian Ocean are overblown. Instead the Chinese navy has to co-operate with its neighbours to share information and rules of engagement, improve interoperability and enhance joint operational capabilities. That's why the Chinese task forces participate in joint naval operations with other countries and in the Bahrain-based Shared Awareness and Deconfliction platform that combats piracy in the Indian Ocean.

The more the Chinese naval ships sail around the globe, the more likely they are to encounter US naval ships. This could mean either contention or co-operation. Some in China worry that the US could block the Strait of Malacca, which supplies more than 80 per cent of China's oil imports. Meanwhile some Americans fear China is trying to drive the US out of the Indo-Pacific.

Both China and the US have nuclear weapons, so the chances of a decisive sea battle between them are slim. But dangers lie in the South China Sea, where tense encounters between the US and Chinese navies have become common. John Richardson, who heads the US Navy, recently announced that the US will react to provocations from the Chinese coast guard and fishing boats as it would from the Chinese navy. Although it is fair to say neither the Chinese nor the American side wants a fight, the challenge is to ensure the encounters do not spark bigger conflicts.

It would be far better for the two navies to co-operate rather than remaining at loggerheads. The first step would be to agree on a flexible interpretation of freedom of navigation. They could then co-operate elsewhere in international waters. Counter-piracy, which once united 20 navies in the Gulf of Aden, is a brilliant example of how common interests may bind unlikely partners. It is also a good place to start.

THE US RISKS MAKING A STRATEGIC
BLUNDER OVER CHINA

First published in *Financial Times*, 25 February 2018

If China's reform and opening-up since 1979 has succeeded in bringing the country to the centre of the global stage, it has also allowed the US to see whether the communist state would become more "like us" in the course of liberalisation.

The results of this experiment have been disappointing from a US point of view. Liberalisation has not changed China as the Americans had hoped.

Jim Mattis, the US defence secretary, used the unveiling in January of a new national defence strategy, following the national security strategy published at the end of 2017, to underline American discontent. "Great power competition— not terrorism," he said, "is now the primary focus of US national security".

The new strategy argues that China has become America's main strategic competitor by "using predatory economics to intimidate its neighbours while militarising features in the South China Sea".

But the Pentagon fails to explain how, if China is so predatory, it has managed to become the largest trading partner of 130 countries and regions including most of its neighbours and the US, given that trade is generally mutually beneficial. True, China provoked worries by engaging in land reclamation in disputed areas of the South China Sea. But no international law forbids land reclamation, and other countries have also engaged in it.

The US further claims that China seeks to displace American military influence, particularly in the Indo-Pacific region. How can China possibly do that when it has just one overseas post, a logistic supply station in Djibouti, while the US has dozens, if not hundreds, of overseas military bases, including some in China's neighbours?

By viewing its relationship with China as a competition between great powers, the US is making another, far more consequential, misjudgment following its wars in Iraq and Afghanistan. While economic security is indeed part of national security, an all-out trade war with China will only invite retaliation. And faced with a common threat, China might opt to become closer to Russia.

Besides, maintaining economic dominance is easier said than done. Under President Donald Trump's predecessor, Barack Obama, the US tried to forge the Trans-Pacific Partnership, a collective effort to check Chinese influence in the region disguised as a trade agreement. But none of the putative members appeared willing to sacrifice their bilateral relationships with China. The pact is yet to come into force.

Today, the world faces two important questions: has the US gone into decline, and can a stronger China make the world a better place?

Although China has no intention to replace Pax Americana with Pax Sinica, the world's centre of gravity is undoubtedly moving east. According to a Gallup poll in January, China has a higher worldwide approval rating, albeit by a slight margin, than the US. And although Chinese president Xi Jinping skipped the World Economic Forum in Davos this year, its theme of "creating a shared future in a fractured world" very much resonates with what he told the gathering in 2017.

Despite US claims to the contrary, China's achievements cannot in any way be attributed to American support. Rather, the country's growing influence stems in large part from its patient handling of the relationship with the US—despite serious incidents such as the Nato bombing of the Chinese embassy in Belgrade in 1999 and the collision in 2001 of Chinese and American aircraft above islands that are part of China's exclusive economic zone.

For years now, China has been able to manage the uncertainty that tends to surround a new American presidency. And by the end of each administration, relations between the two countries have generally improved.

The question today is how the US will behave towards China, now that Mr Trump sees it as a strategic competitor. One American media outlet described the national security strategy as "dead on arrival". But if this is a serious policy document, the whiff of a new cold war, it may well prove to be a watershed in America's irreversible decline.

WHY CHINA CAN REST EASY IF TRUMP IS RE-ELECTED US PRESIDENT

First published in *South China Morning Post*, 21 March 2024

With Donald Trump pulling slightly ahead of Joe Biden in some national polls as the US prepares to vote for its next president, what might America's China policy look like if Trump is reelected? My answer is simple: a Trump 2.0 administration will look a lot like Biden's.

America's China policy took a U-turn when Trump became president in 2017. But his major legacy is not decoupling—which Biden has continued in the name of "de-risking". It is something ideological: a bipartisan consensus against China that has taken root.

To be fair, Trump is not an ideologist. But once bilateral relations are hijacked by ideology, the room for flexibility drastically shrinks. Can Trump break camp? A good example is Richard Nixon. Once a diehard anti-communist rightist, the former US president is best remembered for his icebreaking trip to China.

Nixon, however, is well-recognised as a strategist while Trump is a self-described "deal-maker". In his first book, *Trump:*

The Art of the Deal, he wrote: "My style of deal-making is quite simple and straightforward. I aim very high, and then I just keep pushing and pushing to get what I'm after."

Such a strategy, ironically, seems to work best on American allies. They are appalled by his remarks that he would encourage the Russians to "do whatever the hell they want" to any Nato country that doesn't fulfil its financial obligations to the military alliance.

Should Trump win a second term, it is almost certain that more Nato members would hurry to meet the target defence spending of 2 per cent of gross domestic product so as to avoid the worst-case scenario—America's withdrawal from Nato. If this is a stick, it is expected to work much better than Biden's carrot.

It won't work on China, though. Trump has threatened to place a tariff of 60 per cent or more on all Chinese imports. But this would slash the share of US imports from China to near-zero. US manufacturers in China would take a hit. US financial markets would tumble. And Americans would pay higher prices for imports from elsewhere.

Therefore, Trump wouldn't differ very much from Biden and his administration's "small yard, high fence" restrictions on the flow of key technologies to China. But neither man can stem the flow of global, including US-trained, tech talent to China. Beijing is making massive investments in innovation and, in 2022, China filed for more intellectual property than the rest of the world combined.

Would Trump make a difference on the Taiwan issue, Beijing's primary concern? Unlike Biden, Trump has never openly vowed to defend Taiwan. But Beijing won't be complacent. Nancy Pelosi's Taiwan visit in 2022 triggered People's Liberation Army live-fire drills around the island. Beijing's reaction has to increase with each provocation and each reaction will create a new status quo. Now Chinese military jets regularly fly over the Taiwan Strait's median line regardless of the Taiwanese authorities' protests.

Trump's China policy would also depend on how he could garner domestic and international support. An ABC News/Ipsos poll last year found that three-quarters of Americans believe the country is heading in the wrong direction. A divided America simply cannot have robust diplomacy.

The wars in Ukraine and the Middle East will surely distract the next American president from Beijing. Trump claims that, as president, he could end the Russian-Ukraine war in a day. This is self-praise, but also telling that it is Washington's support for Kyiv that is the key to resolving the conflict.

Ukraine, having failed in a counteroffensive fully supported by Nato, has lost hope of taking back all lost territories while Russia will have to bear with an enlarged Nato. The most likely outcome is an armistice in the heart of Europe that no one likes.

In the Middle East, Trump's most significant diplomatic achievement, the Abraham Accords that aim to improve relations between Israel and several Arab countries, has been squandered. Unlike Biden who has frosty relations with Israeli Prime Minister Benjamin Netanyahu, Trump was Netanyahu's closest political ally during the four years they overlapped in office. He could give Israel a freer hand than Biden, however much that stirs up regional conflict.

Iran's nuclear issue would only worsen with another Trump presidency. So far, Tehran hasn't made the political decision to produce a nuclear bomb, but the more turbulent the Middle East, the more attractive it will be for Iranians to do that. It has already sped up its production of 60 per cent enriched uranium. It can quickly upgrade this to the 90 per cent needed for a nuclear bomb. Saudi Arabia has pledged to create a nuclear bomb if Iran does.

The losers in the two wars are not just the warring parties. It also includes the United States, which has very much lost its credibility and moral authority thanks to the double standards in its contrasting responses to Ukraine and Gaza. Such glaring hypocrisy is widely criticised in the Global South. The damage cannot be easily repaired, particularly by a deal-maker who doesn't give a damn about winning hearts and minds.

That Trump may once again be president will further speed up what US representative Marjorie Taylor Greene calls the "national divorce". Whoever becomes the next president will find it harder to sell the so-called rules-based international order, will find few countries in the Global South wishing to buy into the "democracy vs autocracy" divide, will find even America's allies reluctant to take sides, and will have a longer to-do list to discuss with Beijing. Then, why should China worry?

A GOOD BEGINNING, BUT ONLY HALFWAY DONE

First published in China-US Focus, 8 January 2015

During President Obama's October visit to China, the two heads of state announced that the two militaries had signed a Memorandum of Understanding (MOU) regarding the Rules of Behavior for Safety of Air and Maritime Encounters. This is the first time that the two militaries have been able to conclude some Confidence-Building Measures (CBMs).

The most vulnerable part in Sino-US relations is military relations. The MOU is a great effort from both sides to "develop a new model of military-to-military relations". Although the Chinese military lags well behind the US military, the memorandum somehow puts Chinese and US militaries on an equal footing. It is American recognition of the growing strength of the PLA and the need to avoid confrontation with China. Historically only the Soviet Union and the US, two giants with almost equal strength, signed a similar, US-Soviet Incidents at Sea Agreement, with many of the articles similar to the MOU. During the Cold War, the US-Soviet Incidents at Sea

Agreement helped to significantly reduce incidents between the Soviet Union and the US.

The beauty of the MOU is that it is tactical, more than strategic. At present, there are quite a few mechanisms between the two militaries, such as Defense Consultative Talks, Defense Policy Consultative Talks, Strategic Security Dialogue and a hotline, but they are all at strategic levels whereby only strategic issues are discussed by the two sides. But Rules of Behavior for Safety of Air and Maritime Encounters are tailor-made for officers, sailors and airmen from both sides. It is them who deal with one another every day.

Another credit of the MOU is that it doesn't specify where these encounters might be. Previously many consultations were encounters on the "high seas". Now the MOU doesn't specify any geographic locations, therefore it can actually apply wherever Chinese and American military vessels and military aircraft meet. Given the growing strength of the PLA Navy and its increasing involvement overseas, Chinese and US military vessels will simply meet more often in different waters. A broader rather than prohibitive application of these rules is certainly helpful in defusing any possible misunderstandings or miscalculations.

There are international conventions of maritime and air rules and regulations, such as those in the United Nations Convention on the Law of the Sea, Convention on International Civil Aviation, Convention on the International Regulations for Preventing Collisions at Sea, 1972, Collision Regulations (COLREGs), and Code for Unplanned Encounters at Sea (CUES). Now, with new rules of behavior in place, people may simply hope that these rules could reduce or even eliminate dangerous situations between the two countries, such as the Chinese and American aircraft collision in 2001, the standoff of the USSS *Impeccable* and the USS *Cowpens* with Chinese ships in 2009 and 2013, and the close encounter between a Chinese J-11B fighter jet and an American P-8 in August 2014.

However all lethally dangerous encounters occurred only in China's Exclusive Economic Zone (EEZ), as a result of the US Navy's intelligence, surveillance and reconnaissance activities. For China, there would be no incidents if the US military vessels or aircraft didn't come close to the door at all. Mark Valencia, a maritime policy analyst, pointed out that these encounters in China's EEZ between the Chinese and American military vessels are not really "unplanned". They are "unfriendly" acts in response to what is perceived as "unfriendly" behavior.

Therefore a question arises: with such rules of behavior recognized, will PLA Navy justify American probing, tracking and targeting in China's EEZ? In other words, should the PLA Navy keep a safe distance when it believes that the American military vessels or aircraft are doing damage to China?

There is no easy answer to the question, but the American response so far sounds like: you are welcome to conduct reconnaissance on us if you want. The Chinese are not convinced. The latest example is that on September 17, 2014, Russian military planes were intercepted by USAF F-22 fighters 55 miles from the coast of Alaska. Many in China believe that the US is hypocritical in such remarks, because it knows that China doesn't have such capabilities or even intentions to conduct reconnaissance on the continental USA.

The MOU includes practical operational guidelines, but they won't be able to resolve a strategic issue, i.e., lack of sufficient trust between China and the US. For China, the US Navy is an intruder breaking into its courtyard without permission. Therefore no matter how the US tries to "whitewash" its activities in the name of "freedom of navigation", no Chinese would buy it. China won't "legalize" US military activities in China's EEZ, even with such rules of behavior.

Unlike the US-Soviet relationship, which was characterized by nothing more than hostility, China and the US are described by many strategists as neither friends nor foes. Thus, the Sino-US relationship makes the bilateral ties extremely complicated or even unpredictable. But one thing is clear: so long as the two countries don't have enough confidence in each other, there can only be more and more CBMs to come. This is just the beginning.

CHINA'S ABSENCE IN RIMPAC MARITIME WAR EXERCISE BENEFITS NO ONE, LEAST OF ALL AMERICA

First published in *South China Morning Post*, 11 July 2018

Exercise Rimpac, the world's largest biennial international maritime warfare exercise, held off Hawaii from June through July, is without China this year. The US decision to disinvite China to the Rim of the Pacific drill was announced in May and mentioned by Secretary of Defence James Mattis at the Shangri-La Dialogue held in early June in Singapore. The decision was based on what the US sees as Beijing's militarisation of islands in the South China Sea.

Does Rimpac matter for China? The answer is: not really.

Chinese naval vessels participated in Rimpac in 2014 and 2016, but were only allowed to take part in the humanitarian part of the exercise, such as counter-piracy, disaster relief and onboard inspections. These activities are not professionally challenging for the Chinese navy, which has performed similar drills quite often, either by itself or with other countries, including the US.

The restrictions on operations were made in accordance with a bill passed in 2000, which does not allow exchanges between the US military and the People's Liberation Army in areas other than humanitarian operations, for fear that any exchanges beyond these could contribute to the PLA's warfighting capabilities and create a national security risk.

This is narcissism. Neither Western arms embargoes nor any American restrictions have proven capable of deterring the awesome progress of the PLA, especially in the past two decades.

A report published by the International Institute for Strategic Studies in February cited China's J-20 stealth combat aircraft and the PL-15 air-to-air missile as examples of how the US and its allies are starting to lose air dominance. It also said that "since 2000, China has built more submarines, destroyers, frigates and corvettes than Japan, South Korea and India combined", and "the total amount of new warships launched by China in just the last four years is significantly greater than the entire French navy itself".

The PLA, apart from its own increasingly sophisticated exercises often held off China's coast, is also conducting more and more joint exercises with other countries. But the most valuable ones are those held with member states of the Shanghai Cooperation Organisation (SCO), especially Russia.

Since 2002, when China held its first joint exercise with Kyrgyzstan, the SCO member states have taken part in almost annual exercises. In 2005, about 10,000 troops from China and Russia gathered in the Shandong peninsula to practise air and naval blockades, an amphibious assault, and occupying a region.

In 2016 and 2017, China and Russia held computer-assisted missile defence drills. Their joint exercises in the Mediterranean and the South China Sea were taken in the West as an alarming sign that the two countries are more willing to take care of each other's security concerns.

By disinviting the Chinese navy to Rimpac, the US has not necessarily benefited. First, it loses a routine chance to observe the PLA's professionalism and technological advances. Secondly, it loses a good opportunity to practise good airmanship and seamanship with the Chinese navy, as set out in the memorandum of understanding on the "rules of behaviour for safety of air and maritime encounters", which the two countries signed in 2014 to head off potentially dangerous conflict.

In fact, the top priority in the China-US military-to-military relationship is crisis management. In 2017, a total of five ships of the Seventh Fleet of the US Navy collided with other vessels at different times and in different areas, resulting in the death of 17 American officers and sailors.

This raises two questions. First, how could the strongest navy in the world behave so unprofessionally?

Second, if a Chinese naval vessel meets such an "unprofessional" American naval vessel in an unplanned encounter, how can the Chinese commander distinguish between deliberate provocation and bad seamanship on the American side?

A US Navy caught napping is no reason for China to cheer. A worst-case scenario is an American warship colliding with a Chinese warship, say, in the South China Sea.

This is not impossible. A Chinese J-8 fighter and an American EP-3 aircraft collided in 2001 and the Chinese pilot died. It was not the only stand-off that has occurred; Chinese and American ships have been involved, too.

The value of joint exercises with the US is more political than military: to indicate that the two giants are still able to "cooperate wherever possible", as Mattis would say.

However, this is easier said than done, especially at a time when the current US security strategy regards China as one of America's top strategic competitors and a trade war between the two countries is raging. During President Xi Jinping's meeting with Mattis, Xi said he hoped that the military-to-military relationship could become a stabiliser in bilateral ties.

The fact that Beijing still invited Mattis to visit China after the US withdrew its invitation to China to attend Rimpac 2018 demonstrates both goodwill and self-confidence on the Chinese part.

If one good turn really deserves another, the question is: will the US invite China to attend 2020 Rimpac? Let's wait and see.

WHY CHINA-RUSSIA MILITARY EXERCISES SHOULD PROVOKE SOUL-SEARCHING IN THE WEST

First published in *South China Morning Post*, 19 September 2018

Vostok 2018, Russia's biggest war games in nearly 40 years involving almost 300,000 troops, over 1,000 military aircraft and two Russian naval fleets, took place from September 11 to 15 in Russia's central and eastern military districts.

What made it more exceptional is that it was attended by 3,200 troops with 30 fixed-wing aircraft and helicopters, and a great deal of armour and artillery from China. Never before has the People's Liberation Army (PLA) been involved so massively in a joint exercise overseas.

Such exercises are significant to the PLA primarily for two reasons. First, only large-scale exercises can truly reveal the capacity of a military in terms of strategic planning, power projection, command, control and communication. Therefore, the more sophisticated the exercises, the better.

Since the PLA has not been involved in wars since 1979, its capacity building and operational readiness can only be verified through military drills. Russia was once a superpower. Its military doctrine and lessons learned from wars in Chechnya, Georgia and Syria could be useful to the PLA.

Secondly, these exercises are meant to address large conflicts rather than non-traditional threats such as terrorism, piracy and natural disasters. The PLA's military exercises with foreign armed forces are nothing new—China and Kyrgyzstan started a joint drill in 2002—but most are still focused on preparing for non-traditional threats.

Today, China is still not fully reunified, as some Chinese territories remain occupied by other countries. If large-scale conflicts or wars cannot be ruled out in the future, then such sophisticated exercises with Russia involving different services and arms are certainly good practice for the PLA.

However, the gains of China's participation in the Russia-led military exercises should not be seen as one-sided. Thanks to China's ever stronger defence industry, the PLA is growing rapidly. For example, tanks and armoured vehicles made in China have proven to be as good as those made in Russia in multinational military contests.

Some Russian media has pointed out that, one day, Russia may have to buy warships from China given the decline in Russia's shipbuilding industry.

Being one of the leaders in artificial intelligence technology, China has vowed to build an "intelligent military" and the road map of the PLA, as laid out in the report of the 19th party congress, is clear—to become mechanised by 2020, modernised by 2035 and world-class by 2050.

China and Russia did not just reap military rewards from Vostok 2018. If Carl von Clausewitz is right in saying that "war is but the continuation of politics by different means", then a joint military exercise looks like a natural extension of the political rapprochement of the countries involved.

The fact that Russia invited China—and Mongolia—to attend its largest exercise clearly indicates that Moscow views Beijing positively as a political partner in the international arena and vice versa.

In fact, at the time of the exercise, Chinese President Xi Jinping was attending the fourth Eastern Economic Forum in Vladivostok at the invitation of Russian President Vladimir Putin.

The warming of ties between China and Russia is in part a response to the pressure they both face from the West, albeit to varying degrees and for different reasons, and in part because of their similar views on the international order.

These views are best reflected in the Shanghai Cooperation Organisation, which has Chinese and Russian as the official languages. The Organisation stresses the "Shanghai spirit" of mutual trust, mutual benefits and consultation.

Does this comes as a relief to the West, whose worst nightmare is a China-Russia alliance? If Vostok 2018 worries the West, it should also provide a moment for soul-searching as to why China and Russia are getting ever closer.

GERMANY'S TURNING POINT IN THE WRONG DIRECTION

First published in *Die Zeit*, 20 April 2022

The abrupt announcement of Chancellor Olaf Scholz in February on the creation of a 100-billion-euro fund for the Bundeswehr and spending more than 2 percent of GDP on defense every year from now on invite a natural question: Does Germany have to make such a U-turn?

The standing ovation to Scholz's remarks in Bundestag doesn't necessarily justify the seismic shift in German foreign policy made by the strongest economy in Europe. Yes it will serve to substantiate European Strategic Autonomy which so far is a French slogan and revive a "brain-dead NATO", but the costs are Germany's image as a pacifist country and Europe's security.

Given that Europe's security will only worsen—be it a continuing hot war in Ukraine or a cold war afterwards across the continent, a traditionally low-profile Germany with pro-Russian Ostpolitik could have been best positioned to lead in negotiations with Russia on Europe's future. This is now doomed. A militarized Germany will also invite some imagination if not fear of the world given Germany's Nazi past. At least one of the reasons Russia gave in invading Ukraine is "denazification".

Imagine for a moment that all those countries aspiring to join NATO are accepted, will Europe become safer? If Finland joins NATO, the Alliance's troops would be a stone's throw from St. Petersburg. What will Russia think, and perhaps, act? Russia is now described by the west as a pariah. But a frustrated pariah with the largest nuclear arsenal is most dangerous. President Putin has (in)famously asked "why do we need a world without Russia in it?".

Only Putin can decide how long the Russo-Ukrainian war will last. He will fight till he could declare a "victory". That presumably means Ukraine's formal acceptance of Crimea being part of Russia, Ukraine not entering NATO and the independence of the two "republics" of Donetsk and Luhansk. If this is difficult for Ukraine to swallow, the war will simply continue.

In the long run, a security arrangement between Russia and NATO has to be made. NATO's continuing expansion may prove its popularity, but it will only make Europe more insecure should Russia feel threatened. Europe's security could only be achieved with Russia.

Defense spending tells best how a country views its security environment. Unfortunately, Germany's drastic increase in defense spending is a panic-driven overreaction. It is a *Zeitenwende* ("turning point") in the wrong direction.

AS THE US FOCUSES ON 'EXTREME COMPETITION' WITH CHINA, CONFLICT IS JUST A STEP AWAY

First published in *South China Morning Post*, 28 September 2021

The dust of Afghan war hasn't settled completely. But the fallout is already clear. With the ending of the US global crusade on terrorism, the prelude of Biden's "extreme competition" with China has opened. This question is: how long will it last?

If twenty years' war in Afghanistan is "forever war" for the US, then its competition with China could be described as "forever competition", because it will surely last longer than the Afghanistan war. Gone are the days when China could "hide your strength and bide your time". The second largest economy in the world is simply too big to hide. And it is impossible for Beijing to bide time when Washington has taken her as the primary strategic competitor.

However, in the economic field, the die is cast. By the end of 2020, China's economy was 70% of that of the US. It is widely assumed that by 2030, China will overtake America to become the world's largest economy in terms of GDP. According to Yale professor Paul Kennedy, this is a condition that has not existed since the 1880s when America's economy overtook Britain's. For the entire 20th century, the American economy was about two to four times larger than that of any of the other great powers.

When China emerges as the world's largest economy, as former Australian prime minister Kevin Rudd pointed out, this will be the first time since George III (1738-1820) that the world will have a non-English speaking, non-democratic, non-Western state as the largest economy. This will be a seismic change to Americans who were fed with a myth since they were born that America was "exceptional" or "indispensable". Now they have to come to terms with common sense: nations rise and fall; Americans are like everyone else.

When the economy of an "authoritarian state" like China surpasses that of the US, the influence of western democracy will reach its nadir. According to Freedom House, democracy around the globe has been declining since 2006. Polls show a 55 percent majority of Americans are dissatisfied with their system of government. Winston Churchill famously said "democracy is the worst form of government except all the others that have been tried". If this suggests that in spite of its problems, democracy is still better than other governments, then the insurrection at Capitol Hill on January 6, 2021 shows how democracy can be vitriolic or even deadly violent. It is hard to believe the Capitol building—the supreme seat of American democracy, would be violently attacked by a mob of supporters at the call of President Donald Trump with false allegations of fraud in the election.

From now until 2030, the China-US competition will most certainly intensify in that the US will take it as the last chance to bring down a rising power. The AUKUS agreement made recently among the US, UK and Australia allows the US to share its jealously guarded nuclear-powered submarine technology with Australia in breach of a previous A$50 billion ($35 billion)

Franco-Australian deal. Such an unusual move, described by French foreign minister Jean-Yves Le Drian as "a stab in the back", shows how the US could resort to desperate measures against a competitor at the cost of an important ally.

The problem is a few nuclear subs might indeed complicate decision-making in Beijing, but they won't necessarily become game changers. For Australia, balancing is probably an art that is too delicate to learn. Historically, Australian soldiers always fought other people's wars away from home as junior partners. This time, the Morrison government has obviously decided to take the risk of taking sides with the US in a military conflict with China. Given Australia's inevitable reliance on American and British nuclear technologies in decades to come, the Morrison government has actually taken succeeding Australian governments as hostages for its decision.

Even with some British and Australian help, time is not on America's side. The Pentagon's war games over Taiwan showed the US loses again and again to China. Of course this is no reason for China to be complacent, but should a conflict occur in China's periphery, the PLA has all the advantages of being on "home turf". Today, America's armed forces are considerably smaller than they were in the 1980s. The PLA is just the opposite. By 2019, the PLA navy has approximately 350 ships, outnumbering the US Navy which has around 293 ships. Although quantity is not quality, it has a quality all of its own.

Nothing speaks of a country's security assessment more than her defense expenditure. For three decades, China's military expenditure is below 2% of her GDP. It speaks volume about China's self-confidence against security challenges. If China feels threatened to the extent that she has to increase defense spending, the second largest economy can easily afford to double the defense budget, but could the US double its military spending that is three times larger than that of China?

Biden said the US rivalry with China will take the form of "extreme competition" rather than conflict. But when competition becomes extreme, it is one step away from conflict. Contrary to the US which emphasizes competition, China has righteously called for cooperation. But it takes two to tango. A country cannot compete without strength, likewise, it can only cooperate with strength.

The pendulum of US foreign and defense policy traditionally swings between assertiveness and pull backs. The question is when will America in retrenchment swing back, or will it swing back at all? Biden uses US pullout as an alibi to justify America's competition with China. Only time will tell whether this is a wise decision. But if it is a boneheaded strategic blunder, then it is a monumental error that is more consequential than the Vietnam war, Iraq war and Afghan war combined. It will doom America's hegemonic status since late 19th century, for good.

WITH THE CLIMATE CRISIS THREATENING US ALL, THIS IS A TIME FOR US–CHINA COEXISTENCE, NOT COMPETITION

First published in *South China Morning Post*, 24 November 2021

The joint pledge of China and the US at the COP26 conference in Glasgow to cut emissions is like an oasis in a desert, considering the badly strained ties between Washington and Beijing now. But it shouldn't be a surprise. In facing a common threat looming large over their own survival, major powers know when they need to act together.

The climate change raises a question: if indeed time is running out—the most important consensus of the conference, do we still have time to compete against each other? If human nature is intrinsically flawed such that people only stop jostling each other before doomsday, then climate change provides us a way of looking at our relations from a perspective of coexistence: we cooperate to survive, we don't survive to compete.

Coexistence is not easy, especially between two giants of almost equal weight. During the Cold War, strategic equilibrium was eventually achieved through mutually assured destruction between two superpowers. Admittedly what is happening today is quite different from the Cold War if one thinks of the colossal amount of economic interdependence and entanglement between China and the US. But almost like in the early days of the Cold War, what we are seeing is ever intensifying competition to the extent that President Joe Biden suggested to President Xi Jinping to "establish a commonsense guardrail" in a virtual summit on 16 November.

The question is how. Both China and the US vow not to slide into a new cold war. But there is no guarantee of that. Presumably coexistence with the US should be easier for China, not only because China's time-honored foreign policy is called "five principles of peaceful coexistence", but also because apart from what China views as her sovereignty rights over Taiwan, in the East China Sea and the South China Sea that she has to defend, there is no possibility of a military conflict between China and the US elsewhere. Against a bigger back drop, Beijing doesn't wish to challenge the international system that has tremendously benefited her in recent decades.

Coexistence with Beijing looks more like a bitter fruit for Washington to swallow which takes the relationship very much like a duel of democracy vs autocracy. Ever since the establishment of diplomatic ties between the US and China, it is not rare to hear American presidents saying how the US would wish China to be strong and prosperous, but there was an undertone which was eventually voiced by Vice President Mike Pence at the Hudson Institute in 2018 that "After the fall of the Soviet Union, we assumed that a free China was inevitable". Such hope was dashed. China is getting much stronger but is still different. During the Trump administration, the US took all drastic measures to bash China, ranging from a trade war to increased operations by the US Navy in Chinese waters in the South China Sea and lifting almost all legal restrictions on exchanges with Taiwan.

The Biden administration's policy towards China is very much a follow-up of Trump's great power rivalry. But things seem to be starting to change. In a recent interview with CNN's Fareed Zakaria, US National Security Advisor Jake Sullivan admitted that "one of the errors of previous approaches to policy toward China has been a view that through US policy, we would bring about a fundamental transformation of the Chinese system" which is not the object of the Biden administration. He even mentioned "coexistence".

Even if the summit signals a watershed from the past, in a way, coexistence between Beijing and Washington is more difficult than between Washington and Moscow during the Cold War. Unlike during the Cold War when coexistence between two superpowers was marked by clearly defined spheres of influence, there aren't even buffer zones between China and the US. The US Navy regularly send ships to sail provocatively in Taiwan straits and near the Chinese islands and rocks in the South China Sea while asking the Chinese PLA naval ships to keep a safe distance. Such brinkmanship risks veering into exactly what Biden tries to avoid: a conflict intended or unintended.

To stare into the abyss helps one to step back. Should a conflict occur, with the possible exception of Japan and Australia, no American allies would wish to take America's side. One can hardly imagine Thailand, an American ally and a friend of China would follow the US in a war with China in any circumstances. If the US has succeeded in sweet talking Australia into antagonizing China, as was proved in the AUKUS submarine deal, it has lost the trust of France, another important ally. The immediate outcome is zero, the long-term benefit is inconsequential.

The damage by the Afghan war to the image and credibility of the US can only be matched by the Vietnam war. Some people have argued that America will rise from the ashes and prosper like it did ten years after the Vietnam war. Perhaps. But even if this might be true, the moment will still come around, or even before 2030 when China surpasses the US in terms of GDP as the largest economy in the world.

I call it the "2030 moment". It is more epochal than the "sputnik moment" when the Soviets stunned the Americans in sending the first satellite into orbit or the "1945 moment" described by UN chief Antonio Guterres referring to the beginning of the Cold War. For China, it is a return of history, a reconnection through a time tunnel with the heyday in the past. For America, it will be the first time that she has to accept mutually assured coexistence with a rival since it became a global power after the war with Spain in 1898. And for the whole world, it is a return of common sense: nations rise and fall, the story about rivalry between democracy and autocracy is a myth.

TO AVOID THE FOLLY OF A US-CHINA SPACE RACE, THE TWO COMPETITORS SHOULD LEARN SOME SOVIET-ERA COOPERATION

First published in *South China Morning Post*, 11 March 2021

It is interesting to see how in one month, the planet Mars suddenly had three visitors from Earth: first the United Arab Emirates' "Hope" probe, then a day later, China's spacecraft "Tianwen-I", entered its orbit; and finally Perseverance, Nasa's newest rover landed on the red planet's surface on February 18. The question is: why can't nations pool resources and knowledge on such gargantuan tasks that are extremely difficult and expensive?

In outer space, basically all issues boil down to two categories: peaceful use of space and de-militarization of space. No matter how desirable the former sounds, the latter proves to be the real challenge. US Secretary of Defense Lloyd Austin described space as "an arena of great power competition". But during the Cold War, the two superpowers of US and Soviet Union had managed to cooperate on the Apollo-Soyuz Test Project, the first international partnership in space. On July 17, 1975, the

American Apollo spacecraft launched two days earlier docked with a Soviet Soyuz spacecraft.

Sadly, this won't happen between China and the US, the two largest economies today. The Wolf Amendment limits US government agencies such as NASA from working with Chinese commercial or governmental agencies. But a prosperous China can afford to invest lavishly in the Chinese space industry that is self-propelled and self-sustainable. In some areas, China has already overtaken the United States. China's Five-hundred-meter Aperture Spherical Telescope, larger than the US-run Arecibo spherical reflector dish in Puerto Rico, is the largest in the world. Ironically, on December 1, 2020, the same day that a Chinese lunar probe landed on the moon, the Arecibo dish collapsed.

Contrary to Washington which has refused entry of Chinese astronauts into the America-built International Space Station, Beijing appears more open-minded about space cooperation with other nations. Beijing has announced that it is ready to share her moon samples with international institutions and scientists for "space belongs to everyone." It has also declared in a memorandum with the UN that the Chinese Space Station, due to be completed in 2022, would be used for international scientific experiments and flights of international astronauts. The International Space Station is due to expire in 2024. But even after life-extension to 2030, as authorized by the US Senate, the Chinese space station might still be the only station in orbit. Will Americans ask Beijing for a ride then?

Avoiding militarization of outer space, however lofty in its aim, is easier said than done. The 1967 Outer Space Treaty prohibits placing any weapons of mass destruction in orbit; establishing military bases or installations, testing any type of weapons or conducting military exercises on the moon and other celestial bodies. Ever since 1980s, the UN has had endless debates on avoiding a space arms race with different proposals.

But so far countries have failed to negotiate another treaty for the purpose. In 2018, the US voted "no" on four UN resolutions which included prevention of an arms race in outer space and no first placement of weapons in outer space.

An outstanding problem is how to define what constitutes a space weapon or the weaponization of space. Most space technologies are duel-use in nature, that is, the same technology can be used alternatively for military and civilian purposes. Even a satellite that maneuvers close enough to another satellite can pose a threat. Besides, lasers, electronic jamming, directed energy weapons, and offensive cyber tools can all become "weapons" that threaten satellites.

But difference in interpretations should not be an insurmountable barrier if all countries agree that there won't be winners in a space arms race. The US, Russia, China and India successfully conducted their anti-satellites tests. The US is more vulnerable than any other country simply because it has more civilian and military assets in space that are subject to potential attacks from adversaries. Beijing is vulnerable too. In the last three years, China had more rocket launches than any other country. Space is becoming increasingly crowded. In a single launch in January, a SpaceX Falcon 9 sent 143 small satellites into orbit; thousands of new satellites will be sent to orbit in the coming decade. Every nation has a stake in space security.

The lessons learnt from the Cold War might provide useful revelations. During the Cold War, it was mutually assured destruction (MAD) that prevented an all-out nuclear war. But this concept only came into being when Washington and Moscow concluded they could not have an edge over the other in the arms race and a strategic equilibrium, even balanced by terror, is more desirable than war. Similarly, in avoiding militarization or weaponization in space, perhaps the way out is first recognition of mutually assured vulnerability by major space-faring nations that eventually leads to a treaty of not deploying any weapons in outer space.

If enemies could cooperate during the Cold War, why not competitors today? It is a relief that the Biden administration has renewed the New START nuclear arms control agreement. The agreement prohibited, among others, either country from interfering with the other side's "National Technical Means" for monitoring compliance. This is understood to include satellite reconnaissance systems.

China-US cooperation in selected civil space projects will steer more countries to join the effort to develop space. And it is possible, too. During China's 2019 moon exploration mission, NASA got congressional approval for a specific interaction with China National Space Administration to monitor China's landing of a lunar probe on the dark side of the moon using NASA's Lunar Reconnaissance Orbiter.

Competition is part of human nature. But no human folly is more monumental than attempting to place weapons in orbit to strike back on Earth, our only homeland, to eliminate adversaries. Astronaut Michael Collins once suggested the political leaders of the world should see their planet from a distance of 100,000 miles to change their outlook. And what could they see? "The all-important border would be invisible, that noisy argument suddenly silenced".

THE RISK OF CHINA-US MILITARY CONFLICT IS WORRYINGLY HIGH

First published in *Financial Times*, 25 August 2020

The relationship between China and the US is in freefall. That is dangerous. US defence secretary Mark Esper has said he wants to visit China this year, which shows the Pentagon is worried. That Wei Fenghe, China's defence minister, spoke at length with Mr Esper in August shows that Beijing is worried too. Both men have agreed to keep communications open and to work to reduce risks as they arise.

The crucial question is: how?

In July, US secretary of state Mike Pompeo inverted a famous line of Ronald Reagan's about the Soviet Union and applied it to China: "trust but verify" became "distrust but verify". Washington suspects that an increasingly coercive China wants to drive the US out of the Indo-Pacific.

Beijing meanwhile believes that the US, worried about its global primacy, has fully abandoned its supposed neutrality on the South China Sea. Haunted by economic recession and the pandemic, and desperate for re-election, President Donald

Trump has also made confronting China his last-straw strategy to beat his opponent, Joe Biden.

The risk of a mistake is therefore high. It is one thing for the two countries to point their fingers at each other. It is quite another if naval vessels collide in the South China Sea, triggering a direct conflict. In 2019, the US navy conducted a record number of freedom of navigation operations there. Mr Esper has vowed to keep up the pace this year.

So far, whenever a US ship has come close to China-controlled islands, Chinese naval ships have monitored it and warned it to leave.

This pattern might continue without accident, allowing both sides to "save face". The US can claim its freedom of navigation operations have challenged China's "militarisation" of the area. China can also say it has driven away intruders from its waters.

But that ignores the chance of mishap. The air collision in 2001 between a Chinese jet fighter and a US reconnaissance plane caused the death of one Chinese pilot. In 2018, the USS *Decatur* and Chinese destroyer *Lanzhou* escaped collision by just 41 metres.

Both sides have pledged to keep at a safe distance during these encounters. Yet what is a safe distance exactly?

For the US, the Chinese islands are artificial land reclamations, so a US warship can legally sail as close as 500 metres. But for Beijing, these are natural Chinese territories that China has chosen to enlarge, and the fact they had names before land reclamation are proof they are not artificial. Under Chinese law, a foreign military vessel's entry into territorial seas needs government approval.

China and the US could then even fight each other under the same international laws. Washington cites Article 58 of the UN convention on the law of the sea to justify its right of freedom of navigation and overflight. But Beijing can quote the same article, which says: "States shall have due regard to the rights and duties of the coastal State."

How to de-risk the chance of a conflict that neither side wants but which they could nevertheless sleepwalk into?

During the Cold War, the US and USSR competed via proxy wars, avoiding direct conflict. Should a similar competition arise today, America's Asian allies most probably wouldn't follow the US into war with a neighbour that has nuclear weapons and is their biggest trading partner.

Meanwhile, if US ships and aircraft continue to maintain high-intensity surveillance of the South China Sea, there is always the potential for a confrontation. Beijing has no plan to take on Washington. From Beijing's point of view, it is the US that comes provocatively close to China.

Eventually, it may be that the sheer size of China's military prompts a US rethink. The Chinese army enjoys the convenience of geography, to say the least. Its navy also outnumbers the US navy in terms of warships and submarines, although the US fleet is more heavily armed. Admiral Philip S Davidson, commander of the US's Indo-Pacific Command, has acknowledged that there is "no guarantee" the US would win a future conflict against China.

China's foreign minister Wang Yi has said Beijing will remain "cool headed" whenever there are "impulsive moves" from the US. But in many ways, China hawks such as Mr Pompeo have made it hard for subsequent administrations to de-escalate US competition with China.

It is therefore reasonable to ask: what difference will Mr Esper's trip to China this year make? But the visit itself is a valuable step forward in communication and risk reduction. Talking past each other is better than not talking at all.

CHINA HAS RISEN PEACEFULLY, BUT WILL AMERICA GO DOWN WITHOUT A FIGHT?

First published in *South China Morning Post*, 12 January 2019

What is the greatest challenge we face in the 21st century? It is not China's rise but America's decline.

The decline, albeit relative, is obvious. The United States' share of global GDP has dropped from an estimated 50 per cent at the end of the Second World War to 22.4 per cent in 1985 and to 15.2 per cent today. The International Monetary Fund expects it to slide to 13.9 per cent by 2023.

America's decline started before Donald Trump became president, dating from the apogee of triumphalism at the end of the Cold War, and will probably continue after him. But he is accelerating it with his "America first" agenda.

But is Trump an accident or the inevitable? When asked what he thought of the French Revolution of 1789, Chinese premier Zhou Enlai famously said it was too soon to say.

History will judge Trump, but probably not in two or six years. Accountability and credibility don't seem to matter to the unpredictable US president, who prefers to play with fire.

Even those most critical of China have to admit its rise in the past 40 years has been peaceful, but could America's decline, if inevitable, be equally peaceful?

First, use common sense rather than believe in myths. One doesn't need to read Paul Kennedy's classic, *The Rise and Fall of the Great Powers*, to know great powers are rising and falling all the time.

Brushing aside the rhetoric, America is neither "exceptional" nor "indispensable", nor are Americans God's "almost chosen peoples".

An American is not necessarily more proud of his country than a Maldivian who is greeted every day by tourists coming from all corners of the world. If all men are created equal, so are all countries.

The US still has good reason for self-confidence. It has rich natural resources, an attractive culture, a strong educational system, creative entrepreneurs and favourable demographics.

US military power is unchallenged anywhere and will remain so for a long time. The world still looks to the US for engagement, although not necessarily leadership, on many global issues.

If life is about making the right choices, then the US doesn't need to have so many "vital national interests". It has to be selective, but should not pursue unilateralism and protectionism at the cost of others.

If "the United States cannot continue to be the policeman of the world", as Trump declared in December to US troops in Iraq, he should encourage the United Nations to play a bigger role.

The usefulness of the UN can be best ascertained by asking: what would the world become without the UN taking care of issues ranging from conflict and poverty to social and economic development and human rights?

Although the UN is sometimes criticised for bureaucracy and low efficiency, it best represents collective decisions and actions on global issues.

The UN remains on American soil. As one of the creators of the UN and the largest financial contributor, the US should join others in reforming it, instead of weakening the largest intergovernmental organisation on the planet.

The relationship between the US and China, the world's two largest economies, is understandably complicated, especially given that China is widely expected to overtake the US economically by around 2030.

For China, the challenge is how to continue rising peacefully when the US sees it as a top strategic competitor.

Like it or not, the People's Republic of China has retained its identity as a socialist country.

But today, it is much stronger and more comfortable with the current international system. Beijing's offer to share its stories of economic success with those who are interested should not be taken as an attempt to promote its ideology abroad.

That America takes China to be a strategic competitor is not strategic orientation; rather, it looks like a loss of direction as self-confidence wanes and angst prevails over rationale. Could the two giants sleepwalk into a conflict, say, in the South China Sea?

The situation currently resembles an "atypical security dilemma" in that the US—a third party that claims to take no position on the South China Sea issue—has stepped in and is standing eyeball to eyeball with China, with Asean watching anxiously.

How might Trump tweet about this? "Very bad!"

US AND CHINA SHOULD LEARN FROM THE COLD WAR TO AVOID AN ARMS RACE AND CONFLICT

First published in *South China Morning Post*, 5 February 2021

Last October, US and Chinese defence officials convened their first Crisis Communications Working Group to discuss crisis prevention and management. The meeting was unusual in discussing "crisis" for the first time, rather than "accidents". It showed that the two militaries have begun to worry about things getting out of hand when bilateral ties go into free fall.

For over two decades, China-US military discussions have often been in a Catch-22 situation: Americans wanted technical discussions, say, on how to avoid close and dangerous encounters between ships and aircraft, while the Chinese would point out that these encounters in Chinese waters should simply stop.

Americans would then cite their right to freedom of navigation and overflight, and ask Chinese ships monitoring American vessels to keep a safe distance. The Chinese response? You are safest when you stay away.

So, how can they avoid unwanted confrontation? The answer is: professionalism. During the Cold War, professionalism helped to avoid a nuclear fallout between two bitter enemies. This is reflected in the growing list of confidence-building measures that include the Strategic Arms Limitation Talks, the Anti-Ballistic Missile Treaty and Strategic Arms Reduction Treaty.

China and the US are not enemies. But reducing the risks between them could be more challenging than it was for the US and the Soviet Union. First, there were clearly defined spheres of influence between Washington and Moscow, which allowed them to avoid direct confrontation.

But there isn't even a buffer zone between Beijing and Washington. American naval vessels regularly sail through the waters off Chinese islands and rocks in the South China Sea and the Taiwan Strait.

Secondly, the US and the Soviet Union were balanced by mutually assured destruction. This is not the situation with Beijing and Washington.

The People's Liberation Army lags far behind the US military, although in the Western Pacific, the gap is closing—to the extent that the US believes an ever-confident China wants to drive it out of the Indo-Pacific.

Therefore, Washington is investing more militarily in the region and calling on its global allies and partners to gang up on China. This in turn irks the Chinese and makes the situation more volatile.

For Beijing and Washington to avoid conflict, the first step is to observe the agreements already made. The most dangerous place is at sea. The key is for ships and aircraft to keep a safe distance.

But what exactly is a safe distance? Many factors including visibility, vessel manoeuvrability and an understanding of the manoeuvring intentions of the other vessel have to be considered.

They require not only serious discussions, but also regular training to ensure good seamanship. The two militaries conducted joint drills to avoid unplanned encounters at sea in 2014, 2015 and 2016. Such exercises should continue, in part because a stronger PLA Navy now meets the US Navy more regularly in international waters.

Professionalism is also needed in de-escalating incidents after they occur, such as the deadly collision between two military aircraft in 2001 and a narrowly avoided collision of two naval vessels in 2018.

The most significant discussion of the Crisis Communications Working Group meeting was what to do after an incident, which had not been discussed before. This might help to prevent incidents from happening in the first place.

As the gap in strength between the Chinese and American militaries becomes smaller, both countries need to discuss strategic equilibrium in new areas such as cyber and artificial intelligence, and space. It is difficult to tell whether cyber incidents are espionage or cyberwarfare.

But the bottom line is not to attack critical information networks, such as military command and control systems. In 2013, Washington and Moscow established links between their national computer emergency response teams, agreed to warn each other of cyberexercises through the Nuclear Risk Reduction Centre and set up a direct hotline between the White House and the Kremlin.

Beijing and Washington also have hotlines at governmental and military levels. Eventually, both countries might wish to exchange a list of sensitive targets that should be forbidden from coming under attack in any circumstances.

In artificial intelligence, if preventing AI from being weaponised is not possible, China and the US could lead in building international norms and reducing risks related to AI-enabled military systems. The sooner this is done, the better, while AI is still a nascent development.

As Brookings Institution president John R. Allen put it, once AI is embedded into military systems and applied, there will be less willingness to roll back any new capabilities they afford, particularly given how costly such systems are to develop.

The 2011 Wolf Amendment limits US government agencies such as Nasa from working with Chinese commercial or government agencies, but could not handicap the self-reliant Chinese space industry.

A Chinese space station will be built in 2022, and might be the only space station left in orbit after the International Space Station built by the US comes to the end of its life in 2030.

Will the US, which has refused Chinese astronauts' entry into its space station, ask China for a ride then? And would Beijing agree?

Donald Trump's establishment of the US Space Force in 2019 has ushered in an arms race in space. But in civil space exploration, partnerships are still preferable. Since space belongs to no one, why not make the exploration of Mars a joint effort?

That the Cold War did not become a hot war was not down to sheer luck. In spite of hostilities, professional communications were maintained and strengthened through verifiable confidence-building measures.

No one knows how the China-US relationship might evolve, but for competitors to not become enemies in a new cold war, they need a long list of confidence-building measures. The longer the list, the smaller the risk of war.

WHAT IF CHINESE AND AMERICAN WARSHIPS COLLIDE WITH EACH OTHER?

First published in China-US Focus, 15 September 2017

When the guided-missile destroyer USS *John S. McCain* collided with a heavy oil tanker near the Strait of Malacca on August 21, leaving one sailor dead and nine missing, this was already the fourth similar accident this year for the U.S. Seventh Fleet. The question is: how can what seems impossible occur to the strongest navy in the world?

Before investigators pieced together the causes of the fatal crashes, experts widely assume fatigue and under-training of the seamen are most probably the reasons behind them. According to the *Wall Street Journal*, the American deployable battle force, at 276 ships, is far smaller than what's needed to meet demand. So the ships have to be kept at sea longer. Longer deployments put wear and tear on sailors, their families and the fleet and lead to ships being overused and short of maintenance.

Here comes the worst scenario: what if an American war ship collides with a Chinese war ship, say, in the South China Sea? This is not impossible. A Chinese J-8 fighter and an American

EP-3 aircraft collided in 2001 and the Chinese pilot died. Quite a few standoffs have occurred between Chinese and American ships. In 2013, a Chinese landing ship cut in and stopped less than 500 meters in front of the USS *Cowpens* to prevent it from getting close to the Chinese aircraft carrier *Liaoning* under sea trial. Whenever an American ship conducted freedom of navigation operations (FONOP) up to 12 nautical miles off China-controlled islands in the South China Sea, the Chinese ships are sure to follow and monitor.

It is fair to say that neither China nor the US wants a conflict triggered by an incident at sea. Both China and the US have pledged to observe the Code for Unplanned Encounters at Sea (CUES) and bilateral rules of behavior for unplanned maritime and air encounters. Whenever the US Navy conducted a FONOP off China-controlled islands and reefs to challenge China's sovereignty over the "artificial islands" which China believes are its territories, it praised the Chinese ships following behind being "professional" in keeping distance.

But what if the US ships turn out to be the ones that are not professional? High-tech can never prevent human errors, as demonstrated in the four incidents. And a big issue between China and the US is lack of trust. Since Donald Trump took office, the Seventh Fleet has increased FONOPs in the South China Sea. If a "professional" Chinese naval vessel happens to meet an "unprofessional" US naval vessel next time, how can the Chinese ship commander distinguish between deliberate provocation and bad seamanship on the American side?

Is America's navy in the Western Pacific doing too much with too little, asked *The Economist*. But for America's Navy to answer this, it needs to answer, first of all, what is the dire need to do so much.

The most-mentioned raison d'etre for increased American naval presence in the West Pacific is North Korea and China.

Apparently Kim Jong-un is not deterred by American ships and bombers. Instead, they have actually made Kim more antagonistic. When it comes to China, America needs to search its soul to answer two basic questions: does China really have so many military secrets for the US to justify its daily surveillance and reconnaissance by satellites, aircraft, drones and ships? If not, what is the rationale to maintain such high intensity if these activities are tactically useless and strategically unhelpful to mutual trust?

No matter how the US Navy throws its weight around in the South China Sea, China knows the US won't fight over the reefs and islands for any claimants of ASEAN. Therefore American FONOPs have only face values. And even these face values are questionable. China and the US have different interpretations of the freedom of navigation, but as early as 1998 and in accordance with the UN Convention of the Law of the Sea, China has made freedom of navigation one of the basic principles in PRC Law on the Exclusive Economic Zone and the Continental shelf. In a stark contrast, the US still refuses to ratify the convention.

If freedom of navigation is the mantra of the US Navy, the incidents indicate, however ironically, it is the US that is interfering with freedom of navigation at the cost of the lives of its own sailors and the lives of other innocent people. It adds to people's feeling of America's decline. Is the US really declining? At least President Trump thinks so, otherwise he wouldn't have said to make America great again. But his vow to increase American ships from 276 to 350 sounds more like one of the pledges that he made but doesn't really bother to honor. For the US Navy, it remains to see how long it can still pretend that it is as strong as it was before it reaches its breaking point.

2

LIVING IN AMITY
WITH NEIGHBOURS

IN AFGHANISTAN, CHINA IS READY TO STEP INTO THE VOID

First published in *The New York Times*, 8 August 2021

The speed and scope of the Taliban's takeover in Afghanistan have prompted introspection in the West over what went wrong, and how, after billions of dollars spent on a 20-year war effort, it could all end so ignominiously. China, though, is looking forward. It is ready to step into the void left by the hasty U.S. retreat to seize a golden opportunity.

While Beijing has yet to formally recognize the Taliban as Afghanistan's new government, China issued a statement on Monday saying that it "respects the right of the Afghan people to independently determine their own destiny" and will develop "friendly and cooperative relations with Afghanistan."

The message here is clear: Beijing has few qualms about fostering a closer relationship with the Taliban and is ready to assert itself as the most influential outside player in an Afghanistan now all but abandoned by the United States.

Unlike the United States, China brings no baggage to the table in Afghanistan. China has kept a low profile in the country since the U.S. invasion, not wishing to play second fiddle to the United States in any power politics. Beijing watched as Washington's foray in Afghanistan became a messy and costly morass. In the meantime, China provided Afghanistan millions of dollars in aid for medical assistance, hospitals, a solar power station and more. All the while, Beijing was fostering stronger trade relations, eventually becoming one of Afghanistan's largest trading partners.

With the U.S. withdrawal, Beijing can offer what Kabul needs most: political impartiality and economic investment. Afghanistan in turn has what China most prizes: opportunities in infrastructure and industry building—areas in which China's capabilities are arguably unmatched—and access to $1 trillion in untapped mineral deposits, including critical industrial metals such as lithium, iron, copper and cobalt. Though critics have raised the point that Chinese investment is not a strategic priority in a less secure Afghanistan, I believe otherwise.

Chinese companies have a reputation for investing in less stable countries if it means they can reap the rewards. That doesn't always happen so smoothly, but China has patience. Although the presence of U.S. troops went some way toward preventing armed groups from using Afghanistan as a haven, their exit also means that a 20-year war with the Taliban has ended. Therefore the barriers for Chinese investment on a large scale are removed. China is of course a major buyer of the world's industrial metals and minerals to fund its economic engine.

One of China's current long-term strategic investment plans is the Belt-and-Road Initiative, an effort to finance and build infrastructure across the region. And Afghanistan until now has been an attractive but a missing piece of the enormous puzzle. If China were able to extend the Belt-and-Road from Pakistan through to Afghanistan—for example, with a Peshawar-to-Kabul motorway—it would open up a shorter land route to gain access to markets in the Middle East. A new route through Kabul would also make India's resistance to joining the Belt-and-Road less consequential.

Even before its takeover of Kabul, the Taliban had promised to protect Chinese investments in Afghanistan.

Beijing is now also positioned to hold greater influence over the country's political landscape. Afghanistan's history tells us that one group is rarely in control of the entire country, and given the Taliban's lightning takeover, it's reasonable to expect some civil strife. China—already the largest troop contributor to U.N. peacekeeping missions among the five permanent members of the United Nations Security Council—has also registered a peacekeeping standby force of 8,000 troops—a move that could make it one of the largest contributors overall. If a U.N. peacekeeping mission is deployed to Afghanistan, Chinese peacekeepers, coming from a friendly neighboring country, will almost certainly be more welcome than those from afar.

Becoming an influential player in Afghanistan also means that Beijing is better positioned to prevent what it considers anti-Chinese groups from gaining a foothold in the country. A primary concern of China is the East Turkestan Islamic Movement. According to a Chinese government report, the group had early roots in Afghanistan. According to the U.N., it received Taliban and Al Qaeda support in the 2000s. Some scholars and experts question whether the group has the capacity to instigate violence, or whether it even continues to exist. Still, China's foreign minister, Wang Yi, said in a July meeting with Mullah Abdul Ghani Baradar, the deputy leader of the Taliban, that he hoped the Taliban would "make a clean break" with the East Turkestan group because it "poses a direct threat to China's national security and territorial integrity." Mr. Wang also expressed hope that the Taliban would "build a positive image and pursue an inclusive policy"—a signal that China wants the Taliban to make good on its promise of "inclusive" governance.

In response, Mr. Baradar promised that the Taliban would never allow any group to use Afghan territory to engage in acts harmful to China.

The key to Afghanistan's peace and stability, of course, also lies partly in Pakistan. Despite their proximity, the "conjoined twins," as described by the former Afghan president Hamid Karzai, don't always look in the same direction. Pakistan's Afghanistan policy is driven largely by the strategic goals of ensuring a friendly government in Kabul and undercutting India's increasing influence in Afghanistan. It is in Beijing's own interest—not least for the success of Belt-and-Road—to ensure that Pakistan and Afghanistan are on good terms.

It is no secret that China already enjoys strong influence in Pakistan. Anticipating a more prominent role and future necessity, Beijing pledged in June to continue helping develop and improve relations between the two countries.

Finally, even though the United States is leaving, there is an opportunity for Beijing and Washington to work together for a stable Afghanistan. China and the United States, despite their differences, have enjoyed some cooperation in Afghanistan already—for example, jointly training diplomats and technicians. Neither country wishes to see Afghanistan slide into a civil war. Both of them support a political solution that is Afghan-led and Afghan-owned. Therefore, Afghanistan provides an area for the two competing giants to find some common cause.

When Mr. Wang spoke to Secretary of State Antony Blinken on Monday, he said China stood ready to work with the United States to "push for a soft landing of the Afghan issue."

Afghanistan has long been considered a graveyard for conquerors—Alexander the Great, the British Empire, the Soviet Union and now the United States. Now China enters—armed not with bombs but construction blueprints, and a chance to prove the curse can be broken.

WHO CAN THE US REALLY COUNT ON IN A WAR WITH CHINA OVER TAIWAN?

First published in *South China Morning Post*, 15 May 2024

In the worst-case scenario of a China-US showdown over Taiwan, will America's allies stand with it back to back? My answer is: not necessarily. America has over 60 allies and partners around the globe. But when it comes to a war with China, those that are helpful to the US won't be more than a handful.

Take Thailand for example. Since King Rama IV (1851-1868), Thailand's foreign policy has been one of "bending with the wind". This "bamboo diplomacy" allowed Siam to be the only Southeast Asian country to escape colonisation.

Today, the Beijing-Bangkok relationship is described by both governments "as close as one family". In the past few years, China has surpassed the United States as the primary supplier of Thai military equipment such as tanks and an amphibious dock ship.

It's a similar situation with South Korea. Deeply worried about a nuclearised North Korea, Seoul cannot afford to show any hostility towards Beijing, which has a latent treaty obligation of military help for North Korea.

The best example is that President Yoon Suk-yeol, a seemingly diehard pro-American president, decided not to meet the visiting then-US House speaker Nancy Pelosi after her Taiwan visit in 2022, which triggered live-firing by the People's Liberation Army (PLA) around the island. It speaks volume about Seoul's tiptoeing between China and the US.

Japan has treaty obligations to provide logistical support to the American military in a conflict. It might let the US use bases in Japan, too, but its own participation is unlikely. Public opinion in Japan is generally against getting ensnared in a Taiwan Strait conflict. According to a poll for the *Asahi Shimbun* last year, just 11 per cent of Japanese respondents said their armed forces should join the US in the fighting, and 27 per cent said their forces should not work with the US military at all.

Having fought in every major US war since the second world war, Australia looks the most reliable ally. In recent years, Australia has pushed Washington to curb the influence of Huawei Technologies, and supported the creation of security groupings such as Aukus (between Australia, Britain and the US) and the reinvigoration of the Quadrilateral Security Dialogue (between the US, Japan, Australia and India).

In a war in the Taiwan Strait, Australia, too, is likely to let the US use its military bases. But Canberra also makes clear it has not promised the US to take part in any Taiwan conflict in exchange for American nuclear-powered submarines.

In the Philippines, President Ferdinand Marcos Jnr seems determined to join the American camp, something other Asean leaders have tried their utmost to avoid. US access has been granted to nine military bases that would be most useful in strengthening America's badly needed forward military presence along the so-called first chain of islands. Recently, the US Army's mid-range capability ground-based missile system was deployed to exercises in the Philippines.

But Foreign Affairs Secretary Enrique Manalo also said last April that the Philippines will not let the US stockpile weapons for use in any Taiwan operation. US troops will also not be allowed to refuel, repair, and reload at those sites. Time will tell whether these promises are reliable.

Then, can the US develop a "mini Nato" in the Indo-Pacific as some have argued? Well, Aukus looks too mini and Britain won't be a major player in the region. Even if Japan joins, the glue that binds still won't be strong enough.

As for the Quad, it has a security element, which is reflected in its joint military exercises, but it won't become a military alliance because of India. As a rising power and a founder of the Non-Aligned Movement, India is too proud to be dependent on any major power. Its ambition is to become a global power like China one day. It shouldn't wish to be seen to be antagonising its northern neighbour, whose economic and military strength far outweighs its own.

Whether American allies join the US in a war with China depends first on whether the US gets involved. If Washington concludes that the latest Taiwanese leader is a troublemaker—as president George W. Bush was rumoured to have referred to former president Chen Shui-bien—then why would it write a blank cheque with American blood?

The conflict in Ukraine is also giving people second thoughts. If Nato, an alliance of 32 states, can hesitate to take on Russia, then what gives the US the confidence to fight China with a few half-hearted allies? Yes, Russia has more nuclear bombs than China. But the PLA has a military budget over three times bigger. The PLA is also known to have better drones, early warning aircraft and other force multipliers such as hypersonic weapons.

Much has been said about America's "strategic ambiguity"—not specifying whether it would assist Taiwan militarily in a conflict—but for Washington, the biggest strategic ambiguity comes from Beijing: will a stronger China become more confident in an eventual peaceful reunification or will it become more impatient and resort to force?

Quite a few American generals have publicly predicted some worst-case scenarios, but so far, Beijing is still talking about a peaceful reunification, even as Taiwan's Democratic Progressive Party has been re-elected.

That Washington can count on its allies is a best-case scenario—and more likely, wishful thinking. Alliance is a marriage of convenience. America's alliances in the region are more the sort of marriage described by George Bernard Shaw—between a man who can't sleep with the window shut and a woman who can't sleep with the window open.

CHINA AND INDIA SHOULD BE GLOBAL SOUTH ANCHORS, NOT POWER COMPETITORS

First published in *South China Morning Post*, 2 February 2024

Much has been said about how China and India are jostling for leadership of the Global South. This is bunkum. China harbours no intention of becoming the Global South leader, and India is unlikely to become one even if it wants to. China describes itself only as "a natural member of the Global South", in line with what it calls itself: a developing country. But while India has not yet declared itself the leader of the Global South, its ambition is hardly veiled.

Last year, with New Delhi hosting the G20 summit, Prime Minister Narendra Modi convened two Voice of Global South Summits for 125 developing countries without inviting China, Brazil or South Africa. This is almost understandable: India could hardly puff up with self-importance as the voice of the Global South in the presence of these leading G20 developing nations.

China and India have the same problem in trying to convince others to see them as they see themselves. As China gets stronger, despite the late Deng Xiaoping's mantra of *tao guang yang hui*, meaning to hide your strength, bide your time, it can hardly hide its strength any more.

For example, China has said it will remain a developing country forever. There is indeed no strictly agreed definition for a developing or developed country. But if China overtakes the United States in 10 years to become the world's largest economy, could it then still be a developing country? Some are already calling China a superpower. For India, the challenge is to encourage a belief that it is bigger than it actually is. With liberal democracy in steady decline, India's self-description as the world's largest democracy adds little dazzle. Besides, there are doubts that India is a full democracy and many consider Modi's government repressive.

India's latest self-branding is "Vishwaguru", or world teacher. The question is what India can teach the world. While India has outpaced China in economic growth over the past few years, China's economy remains five times as large. Even if India could sustain an average annual growth of about 5 per cent, its gross domestic product will still only be where China's is today in around 2050.

China, which spent four decades lifting 800 million of its people out of poverty, is more qualified to share its lessons learned with other developing countries. In diplomacy, India has yet to set a better example than Beijing's successful mediation between Saudi Arabia and Iran. The war in Gaza is showing up India's difficulties in trying to assume leadership of the Global South. On October 7, Modi wrote on X: "We stand in solidarity with Israel at this difficult hour" before US President Joe Biden tweeted his support for Israel. India's backing of Israel, one of its biggest weapon suppliers, is probably a reflection of its realpolitik.

But most Global South countries, including China, are more sympathetic to the Palestinians. South Africa, in particular, has launched a case in the International Court of Justice accusing Israel of "genocidal acts" in Gaza.

Perhaps the best narrative India has found for itself is in being a bridge between the Global North and South; this at least carries a grain of modesty. According to Modi, India can serve as a bridge "so that linkages between the North and South can become stronger and the Global South can itself become stronger". But, in a globalised world, why would any Global South country need to reach the Global North through an Indian bridge? The only thing that looks somewhat like a bridge is the India-Middle East-Europe Economic Corridor in which India has a key role. But this is a US-led project. And it will probably never come to fruition due to the Gaza conflict, which threatens to spread across the region.

Modi's government is at best pragmatic and at worst opportunistic. India is drawing closer to the US. With China-US competition intensifying, Washington naturally needs New Delhi, in groupings such as the Quadrilateral Security Dialogue, just as it needed Beijing during the Cold War to counterbalance Moscow. The question is what price India is ready to pay. New Delhi has maintained good relations with Moscow since the Cold War and, for a long time, will continue to depend on Russian oil, gas and spare parts for the Russian weapons that make up the bulk of what's used in its military. But this relationship will cool as India warms up to the US. The challenge is how India can step back gradually from Russia.

The more difficult relationship is with China, India's largest direct neighbour. Their disputed border areas have led to many military stand-offs, including a deadly clash in 2020. In the Indian Ocean, where India considers itself a "net security provider", it frets about China's increased economic and military presence. India repeatedly objected to Sri Lanka allowing Chinese military vessels to dock to replenish supplies, forcing the government to introduce a ban on Chinese ships. China, in contrast, has welcomed India's membership in the Shanghai Cooperation Organisation and BRICS (which also includes Brazil, Russia and South Africa), two organisations in which China has a crucial role.

The future bodes well for both China and India. The Asian century that Deng Xiaoping described to Rajiv Gandhi in the late 1980s is dawning. China has grown into a pole in our multipolar world and India could one day become another. If this is to be a blessing for the Global South, both Asian giants must serve as anchors rather than competitors in our volatile world.

AN INDIA SEEKING GAINS FROM US-CHINA RIVALRY IS NO GURU TO THE WORLD

First published in *South China Morning Post*, 27 September 2023

India is growing in importance. But how much more important will it become? In the lead-up to the Group of 20 summit in New Delhi, major newspapers, billboards and bus stops in every Indian city proclaimed India as a "Vishwaguru", or teacher to the world.

This is baffling. What would India teach the world? It has never been shy to describe itself as the world's largest democracy. But the Indian government, led by Prime Minister Narendra Modi, is increasingly being criticised as authoritarian and repressive. On September 18, Canada's Prime Minister Justin Trudeau told the country's parliament of "credible allegations" that linked the killing of a prominent Canadian Sikh to "agents of the government of India".

While the advance of what is now the world's fifth-largest economy has been impressive, even if India could sustain annual growth of 5 per cent, its gross domestic product per head would reach about 30 per cent of the United States' levels, roughly where China's is today, in 2050. Meanwhile, Beijing has lifted hundreds of millions out of poverty in four decades. Needless to say, China has more to share with other developing countries on ways of achieving economic development.

In January, Modi hosted a virtual Voice of Global South Summit for 125 developing countries, but didn't invite China, Brazil or South Africa. Presumably, in the presence of these leading developing nations, India would have felt embarrassed to describe itself as the voice of the Global South.

India's real advantage is that, as a middle power, it can capitalise on major-power competition. With regard to the war in Ukraine, while both China and India have adopted a studied neutrality, Washington has set aside its frustration at New Delhi because of its long-term strategic need to draw India closer and counter China. This is how India succeeded in persuading the US and Europe to agree to a softened G20 statement on the Russian invasion of Ukraine. Clearly, such a consensus would have been harder to reach with China as G20 host.

However, India is unable to play a "central role" in facilitating an end to the hostilities in Ukraine, despite what Italian Prime Minister Giorgia Meloni suggested. There are already several peace plans on the table, including one from China. None of them will work unless Moscow and Washington, rather than Moscow and Kyiv, can agree a deal. If Russia will listen to anyone, it is more likely China than India.

India depends on Russia for weaponry and energy. But, according to Alexander Gabuev, director of the Carnegie Russia Eurasia Centre, Russia's reliance on China will outlast Vladimir Putin, in that Russia is increasingly dependent on China as a market for its commodities, as a source of critical imports, and as its most important diplomatic partner.

In the long term, the Indian-Russian relationship is on a downward trend, although it won't break. For decades to come, India will still need Russian oil and gas, but it will reduce its dependence on Russian arms. Due to the war in Ukraine, Russia has already fallen behind schedule in delivering Talwar-class stealth frigates to India.

Washington would be only too happy to wean New Delhi off Russian dependency. It remains to be seen whether increasing US-India defence industrial cooperation can really bolster New Delhi's defence manufacturing capabilities, or if India's defence sector will end up a bigger hodgepodge of everything from everywhere.

New Delhi's biggest challenge is maximising gains from its relations with a faraway Washington without irking Beijing, its stronger neighbour. India is now being wooed by the US as China was once cozied up to by the US against the Soviet Union during the Cold War. This is certainly an opportune moment for New Delhi to seize. If pretending is an art, then Modi is a guru second to none.

For example, he has echoed the US's call for a "free and open Indo-Pacific", even though India's position on maritime law is closer to China's than the US's. Both China and India have been challenged by the US Navy with its freedom of navigation operations in their exclusive economic zones. The difference is that the Chinese Navy will definitely react, while the Indian Navy will pretend nothing has happened.

Detente between China and India would serve both countries' interests. For instance, India's pharmaceutical industry, a big exporter, gets 70 per cent of active ingredients from China. Likewise, India is a vast market for China. This explains why, in spite of complaints about India's domestic environment, Chinese companies are still considering investing in India.

Unless there is a border war between China and India, New Delhi won't be a willing pawn for Washington. The likelihood of a conflict between China and India is low. While it is true that the two sides had a deadly brawl in the Galwan Valley in June 2020, it was the first case with casualties in over 40 years.

The fact that the soldiers from both sides were fighting with stones and clubs tells us that they knew they shouldn't shoot at each other in any circumstances. If a lesson has truly been learned, it is entirely possible for both sides to maintain peace in the border area, at least for four more decades.

India's foreign policy is at best pragmatic and at worst opportunistic, but trying to be all things to all people won't make India a "Vishwaguru". Instead, India comes across more as the bat from Aesop's fable, which describes itself as a bird or a beast depending on its assessment of an impending war between birds and beasts. But India is not alone in this. In a world of intensifying major-power competition, there are more bats than birds or beasts.

WHY INDIA'S MARITIME INTERESTS ARE CLOSER TO CHINA THAN THE US

First published in *South China Morning Post*, 6 May 2021

India was caught totally unprepared when the USS *John Paul Jones*, a 9,000-tonne guided missile destroyer asserted navigational rights and freedoms approximately 130 nautical miles west of the Lakshadweep Islands on April 7, inside India's Exclusive Economic Zone (EEZ), without requesting India's prior consent.

Pricked by the suddenness of the operation, India's Ministry of External Affairs made a mild protest saying that the operation was unauthorised, adding that its concerns had been conveyed to Washington "through diplomatic channels".

Should India have a choice, that is, if the US Navy didn't announce this at all, most probably the Indian government would pretend nothing had happened. But this slap in New Delhi's face—less than a month after the first-ever Quad summit and during US presidential climate envoy John Kerry's visit in the Indian capital, was too loud to ignore.

Recent years found New Delhi and Washington in a duet chanting "free and open Indo-Pacific", a thinly-veiled finger-pointing at China. But they are not birds of a feather that flock together. If Washington decides to challenge India's EEZ, that means at least the water area of around 2,300,000 km² in the Indian Ocean is not "free and open" for Washington.

Otto von Bismarck famously said, "Laws are like sausages, it is better not to see them being made". The UN Convention on the Law of the Sea (UNCLOS) is probably the longest sausage ever made. It was negotiated for nine years, making it the longest-running international law negotiation in history. Understandably, compromises are made and ambiguities that could be flexibly interpreted found.

Four decades passed after the UNCLOS was adopted in 1982. It is hilarious to see the US that still hasn't ratified the Convention would behave as if it is the guardian of maritime law. From October 1, 2019 to September 30, 2020, U.S. forces operationally challenged "28 different excessive maritime claims made by 19 different claimants throughout the world", according to the Pentagon. Therefore, a simple question arises: If the Convention is good, why don't you ratify it? And if it is not, why would you challenge others in the name of it?

It is no secret that India is not happy with China's growing influence in the Indian Ocean which it jealously guards as its own backyard. Also, the deadly brawl between Chinese and Indian soldiers in the Galwan Valley in the border areas last year made its trust towards China "profoundly disturbed", as Indian Minister of External Affairs S. Jaishankar said. But when New Delhi mimics Washington to tout about "free and open Indo-Pacific", it almost has a black humor effect in that India has more in common with China than with the US when it comes to international maritime law.

For example, China does not accept arbitration on all disputes referred to in Article 298 of the Convention. India has reservations for the same article, too. In its protest to the US,

India said it believed "the convention does not authorise other states to carry out military exercises or manoeuvres, in particular those involving weapons or explosives, without the consent of the coastal state in the Exclusive Economic Zone and on the continental shelf".

Like India, China is equally concerned with foreign military activities in her EEZs. The Chinese spokesmen criticized America's close-in reconnaissance of "high intensity and large scale" from time to time. And China and India are not alone. More than 20 countries in the world have restrictions on foreign military activities in their EEZs to varying degrees.

A key difference though, is that Beijing's response to America's provocations is robust, unlike New Delhi. The United States has conducted FONOPs directed at Indian maritime claims since at least 1992, but "the (Indian) government and navy prefer to remain silent on US operations in the EEZ," the Indian analyst Manoj Joshi wrote, "There is no record of the Indian Navy having attempted to thwart US Navy ships."

But China's response ranges from assured protests, ship-to-ship warnings to even interceptions, particularly when the American ships enter into the 12 nautical mile territorial waters off Chinese rocks and islands in the South China Sea. There was a deadly aircraft collision in 2001 and a number of dangerous encounters at sea.

I once asked a senior American naval officer at an international conference how China and the US might deconflict from accidents that neither wants in the South China Sea. Without hesitation, he said, "The Chinese ship commander can say whatever he wants, but don't sail in my way." This is impossible. If American FONOPs increase in China's EEZ or territorial waters in the South China Sea, a stronger PLA can only become more determined to check them. Therefore at least in theory, it is only a matter of time before the next crisis occurs.

In Kishore Mabubani's book *Has China Won?*, he assumes that by 2050, when the Chinese economy could effectively be twice as large as the American economy, America could withdraw from the Western Pacific Ocean and retreat back into its hemisphere and live seven thousand miles away from China. Maybe. But what would have happened before that? For Beijing, the fundamental problem exists from the very beginning: if the US doesn't want the water to boil, why keep throwing wood into the fire? It is the American ships that have come regularly to China's doorstep and not the other way round.

It is not clear why the US Navy chose to publicize its operation in India's EEZ at a time when Washington badly wants New Delhi to take its side in its competition with China. But it is a useful lesson for India: expediency might sell in the short term, but it seldom pays off in the long run. Worse still, it might backfire.

CHINA AND INDIA SHOULD LOOK BACK TO MOVE FORWARD ON BORDER IMPASSE

First published in *South China Morning Post*, 15 June 2021

One year has passed since a deadly brawl between Chinese and Indian troops in the Galwan Valley in the China-Indian border areas, which resulted in the death of 20 Indian soldiers and four Chinese troops. The aftermath is still being felt today.

Beijing was given the cold shoulder when it offered to help pandemic-devastated India. Such resentment speaks volumes of the frosty relationship, which was described by Indian Minister of External Affairs S. Jaishankar as "profoundly disturbed".

In a few meetings with Indian scholars, I was surprised to learn how they almost invariably believed that the Galwan clash was the result of a planned attack by China. This is impossible. If China has to compete in an America-initiated great power competition, why would it suddenly divert its attention and strength away from that to take on India?

Since the Line of Actual Control (LAC) in the border areas is not demarcated, it is not rare for face-offs between Chinese and Indian troops. According to the Chinese, Indian troops started to unilaterally build roads and bridges in the valley in April 2020, despite Chinese protests.

The deadly incident was dreadful in that it came closest to breaking a decades-old tacit agreement between the two countries not to use force. "In the last 40 years, not a single bullet has been fired because of [the border dispute]," Indian Prime Minister Narendra Modi said in 2017. But the Galwan clash, even though no bullet was fired, has changed the whole atmosphere.

The complexity of the China-India border dispute is daunting. Even the length of the border is not necessarily agreed on. China believes it is 2,000km long, while India believes it is 3,488km. According to New Delhi, Pakistan illegally ceded 5,180 sq km of Indian territory in Pakistan-controlled Kashmir to China in 1963. Both China and India maintained that the valley is their own territory.

To makes things worse, the LAC is not verified. A 1993 agreement between the two governments stipulates that "when necessary, the two sides jointly check and determine the segments of the Line of Actual Control where they have different views as to its alignment". But when is it necessary?

The approaches of China and India seem irreconcilable. China prefers a top-down approach, which is basically a land swap based on mutual accommodation, while India insists on a bottom-up approach of verifying the LAC as the priority.

Beijing suspects that, once the alignment of the LAC is verified, India would take it as a de facto border and refuse further negotiations. Such suspicion is not entirely groundless. India has refused any talks on the position of Arunachal Pradesh, which China holds is part of southern Tibet, citing the reason that Tawang is the birthplace of the 6th Dalai Lama.

How to prevent the dispute from spilling over into a conflict? The way forward is to look back. Between 1993 and 2013, China and India reached five agreements on confidence-building measures at governmental and military levels. This is more than any bilateral agreements China has signed with other countries.

And they are substantive, too, which is impressive. Both reaffirm that they shall reduce or limit their respective military forces along the LAC to minimum levels; major categories of armaments such as combat tanks, infantry combat vehicles, large-calibre guns, surface-to-surface missiles and surface-to-air missiles are to be reduced; large-scale military exercises involving more than one division in the proximity of the LAC shall be avoided; and combat aircraft should not fly within 10km of the LAC.

If only these measures were being implemented. In fact, both sides are strengthening their military presence in the region. This is no surprise in the wake of a crisis. But when the situation cools down, both countries will have to think about how they can best make the border areas peaceful and tranquil.

One way is to resume the joint working group and ask the diplomatic and military experts working under it to find the low-hanging fruit in the confidence-building agreements. New confidence-building measures could also be ushered in. In the wake of the incident, at least 11 rounds of corps-commander-level talks were held, which helped to de-escalate the situation. Such regular meetings of front-line senior military officers should be maintained.

Both sides should also consider establishing hotlines for real-time communication. China has military hotlines with Russia, the United States, South Korea and Vietnam. Reportedly, China and Japan are considering establishing one as well. India often uses its hotline with Pakistan. There is no reason the two immediate neighbours with territorial disputes should not have similar instruments.

Perhaps the boldest step might be to establish buffer zones in the most dangerous areas along the LAC. Without prejudicing their respective positions on the boundary question, this is the most effective way to disengage and prevent conflict. Both sides agree they shall not follow or tail patrols of the other side in areas where there is no common understanding of the LAC.

Building buffer zones is a step further. And it is possible, too. From the mountains around Pangong Lake, a de facto buffer zone has already been established after the mutual withdrawal of troops.

It is ridiculous if, in the 21st century, Beijing and New Delhi are still hijacked by a dispute that is a colonial remnant, not least because apart from this dispute, they have no outstanding problems with each other.

Gone are the days when India said "*Hindi Chini bhai bhai*", which means, in Hindi, "Indians and Chinese are brothers". But China and India have every reason not to become foes. The border issue should not be a perennial curse. The two nuclear neighbours can ill-afford even a conventional war.

SINO-INDIA TIES AND LESSONS FROM THE GALWAN VALLEY BRAWL

First published in *The Straits Times*, 5 August 2020

On June 1, 2018, I was invited to speak as a panelist along with Mr. Ram Madhav, the National General Secretary of the Indian Bharatiya Janata Party, at a special session of the Shangri-La Dialogue entitled "competition and cooperation in China-India relations", right before Indian Prime Minister Narendra Modi's keynote speech in the evening. I was surprised to find how much we both focused on cooperation rather than competition as if the different speeches were written by the same person.

But what happened on 15 June at Galwan Valley along the Line of Actual Control between China and India is another story. As a follow-up to tense military standoffs since April, a brawl involving fists, rocks and wooden clubs between Chinese and Indian soldiers killed 20 Indian servicemen on June 15. The Chinese side didn't report casualties, but maintained that the Galwan Valley was located on the Chinese side of the Line of Actual Control and that it was the Indian border troops that had trespassed into China's territory to build fortifications and barricades which triggered fierce physical conflicts and caused casualties.

The border that led to war between China and India in 1962 has never been demarcated. What lies instead is the Line of Actual Control, a line not verified in terms of alignment. This explains why some areas are perceived by the other side to be its own territory. Quite a few standoffs have occurred since the 1980s. But none more deadly than this one.

It's fair to say both governments have made great efforts in maintaining stability. Since 1993, at least five agreements have been made both at governmental and military levels, more comprehensive than any similar measures that China has made with any other countries. But the challenge is how to maintain stability while the Line of Actual Control is not demarcated.

For example, according to the 1993 Agreement, "In case personnel of one side cross the line of actual control, upon being cautioned by the other side, they shall immediately pull back to their own side of the line of actual control." But how could they pull back from the line of actual control if they don't even know where the line of actual control actually lies?

Such a catch-22 situation is caused because Beijing's approach is kind of top-down, that is, rather than discuss the alignment of the line of actual control, both side should discuss the principles for demarcation followed by eventual and mutual accommodation of the disputed territories, but India's approach is more bottom-up, that is, to verify the line of actual control first before talking about anything else. New Delhi so far has shown no interest in any possible adjustment in the disputed territory that is already under India's control. During negotiations, Beijing found that New Delhi had pushed its own recognized line on the map into the Chinese territory to maximize gains in negotiations.

This is why so far negotiations have failed to produce any substantial results. Still, there is a tacit understanding not to shoot at each other in any circumstances to avoid conflict. As Prime Minister Modi said in an interview to *Hindustan Times* in April, 2018, "Over the last four decades, not a single bullet has been fired across the India-China border".

But if the purpose of not shooting at each other is to avoid casualties that might spill over into a conflict, the deadly brawl at the Galwan Valley has breached the understanding, even without shooting. It is sad to see the two largest armed forces in Asia, in an attempt to avoid shooting, were engaged anyway in fist fighting and rock-throwing of the Stone Age. Those soldiers could very much be the same people who would have walked across the border to join the jolly national day celebration of the other side.

The incident provides a chance of reconsidering what new measures both have to take to deconflict. This might include keeping a safe distance from each other, not building any facilities on territories taken by the other side as its own and establishing hotlines between military commands that are critical in a crisis.

But the incident also raises some bigger issues for both. For Beijing, it may wonder whether the nationalistic Indian government that didn't hesitate to revoke Kashmir's special status and suppress the Indian Muslims at home is becoming more antagonistic, even with China. The faceoff at Doklam in 2017 is a good example. Even if India believes Doklam is Bhutanese rather than Chinese territory as China claims, it should not step into a faceoff with China on foreign territory that lasted for 73 days. When asked what lessons India might learn from the Doklam standoff, then Indian defense minister Arun Jaitley said, "India of 2017 is different from India of 1962." In response, the Chinese spokesman only said briefly, "So is China".

The second question is, to what extent could India become a piece on the chessboard of the United States that has taken China as a primary strategic competitor? Although India is one of the founders of the Non-Aligned Movement, recent years have indeed witnessed India getting ever closer to the United States.

How might the Quad—a grouping of The United States, Japan, Australia and India, evolve? Of course none of them would admit it is against China as is widely speculated, but it is most certainly because of China. At the Raisina Dialogue in New Delhi in January 2019, a Chinese scholar asked the Indian panelists: if indeed the Indian-Pacific is free and open, could the Quad accept China as a member? The response was a burst of laughter from the audience.

Likewise, quite a few Indian "strategists" like to consider that China wants to "encircle" India from the border in the north to the Indian Ocean in the south and perhaps with the help of Pakistan. Such worries, fueled by a concern that China may eventually establish "a string of pearls" of military bases in the Indian Ocean, have grown particularly after the Chinese navy started patrolling in the Gulf of Aden and the Somali Basin for counter-piracy at the end of 2008. Furthermore, there are more people who believe in the western media that a stronger China is becoming more assertive and even coercive, say, in the Taiwan Strait, the South China Sea and along the Sino-India border.

Both are wrong. The first question is easy to answer. China's economy is five times larger than India's. And Chinese military strength is well above that of India, too. There is no need for China to encircle India. Such a belief is but the self-importance of a narcissist in another way. The phrase 'String of Pearls' was particularly popular with Indians. But 15 years after it was first coined in 2005, the world only found one Chinese logistic base in Djibouti. It was built in 2017 in support of its counter-piracy operations in the Indian Ocean.

The second question is a billion dollar question. But a simple answer is that an ever stronger China won't necessarily become assertive or coercive since it is in China's own interests to continue to develop peacefully, like in the last four decades. Being the second largest economy, China is the largest beneficiary of its own peaceful rise and the existing international system which is basically designed by the West led by the United States.

For China, nothing down the road is more important than "the great rejuvenation of the Chinese nation". This, described as "China dream", is written into the Chinese constitution and is projected to be realized in 2049 when PRC celebrates its centenary. It is amazing to see how "China Dream" is similar to the Modi government's "New India" blueprint and how China's "Belt & Road" goes west while India's "Act East" extends to the east. They are poised to meet midway.

The real question is: Can "China dream" be realized peacefully, like its peaceful rise? Whether China could continue to develop peacefully is not entirely up to China. Beijing believes the world is undergoing "profound changes unseen in a century". But even though the future is always uncertain, it won't necessarily suggest that it is more dangerous than the past. A stronger China today is in a better position to shape the environment for the better without the use of force. In the "profound changes unseen in a century", the most profound change is China getting ever stronger.

The brawl in the Galwan Valley is unfortunate especially because it is the most violent in decades. The 21st century is often described as "the Asian century", but it won't be unless the dragon and the elephant figure out how to coexist in the same room.

DOKLAM STAND-OFF WITH CHINA

WILL INDIA LEARN THE RIGHT LESSONS OR PAY AS NEHRU DID?

First published in *South China Morning Post*, 8 January 2018

Before the 20th round of China-India talks at the special representative level got under way in December, a spokeswoman from the Chinese Ministry of Foreign Affairs said: "We should learn lessons from this [Doklam stand-off] incident to avoid any further conflict of this kind." The problem is: what exactly are the lessons?

It won't be easy for China and India to draw some common lessons. Beijing and Delhi disagree even on the length of the border: China maintains it is 2,000km while India holds it is 3,488km, including disputed areas in Jammu and Kashmir and Arunachal Pradesh.

The Line of Actual Control in the border areas is not verified. And, without a clear idea of the alignment, patrolling troops sometimes end up entering an area perceived by the other side to be its own "territory". But the Doklam stand-off was a different story. China and India have no territorial dispute in Doklam, which Beijing believes is Chinese territory and India believes is Bhutanese territory.

Delhi referred to the 2007 India-Bhutan Friendship Treaty as the raison d'être for sending troops into Doklam. But the treaty only states that the two countries "shall cooperate closely ... on issues relating to their national interests". There is no clear invitation from the Bhutanese government to the Indian side for military assistance.

The most talked about reason for Delhi's intervention was its fear that, if China controlled the Siliguri corridor "chicken's neck", a thin strip of land just south of Doklam, it would cut off India from its northeastern states, including Arunachal Pradesh—over which China claims sovereignty. But the incident may have occurred against the backdrop of India's strong sense of hopelessness in the face of China's growing economic and military influence in the Indian Ocean and its hallucination of being encircled by China.

China's "Belt and Road Initiative" has been welcomed by all South Asian countries except India and Bhutan, which doesn't have a diplomatic relationship with Beijing. It contrasts sharply with the failure of Indian Prime Minister Narendra Modi's "neighbourhood first" policy which, despite initial success, has drawn resentment from smaller neighbours against Delhi's "big brother" attitude and interference in their sovereignty.

Contrary to how Indian media described it, the Doklam stand-off was not even a tactical victory for India. Indian soldiers withdrew first from the site, as China insisted. Today, Chinese soldiers remain in Doklam. China made it very clear in the wake of disengagement that its troops would continue to patrol its own territory and road construction would have to be completed. Fresh Chinese road construction activity, although not at the exact location of the face-off, began shortly after.

One huge cost of the Doklam crisis is that the Sino-Indian border will not be the same again, to India's disadvantage. For years, the disputed border has not really been on China's strategic radar, in part because of its emphatic victory against India in the 1962 border war, and in part because China's major strategic concerns lie elsewhere.

The Doklam stand-off provided China with a lesson on reconsidering its security concerns. As a result, China will most probably enhance infrastructure construction along the border. India may follow suit, but it will in no way be comparable in either speed or scale—given China's more robust economy and infrastructure development capabilities.

Another cost is that peace and stability along the Line of Actual Control has become less predictable. Cautious optimism prevailed before the stand-off. Although accusations of intrusions into each other's territories were common, violence was rarely seen. Doklam may well prove to be a turning point. During the stand-off, palpable animosity grew to the extent that border troops threw stones at each other in Ladakh, 1,300km away.

Should another stand-off occur, tension, fuelled by animosity and nationalism on both sides, may threaten to spiral out of control.

Any conflict between the second-largest economy and the fifth-largest-to-be are most unfortunate. But reflecting on the probability of a worst-case scenario in the first place may help prevent that from occurring in the end. The fact that China and the former Soviet Union had a skirmish in 1969 means that war is still possible between two nuclear powers. India's military resources cannot sustain a showdown with China. The Indian army's ammunition reserves during the Doklam stand-off were reportedly only capable of lasting 10 days in a war.

It is up to India to figure out what lessons it might take from the crisis. But if the Indian government draws the conclusion that India "won" and China "lost" at Doklam, such triumphalism, if further blended with adventurism, will cost India dearly, as it did the Nehru government—which carried out its "forward policy" in Chinese territory with the complacency that nothing would happen.

When asked what lessons India might learn from the Doklam stand-off, then Indian defence minister Arun Jaitley said: "India of 2017 is different from India of 1962." In response, a Chinese spokesman said briefly but correctly, "so is China".

CHINA AND INDIA NEED TO TALK, NAVY TO NAVY, TO PREVENT INDIAN OCEAN HOSTILITIES

First published in *South China Morning Post*, 13 August 2018

Should China and India talk about confidence-building in the Indian Ocean? On the face of it, this shouldn't be an issue. The Indian Ocean is not India's ocean. And unlike the Line of Actual Control in the border areas between China and India, which has yet to be verified, the two countries have no maritime disputes in the Indian Ocean.

But the waters in the Indian Ocean are getting warmer, in part because China's full-fledged Maritime Silk Road initiative has attracted India's small neighbours (to whom India usually takes a "big brother" attitude) and in part because China has taken a strong foothold in the Indian Ocean with a military supply station in Djibouti.

In 2014, Sri Lanka allowed a Chinese submarine to dock in Colombo, triggering fierce opposition from India. Then, in 2017, New Delhi was widely believed to have put pressure on Sri Lanka, a sovereign state, to reject a request from China to let a Chinese submarine dock in Colombo for resupply.

Behind India's angst is a fear that the Indian military might lose to the Chinese military on all fronts. Indian strategists traditionally believe that in a possible conflict, India may have a disadvantage along the China-India border, but certainly an advantage over China at sea in the Indian Ocean, given the geographic proximity to India.

But such confidence is waning. According to the International Institute for Strategic Studies, China has built more naval surface ships and submarines since 2000 than India, Japan and South Korea combined. The only question is how soon a Chinese carrier strike group will come into India's "backyard".

The rub is how China might possibly convince India that the Chinese military presence in India's traditional sphere of influence is not necessarily to India's detriment. This will take time, but is not impossible.

China should make clear to India about her legitimate rights and interests in the Indian Ocean. As the largest trading nation in the world, China is rightfully concerned over the safety and security of the sea lanes, since 90 per cent of global trade is maritime trade. Besides, China has huge investment in South Asian countries, including India, and in the rim lands of the Indian Ocean. In 2011 and 2015, Chinese warships helped evacuate Chinese nationals and foreigners from Libya and Yemen.

There is no indication that an ever-stronger Chinese navy wants to challenge India's navy in the Indian Ocean. Given China's sensitivity to its own sovereignty and maritime rights and interests, China can be expected to pay equal regard to those of India.

In fact, China and India have joined others in fighting against piracy in the Gulf of Aden and the Somali Basin since the end of 2008. And after the Indian Navy rescued the Chinese ship MV *Full City* when it came under attack by pirates in 2011, China expressed its thanks.

Maybe the best way for China to mollify India is to raise the fact that China has never attempted to meddle in India's relationship with countries in China's "backyard"—Southeast Asia. Modi's "Act East" policy has led to tremendous Indian trade, investment and ever-closer military exchanges with member states of the Association of Southeast Asian Nations, including joint military drills in the South China Sea. Fifty-five per cent of India's international trade goes through the South China Sea, and like any other maritime trade through the region, it doesn't encounter any interference from China.

Now that confidence-building measures have been introduced to ensure overall peace and tranquility in the border areas, it is time for Beijing and New Delhi to think about such measures at sea. The chances of encounters between Chinese and Indian naval vessels are on the rise, be it in the Indian Ocean or in the South China Sea, therefore mutually recognised rules are needed to reduce the chance of misperception and miscalculation and—in the event of an incident—to prevent it from escalating.

One of the most useful instruments to avoid incidents is the Code for Unplanned Encounters at Sea. This code offers safety procedures, a basic communications plan and manoeuvring instructions when naval ships or naval aircraft of one state meet casually or unexpectedly with a naval ship or naval aircraft of another state.

Both navies have agreed to observe the code, but they haven't discussed how it might be applicable to them to ease a conflict. Furthermore, they need to do familiarisation exercises to make sure sailors follow good seamanship.

Finally, Beijing and New Delhi should make good use of the existing consultation mechanisms between the defence and foreign affairs establishments for regular reviews of the situations at sea.

Should these happen, it will be a sea change for the Chinese navy in that this is the first time the Chinese military practises a code of conduct with others in oceans other than the Pacific. This would be a big step forward for a "world class" navy of tomorrow. And it is no less significant for India, which vows to become a "net security provider" in the Indian Ocean and beyond.

INDIA IS RUNNING OUT OF TIME IN DOKLAM DISPUTE WITH CHINA

First published in *South China Morning Post*, 24 July 2017

The stand-off between Chinese and Indian troops in the Doklam area of the Sikkim section of the China-India border since June 18 shows no sign of abating. The question is: who will blink first?

China maintains that the trespass by Indian border troops into Chinese territory took place at the undisputed Sikkim section, defined by a Sino-British treaty relating to Sikkim and Tibet in 1890. A Chinese spokesman was confident enough to quote what Indian prime minister Jawaharlal Nehru wrote to premier Zhou Enlai on September 26, 1959, that: "There is no dispute over the boundary between Sikkim and Xi Zang, China". The Indian government tactically avoided mentioning the 1890 convention, but stated that China unilaterally violated a 2012 agreement on the tri-junction boundary points between India, China and third countries.

India is at a moral disadvantage for two reasons: first, New Delhi admits that this is not a territorial dispute between India and China. Indian army chief General Bipin Rawat told the *Hindustan Times* on June 27 that there was no incursion into India.

Secondly, even if India believes Doklam belongs to Bhutan, which China disagrees with, it sent in troops without notifying Bhutan—a sovereign state.

The question is how would Bhutan look like a sovereign state to India? It is no secret that India can hardly live in amity with most of its neighbours. Bhutan appears to be the only exception, but the rapprochement was, in part, driven by fear and maintained at the cost of Bhutan's sovereignty—if not dignity. According to the 1949 Treaty of Friendship between India and Bhutan, renegotiated in 2007, Bhutan agreed to be "guided" by India in its external relations, an unusual move for any sovereign state.

To some extent, India has succeeded in making use of the stand-off to stall China-Bhutan relations, which had been steadily progressing. China and Bhutan have held 24 rounds of boundary negotiations since the 1980s. Now the two sides have basic consensus on the situation in the border areas, including the boundary alignment. But Bhutan's statement on June 29 that China has changed the status quo will only make negotiations in the future more complicated.

Bhutan chooses to solve the border dispute before establishing diplomatic ties with China. Such an approach can only look strange, given that most neighbouring countries with territorial disputes have diplomatic relations anyway. It is hard to believe that Bhutan does not want to establish normal relations with its immediate northern neighbour, which is also its largest trading partner and the source of over 80 per cent of its tourists. When Indian President Pranab Mukherjee visited Bhutan in 2014, a front-page article in *The Telegraph* of Calcutta said the state visit was about India's anxiety over China-Bhutan border talks. It recalled that India withdrew subsidies in 2013 to warn Bhutan against normalising relation with China.

The stakes in the Doklam area are high for both China and India. India sees Chinese road construction in Doklam as a change of the status quo, with serious security implications. The worry is that if China controls the narrow Siliguri Corridor— or "chicken's neck"—it will cut India off from its northeastern states, including Arunachal Pradesh, over which China claims sovereignty. China believes that if India's trespassing into the undisputed Sikkim section is not checked, a creepingly assertive India will only create more friction with China in the whole border area.

How long will the stand-off last? Nobody knows. But time is not on the Indian side. After all, Indian soldiers standing on foreign soil cannot be as resolute as the Chinese soldiers determined to drive the intruders away. It appears New Delhi has started to tone down its rhetoric. The Indian army spokesperson was cited as saying that the stand-off this time is not the longest since 1962. India's best hope is that China agrees to withdraw at the same time, to save face. This is unlikely. Beijing maintains that India must withdraw from Chinese soil unconditionally before any talks.

Currently, India is struggling not to be the first to blink, but how long can it hold its gaze?

CHINA'S SUBS IN INDIAN OCEAN NO WORRY FOR INDIA

First published in *China Daily*, 20 July 2015

Whenever a Chinese submarine appears in the waters of the Indian Ocean, India's media react immediately. In June, a leading Indian newspaper said a Chinese conventional Yuan-class submarine had entered Karachi port for replenishment. Indian Navy Chief Admiral Robin Dhowan was quoted as saying his force was "minutely and continuously monitoring" the presence of Chinese warships in the region to ascertain "what challenges they could pose for us".

When a Chinese submarine anchored in Colombo last September, rumors had it that the Indian government had warned the Sri Lankan government that this shouldn't happen again.

This is most unfortunate. Chinese submarines in the Indian Ocean are no secret. In fact, they passed visibly through the Strait of Malacca with other Chinese naval ships sailing to the Gulf of Aden. Some in India argue that anti-piracy doesn't need a submarine and China is practicing long-range deployments of its nuclear and conventional submarines on the pretext of anti-piracy.

However, in 2010, a Dutch submarine under NATO command was deployed to combat piracy off the east coast of Africa. The submarine was used to monitor communications between pirate vessels and their warlords on shore.

But even if Chinese naval ships and submarines appear regularly in the Indian Ocean, so what? Ninety percent of world trade is maritime trade. As the largest trading nation in the world, maritime security in the Indo-Pacific cannot be more important for China. The Chinese navy has to protect its overseas interests such as the safety of personnel and security of property and investment. Much of these are along the rim of the Indian Ocean. As one of the largest oil importers itself, India should have a better understanding, say, of the energy needs of China and China's concern over the sea lanes in the Indian Ocean. Four-fifths of China's oil imports pass through the area.

India alone cannot assure the security of the Indian Ocean, even if it regards the Indian Ocean as its backyard and wishes no one to compete with it there. This is why counter-piracy has involved navies from more than 20 countries, including China and India. China is not jostling with India for strategic influence in the Indian Ocean.

The likelihood of a naval clash between the two navies in the Indian Ocean, as some Indian strategists have suggested, cannot be more hypothetical. If there can't be an all-out war between China and India, how can the Chinese and Indian navies have war at sea? And if the disputed border has remained peaceful for more than half a century, how can anyone prove that the two countries are going to have a war at all?

Since 2000 the Chinese and Indian navies have had quite a few reciprocal visits. These visits are part of the exchanges between the two militaries which mirror the growing understanding, if not rapprochement, between the two sides. The Indian navy is not unfamiliar with Chinese waters: it has sent ships to attend fleet reviews in China in 2009 and 2014. As a token of good will, it has invited the Chinese navy to attend an international fleet review in India in 2016.

Maybe one day the submarines of the two countries could also visit each other? Even the most advanced Chinese conventional submarines have received foreign visitors. If a Chinese submarine's visit to India is still a taboo, probably an Indian submarine can be invited to visit China and dock at a Chinese naval base first.

India, like China, is growing in strength. If growth of strength indeed brings confidence, a stronger India should be broad-minded. The Chinese naval vessels in the international waters of the Indian Ocean should not be taken as a threat. If the Pacific Ocean is big enough to accommodate China and the US, so is the Indian Ocean to accommodate India and China.

HOW CHINA-JAPAN RELATIONS
WILL BENEFIT FROM NEW CRISIS
MANAGEMENT AGREEMENT

First published in *South China Morning Post*, 14 May 2018

Premier Li Keqiang's official visit to Japan last week, the first by a Chinese premier since the Japanese government "bought" the Diaoyu Islands in 2012, saw one of the most significant outcomes—the signing of a crisis management agreement on which the two sides spent 10 years of on-and-off negotiations.

The agreement comes as a huge relief. Officially described as a "maritime and air liaison mechanism between the defence ministries of China and Japan", it is meant to defuse tensions arising out of close encounters between Chinese and Japanese military aircraft and naval vessels. Although there is yet to be an incident, the chances of dangerous encounters are on the rise with each passing year.

In 2013, China announced the establishment of an air defence identification zone, which overlaps slightly with Japan's own zone. While Japan strongly protested against the move, it is not legally prohibited.

An air defence identification zone is an airspace that extends beyond a country's territory to give the country more time to respond to possibly hostile aircraft. Since the first such zone was established by the United States in 1950, over 20 countries in China's periphery, including Japan, South Korea, North Korea, India, Pakistan and Russia, have established their own zones.

Japan's zone, created by the US after the second world war, is much larger than Japanese territory and extends to within 130km of China's coast. Thus, Japan's hysterical reaction to China's much smaller zone was strange.

In recent years, the Chinese navy and air force have stepped up military exercises in the country's exclusive economic zones or on the high seas in the Western Pacific Ocean. These exercises, however legitimate, are becoming dangerous. Whenever Chinese military aircraft and ships conduct training in the East China Sea or transit through the international sea lanes in the Japanese straits to the Western Pacific, they are followed and monitored by Japanese military aircraft and ships, sometimes at close quarters. The Japanese media hype adds to the acrimony, leading in turn to Chinese protests.

This is why a mutually agreed code of conduct is needed.

The mechanism reportedly allows direct communication between two pilots or captains if their warships or aircraft come unexpectedly into proximity. It is obvious that such frontline direct contact is crucial to avoid accidents. These tactical communications will be further supported by annual reviews at the higher strategic-level meetings of the defence agencies.

The beauty of the mechanism is that it applies to all situations regardless of location. This is extremely important for China and Japan because their overlapping air defence zones cover the disputed islands which China call "Diaoyu" and Japan call "Senkaku". Therefore, if one country tries to exclude the islands from the mechanism, it means that country insists on its sovereignty over the islands, which would only invite protests from the other country. Thanks to the political wisdom of both sides, the mechanism does not specify geographic scope.

In so doing, it comes into line with the 2014 Code for Unplanned Encounters at Sea approved by 21 navies, including China and Japan, in the Western Pacific, which doesn't specify geographical scope. Instead, with a host of operational and communication procedures, it calls for the maintenance of safe speed and safe distance between naval vessels of different nations to avoid collisions.

The consequences of a possible collision of Chinese and Japanese aircraft or ships would be more catastrophic than might be imagined, given the mistrust between the two countries—due to a troubled history with Japan on China's part and fear of an ever stronger China on Japan's part.

When a Chinese J-8 and an American EP-3 collided in 2001, the two governments showed great flexibility in spite of harsh rhetoric. The American crews were released in 11 days after the US government apologised twice to the Chinese government. Sadly, such flexibility and resilience are not present in China-Japan relations. An incident at sea or in the air may easily inflame relations between the two countries.

Even compared with similar arrangements in the region, such an agreement is long overdue. For example, China has established a series of confidence-building measures with some major powers and neighbouring countries, but noticeably not with Japan. China now has direct telephonic communications with the US, Russia, North Korea and Vietnam.

The Sino-Indian border is managed through such concrete measures as not stalking the patrolling troops of the other side and holding border meetings at regular intervals.

The Chinese and US militaries set up a maritime consultative mechanism as early as 1998. In 2014, the two sides agreed to notify each other of major military activities and observe the rules of behaviour for unplanned air and maritime encounters. China and Vietnam have signed an agreement on principles guiding maritime issues and another agreement on joint patrol between the two navies in the Beibu Gulf. There have even been dialogues between the navies of China and Indonesia, a non-claimant in the South China Sea dispute.

The fact that such a badly needed but not very sophisticated mechanism took 10 years to negotiate reflects how vulnerable China-Japan relations are. This is most unfortunate, not only because they are close neighbours, but also because a persistent less-than-amicable relationship between the two powers would have a negative impact upon the whole region.

In comparison, although the China-US relationship is far from smooth, it is supported by dozens of different mechanisms at various levels, coupled with frequent exchanges and confidence-building measures. China and the US have had a series of joint exercises aimed at avoiding accidents during close encounters. Even China and the Association of Southeast Asian Nations have announced an exercise for unplanned encounters to be held by the end of the year.

The China-Japan maritime and air liaison mechanism is a good beginning, but precisely because it is so hard-won, the best way to avoid incidents is to embark on the next important step—more frank exchanges at all levels and drills on good seamanship and airmanship.

US, DPRK MUST HOLD TALKS BEFORE IT'S TOO LATE

First published in *China Daily*, 18 April 2017

Among the possible, but the least desirable, responses to the Democratic People's Republic of Korea's nuclear and missile tests (although its last one on Sunday was a failure) could be a preemptive strike by the United States. There is no guarantee, though, that the presumed US strike would be precise enough to wipe out all nuclear facilities in the DPRK before Pyongyang launches a nuclear attack in retaliation.

If that happens, the DPRK won't wait to fire its nuclear missiles, and thousands of howitzers and rocket launchers deployed along the 38th parallel Military Demarcation Line into the Republic of Korea. No defense systems, including the US Terminal High Altitude Area Defense anti-missile system, will be able to fend off such a shower of artillery shells. And Pyongyang's missiles could destroy Seoul and even hit Japan.

Since 2006 the United Nations has passed a number of resolutions imposing sanctions on the DPRK. The ever-tougher sanctions have crippled the DPRK's economy but failed to rein in its nuclear and missile programs, revealing an intrinsic loophole in any economic sanctions: they are meant to harm the leader or ruling party but, instead, always end up hurting innocent citizens first and most, leaving the real target to suffer the effects, if at all, last.

Talks are the only way to resolve the issue. But how can the US be persuaded to hold talks with the DPRK? Having fired 59 Tomahawk missiles on Syria on April 6, the Donald Trump administration seems anxious to use force to showcase its political resolve. The US doesn't want to be seen as being blackmailed by a country it has labeled a "rogue state". That is why Washington has rejected all proposals by Pyongyang for bilateral talks. Besides, it believes that the Six-Party Talks were useful only in giving the DPRK the time needed to develop nuclear weapons.

But time is running short. DPRK leader Kim Jong-un said in his New Year's Day address that his country was close to testing an intercontinental ballistic missile which would bring the US within its range. Although Pyongyang has suffered many failures in missile tests (like the one on Sunday), if it can, even theoretically, develop medium range missiles, it can build ICBMs one day. In fact, Pyongyang exhibited two ICBM-sized canisters for the first time at a parade on April 15, the 105th anniversary of the birth of DPRK founder Kim Il-sung.

But why would the DPRK want to develop nuclear weapons? A short answer is: for survival. Its worst fear is a preemptive strike by the US to effect a regime change. Unless attacked, there is no reason why the DPRK should launch a suicidal attack against the ROK. Pyongyang is desperately trying to develop ICBMs because it believes, however wrongly, that if it possesses missiles that can reach the US, its survival would be assured.

Therefore, the first step toward denuclearizing the Korean Peninsula is to reduce the importance of nuclear weapons for the DPRK. For that to happen, the US needs to convince Kim Jong-un that it has no plans to launch a strike on or engineer a regime change in the DPRK. Indeed, US Secretary of State Rex Tillerson has said the Trump administration has no plans for engineering a regime change in Pyongyang, but apparently the deployment of US warships in the region sends a different signal.

That is why China's proposal of suspending hostilities is worth considering. Beijing has suggested that as a first step, the DPRK freeze its nuclear program if, in exchange, the US halts its military exercises with the ROK. The proposal is balanced in that it doesn't ask for any unilateral concession. It saves face for both sides because it is mutually conditional. Above all, it will help cool down the high tensions on the peninsula.

If the US can come to agreements with Cuba and Iran, why can't it do so with the DPRK? A dialogue, be it formal or informal, be it bilateral between the US and the DPRK or multilateral among all stakeholders, as suggested by Beijing, looks like the most affordable price the US can pay when compared with the sad eventuality of the DPRK possessing ICBMs that could reach the US mainland.

THAAD SEEKING A HARE IN A HEN'S COOP

First published in *China Daily*, 12 March 2016

Let's face it, in the wake of the Democratic People's Republic of Korea's fourth nuclear test and launching of a satellite, it is difficult to dissuade the Republic of Korea from taking measures to beef up its military for self-defense. But deployment of the Terminal High-Altitude Area Defense system is not a good option.

The THAAD is an anti-ballistic missile system of the United States Army designed to shoot down short, medium and intermediate range ballistic missiles in their terminal phase using a hit-to-kill approach. The Korean Peninsula is only 1,100 km long and Seoul only 40 km from the demilitarized zone. So most, if not all, of the DPRK's missiles targeting the ROK can only be short-range ballistic missiles with a maximum range of 1,000 km.

The threats from the DPRK to the ROK are not primarily the short-range missiles of the DPRK, just like the THAAD is not primarily designed, if at all, to shoot down missiles flying at low altitude. The missile threat from Pyongyang to Seoul essentially comes from KN-02, Hwasong-5 and Hwasong-6 with ranges from 160 km to 500 km.

If the DPRK missiles carry conventional warheads, the threats from them would not be greater than the Scuds that were fired sporadically and inaccurately by Iraq into Israel during the Gulf War. And the ROK already has Pac-2 deployed against them. Also, it has been developing its own missile-defense system. Besides, the ROK military, thanks to its alliance with the US military, won't wait to fire back until the DPRK fires all its missiles.

Contrary to what the ROK's Ministry of Foreign Affairs has said, a scenario of the DPRK launching a nuclear attack against the ROK is next to impossible in the near future.

Even if the DPRK has short-range nuclear missiles, as it is claiming now, a successful nuclear strike by Pyongyang and successful interception by THAAD from the ROK would still cause unbearable damage to both sides because of the geological proximity between the DPRK and ROK, and the lingering radioactive dust would make either side's victory meaningless.

Such short-range missiles don't appear to be a priority for the DPRK. Its focus is on improving the capability of its nuclear bombs as demonstrated by its fourth underground nuclear test on January 6, and developing intercontinental ballistic missile capability as shown by its satellite launch on February 7. Most probably the DPRK launched the satellite to test the range of the missiles - whether they would reach continental US, in order to create maximum panic among Americans and thus increase its bargaining chips.

The real lethal weapons of the DPRK are its long-range artillery pieces—Koksan 170 mm howitzers and 240 mm multiple rocket launchers—that are capable of bombarding Seoul, a city of over 10 million people. Indeed it is not rare to hear from Pyongyang how its massive and preemptive strike could turn Seoul into "a sea of fire". Admittedly, no defense systems including the THAAD would be able to fend off a shower of artillery shells in such a doomsday scenario.

Citing the need to defend against the DPRK's missiles with the THAAD is either a sign of paranoia that has hijacked people in the ROK or a deliberate ploy of security populism to pacify people or, more likely, a bit of both. But it comes at financial and political costs, too.

Financially one battery of the THAAD system consists of a launcher, interceptors, a fire control and communications unit, and an AN/TPY-2 radar, and costs about $1 billion. This is more than the $866.5 million the ROK government paid in 2014 for the 28,500 US troops stationed on its soil.

ROK defense officials have said at least two THAAD batteries are needed to thwart missile attacks from the DPRK. But who is going to pay, Washington or Seoul? Why the US if the ROK is a free rider? And why the ROK if it is, as claimed, meant more for the protection of US troops? This has been a hot-button issue in recent years.

Politically, the installation of THAAD in the ROK will surely be taken by the DPRK as provocation and accelerate the vicious cycle of action versus reaction.

Moreover, the move has already drawn strong protests from China, which believes THAAD, if deployed, will be integrated into the US missile defense network in East Asia and affect its security interests. Russia, too, believes it will destabilize the strategic equilibrium in the region.

The deployment of THAAD on the Korean Peninsula can only set a bad example, of how anger and angst can overpower and replace rational response. It is like seeking a hare in a hen's coop.

HOW TO AVOID A CHINA-JAPAN CONFLICT AT SEA

First published in *China Daily*, 18 June 2016

On June 9, Japan's Defense Ministry said a Japanese naval destroyer had detected a Chinese frigate entering the waters near Diaoyu Islands (which the Japanese call Senkaku Islands) and lodged a serious protest with the Chinese ambassador to Tokyo. And Japan's Chief Cabinet Secretary Yoshihide Suga said it was the first time a Chinese naval ship had entered the waters contiguous with the island chain.

The truth became clear gradually: the Japanese destroyer had actually seen a Russian flotilla, and it was only after the Japanese ship ventured into the waters off the island chain (apparently to check out the Russian flotilla) that a Chinese frigate did so to monitor the Japanese vessel.

For Japan, a Chinese naval vessel entering the waters off the Diaoyu Islands indicates that Beijing probably wants to take new risks to escalate tensions in the already volatile waters. Japanese media say that if China's actions go unchecked, its naval vessels will one day enter the 12-nautical-mile territorial sea of the islands, leading to a showdown between Beijing and Tokyo.

This assumption is irrational.

First, the entire world knows China and Japan have a sovereignty dispute over the Diaoyu Islands. The Japanese government, however, insists there is no dispute, although it would like to hold talks with China on the issue. This is self-contradictory: if there is no dispute, why should the two sides talk?

Besides, since the Diaoyu Islands are Chinese territory, China could say the Japanese destroyer entered their contiguous waters and claim it to be an unprecedented incident that needs to be addressed seriously.

Second, the incident reveals Japan's double standard when it comes to freedom of navigation. Even if Tokyo believes the Chinese frigate entered "Japan's contiguous zone", no international or Japanese law prohibits it. Also, Japanese EP-3 and P-3C aircraft have entered China's undisputed exclusive economic zone east of Zhoushan Islands in Zhejiang province for surveillance and reconnaissance from time to time, but when Chinese flotillas pass through the international sealanes in any Japanese strait, Japan's Self-Defense Force sends ships and aircraft to track and monitor their movements.

Third, until the June 9 incident only Chinese and Japanese coast guard, not naval, ships patrolled the waters off Diaoyu Islands. If that is a tacit understanding between the two sides to not escalate tensions, then Japan violated it on June 9. The Chinese frigate did enter the contiguous zone of the islands, but it only followed the Japanese destroyer as a counter-measure. This shows Japan, not China, has "unilaterally heightened tensions".

However neither China nor Japan wants such an incident to snowball into a full-blown conflict. So what should be done?

To begin with, China and Japan should follow the Code for Unplanned Encounters at Sea, which both have pledged to honor. CUES has a set of communication and operational procedures, for example, to prevent a ship from getting too close to vessels in formation, and avoid aiming guns, missiles or fire control radars at other vessels or aircraft it encounters.

The Chinese navy has held quite a few exercises with foreign navies, including the US Navy, on how to fully observe CUES. The Chinese and Japanese navies could do the same to build confidence and familiarize themselves with the procedures.

China and Japan should also expedite negotiations to establish the China-Japan Maritime and Air Liaison Mechanism, which, among others, would allow direct communication between captains of ships and pilots of aircraft during "close encounters". The procedures of the mechanism would be similar to those in CUES and the Rules of Behavior for Safety of Maritime and Air Encounter concluded between China and the US.

The Japanese government's decision in 2012 to "nationalize" the Diaoyu Islands caused suspension of the negotiations. Since the Chinese and Japanese "Air Defense Identification Zones" to a large extent overlap with each other and they cover the same islands that both claim as their own territories, the issue has become more complex.

It remains to be seen how the two sides will use their wisdom to move between principle and flexibility, in order to chart out a new and fruitful path, because the June 9 incident is a chilly reminder that the issue has to be settled before it is too late.

CHINA-JAPAN TALKS A SILVER LINING

First published in *China Daily*, 15 January 2015

This is really good news in the beginning of the year: China and Japan resumed talks over a maritime liaison mechanism in Tokyo on January 12. Both sides agreed to initiate the mechanism at the earliest possible date.

This restarts an aborted effort. In June 2012, the Chinese and Japanese militaries almost concluded the mechanism, with the aim to avoid dangerous situations at sea. But the consultation couldn't continue since the Japanese government decided to "nationalize" the Diaoyu Islands in September. Before Japanese Prime Minister Shinzo Abe came to Beijing for the APEC summit in November, 2014, the two governments reached a four-point consensus in which crisis management is stressed. This paved the way for renewed talks.

The danger of misunderstandings and even miscalculations between the second and the third largest economies in the world, however unfortunate, is a worrisome reality. In the last two years, tensions have risen in the waters off the disputed islands. China and Japan now have large overlapping Air Defense Identification

Zones (ADIZ). The chances of dangerous encounters of military aircraft have grown considerably.

Japan's reconnaissance and surveillance in China's exclusive economic zone (EEZ) in the East China Sea, sometimes in tandem with its American ally, have intensified. The Chinese naval flotillas' transit passages through Japanese straits to the West Pacific, although in line with international laws, would always invite Japanese tracking and probing.

In spite of such uncertainty, there is no institutionalized mechanism of crisis management between the two countries, let alone a hotline between the two militaries, such as the one between China and the United States, and the one between China and Russia.

This is why the mechanism is so badly needed. It is the vital first step in defusing a potential crisis. According to Japanese media, the mechanism will include meetings at different levels, direct communication links between military leaders, and most important of all, direct talks between the captains of ships and the pilots of aircraft in close encounters.

Of all China's foreign relations, the Sino-Japanese relationship, although important, is nevertheless the most vulnerable one because of historical issues and territorial disputes. Such vulnerability is most acutely felt in the defense sector. Exchanges between Chinese PLA and Japanese Self Defense Forces are never in full swing. Whenever the relations at government level turned sour, the military-to-military relations came to a stop.

Since the Diaoyu Islands dispute flared up, the two militaries have had virtually no interaction. Nobody can imagine what will ensue should a Chinese and Japanese military aircraft collide in the ADIZ, as happened between a Chinese J-8 and an American EP-3 in 2001.

It remains to be seen how the overall relationship might improve after President Xi Jinping shook hands with Prime

Minister Abe at the APEC meetings in Beijing. But the ongoing consultation gives people hope that the free fall in the Sino-Japanese relationship has been arrested and things are moving in the right direction.

RELATIONSHIP WITH THAILAND IS MODEL CHINA WANTS FOR AUSTRALIA

First published in *The Australian*, 19 January 2018

When Malcolm Turnbull suddenly switched from English to Mandarin to invoke a Chinese slogan—a famous saying of Mao Zedong—that "the Australian people stand up", it clearly showed that something had gone wrong between Australia and China. The day before, December 8, Beijing had expressed shock after the Prime Minister singled out China as a focus for concern and cited "disturbing reports" about Chinese influence in Australian national affairs.

Canberra's angst over a rising China and a decaying Pax Americana is not even thinly disguised. In November, Australia's first foreign policy white paper in 14 years claimed that "the US has been the dominant power in our region throughout Australia's post-Second World War history. Today, China is challenging America's position."

While underlining the US's diminished share of the world economy and contrasting that with China's rapid increase, Canberra vows anyway that Australia will continue strongly to support US global leadership.

This is easier said than done. For the first time in history, Australia's largest trading partner is not its biggest ally. If balancing is a delicate art, Australia has never tried to learn it. Be it Gallipoli, Vietnam or Iraq, to name just a few, Australia has always fought other people's wars. As a junior ally that was called upon, it didn't seem to bother with thinking independently.

Will Australia fight against China as an American ally? This probably is the ultimate question that both China and the US want answered, but that Australia wishes away. In 2014, former US secretary of state Hillary Clinton warned the Abbott government that even more trade with China "makes you dependent, to an extent that can undermine your freedom of movement and your sovereignty, economic and political".

In China's view, the thought is absurd that China could become a country that Australia should stand up against.

The two countries are disconnected geographically. China's major strategic concerns are not in the South Pacific (even China's Maritime Silk Road is not in the direction of Australia).

China accounts for 32 per cent of Australia's goods exports and the two sides have military exchanges that both Beijing and Canberra are keen to enhance. Above all, China never asks Australia, or in fact any countries in the region, to make a choice between China and the US, because China, too, has a huge stake in maintaining a healthy China-US relationship.

Beijing holds that "the Pacific is big enough to accommodate both China and the US".

In the white paper, Canberra expresses concern over the "unprecedented pace and scale of China's activities" in the South China Sea. But no international laws forbid land reclamation or regulate the pace and scale of land reclamation. Two-thirds of Australia's exports pass through the South China Sea—most of them on their way to China. Not a single example can be cited to prove that China is affecting freedom of navigation by any means.

Canberra maintains that the ruling of the Permanent Court of Arbitration is final and binding on both China and The Philippines, but as early as 2006, well before The Philippines took the case to international tribunal in 2013, China informed the UN that it wouldn't accept arbitration on territorial sovereignty referred to in article 298 of the convention.

Beijing is watching Canberra and looking for two signposts.

First, does Australia want to join with the US to become a player in the South China Sea? The Australian military has drastically intensified its military activities there in recent years. From the beginning of September a group of warships spent three months in a series of military exercises called "Indo-Pacific Endeavour" in the South China Sea. This is the biggest Australian task group deployment since the early 1980s.

Secondly, will Australia allow the US to use its soil for further military activities?

No matter how hard Canberra tried to whitewash its decision of allowing 2,500 American marines to be deployed in Darwin, Beijing cannot be easily convinced that this is not part of an American rebalancing against China.

If either of these two happens, it will bring major changes to the China-Australia relationship.

For China, an ideal Australia would be like Thailand, an American ally that is always friendly towards China, and not like Japan, another American ally that jealously guards against any move that might bring China and the US closer together.

For the Turnbull government, it won't be easy to facilitate the peaceful coexistence of China and the US, but it is certainly a more comfortable prospect than tiptoeing between the two.

ASEAN AND THE FINE ART OF BALANCING TIES WITH CHINA AND US

First published in *The Straits Times*, 27 September 2019

The first ASEAN-US Maritime Exercise from 2-6 September is neither politically sensitive nor technically sophisticated. Held in undisputed international waters in the Gulf of Thailand and South China Sea, the US Navy deployed "suspicious boats" in a mock exercise to help its ASEAN counterparts search, verify, and prosecute the boats.

The real significance of the exercise lies in balancing two previous joint maritime exercises ASEAN had with China in October 2018 and April 2019. In the April exercise, ASEAN insisted on using "Southeast Asian Countries" instead of "ASEAN" to indicate that ASEAN only had one exercise with China before conducting a similar exercise with the US.

Such caution is not as ludicrous as it seems. The strategy of the ten Southeast Asian countries is to engage regional powers through the "ASEAN Way", sometimes this compromises on quality in ASEAN-led activities: too many meetings including meetings to discuss how to reduce these meetings; endless declarations that are politically right but hard to remember;

delegates reading pre-prepared statements but refraining from substantive discussions ...

But such a strategy of "comfortable to all", described by Kishore Mahbubani as a crab's move—taking two steps forward, one step backwards and one step sideways, has worked over time. Rather than being sandwiched by regional powers, the regional organization has thrived and even assumed a driver's role in regional security architecture. Countries such as China, the United States, Russia, India, Japan, ROK and Australia all agree to ASEAN's "centrality". Quite a few mechanisms in the region are led by ASEAN, such as East Asia Summit, ASEAN Regional Forum, ASEAN+3 and ADMMPLUS. What an achievement!

Admittedly, ASEAN's centrality is a bit like the emperor's gown. The regional powers nod to it because of mistrust and rivalry among themselves. However, it pales almost immediately with the release of the U.S. free and open Indo-Pacific (FOIP) strategy. FOIP highlights great power competition—specifically between the US and China, as the overarching feature in the region. Amid such rivalry, the regional grouping risks sliding into irrelevance. The ASEAN Outlook on the Indo-Pacific (AOIP), released after more than a year of deliberation, is ASEAN's latest attempt to come back into the spotlight. The key words are "inclusivity" and, of course, "ASEAN centrality".

At the Shangri-la Dialogue this year, Singapore Prime Minister Lee Hsien Loong warned impressively that small states should actively avoid taking sides, but also not be pressured to take sides. Who is more likely to pressure ASEAN to take sides? China doesn't have military alliances with any countries, the US does and George W. Bush pronounced after 9/11: either you are with us or against us.

If China-US competition intensifies, the US is likely to pressurize Singapore, Thailand, Vietnam and the Philippines to station American military ships and aircraft. The US Secretary of Defense Mark T. Esper suggested during an Asian tour in August that the Pentagon would like to deploy intermediate-range American missiles in Asia within months. The question is: where? The answer is: wherever they are, Beijing won't hesitate to "take countermeasures", as it has warned.

It remains to be seen how ASEAN can catch two hares - China's Belt & Road initiative and America's Indo-Pacific strategy, at same time. The former is infrastructure building with strategic ramifications while the latter appears more like a strategy that has yet to be stuffed with substance. The Belt & Road initiative has been accepted by some ASEAN countries to varying degrees. Reading between the lines of AOIP, one feels that ASEAN, apart from adopting the term "Indo-Pacific", has kept a safe distance from America's Indo-Pacific strategy by emphasizing inclusiveness which is devoid of any intention to contain China.

If balancing is a delicate art, then the key to balance is neutrality or more precisely, impartiality. This is easier said than done when it comes to the South China Sea issue. Because some ASEAN countries are also claimants, it is certainly tempting for them to stir non-claimants in to standing up against China. From Beijing's view of point, the risk of ASEAN being hijacked by these claimants cannot be discounted. In 2015, former ASEAN Secretary General Le Luong Minh told *The Manila Times* that China's claim in South China Sea based on the nine-dash-line was illegal, and that the happenings in the South China Sea were further complicating the situation and impeding the development of the ASEAN community. For Beijing, he talked more like a Vietnamese rather than ASEAN Secretary General.

Another test is ASEAN's attitude towards the US Navy's FONOPs in the South China Sea. The Americans believe they are challenges to China's excessive claims while the Chinese believe they are deliberate provocations to her sovereignty.

In spite of rules of behavior for unplanned encounters at sea, Chinese and American warships narrowly missed a collision by a distance of 40 meters in 2018. What might happen next? As Malaysian Prime Minister Mahathir Mohamad told the *South China Morning Post*, "Someday, somebody might make some mistakes and there will be a fight, some ships will be lost, and there might be a war."

Will China and the US split further into another cold war? It is not entirely impossible since GPC (great power competition) has become the Pentagon's newest acronym. Nevertheless, there is a simple ASEAN metric of assessing the relations between Beijing and Washington. If ASEAN's centrality is still talked about; and if ASEAN is still doing joint exercises with China and the US alternately, it means ASEAN still doesn't have to choose sides, and, to everyone's relief, Beijing and Washington haven't come to a showdown yet.

A US INDO-PACIFIC STRATEGY THAT ISOLATES CHINA IS SMALL-MINDED AND DANGEROUS

First published in *South China Morning Post*, 27 June 2019

Ever since US President Donald Trump spoke of a "free and open Indo-Pacific" at the Asia-Pacific Economic Cooperation forum in Vietnam in 2017, the question has been: what is this, a vision, an initiative or a strategy? With the release of the Pentagon's "Indo-Pacific Strategy Report" on June 1, the dust has finally settled.

In the introduction to the paper, then acting defence secretary Patrick M. Shanahan frames "geopolitical rivalry between free and repressive world order visions" as the US's main security concern and singles out China as a country which "seeks to reorder the region to its advantage".

One doesn't need to read the full text to know this strategy has China at its core. In what proved a litmus test, a Chinese scholar attending the Raisina Dialogue, a geopolitical conference in New Delhi, in January 2018, asked Indian panellists: if the Indo-Pacific is indeed free and open, could "the Quad"—the United

States, India, Japan and Australia—accept China as a member? The response from the audience was a burst of laughter.

Here lies the dilemma of the Indo-Pacific strategy: if the geopolitical strategy is aimed at China, few countries would support it overtly; if it isn't, why bother to develop such a strategy at all? As relations between China and the US deteriorate, all countries vowing not to take sides are actually taking sides in a smart way, that is, on issues rather than choosing partners.

For example, Asean countries are widely believed to rely on China economically and on the US militarily. Even the members of the Association of Southeast Asian Nations that want to see a US military presence in the region have joined China's Asian Infrastructure Investment Bank and are open to using Huawei's 5G technology.

The Quad might look like an anti-China club, but this is precisely the perception the US's supposedly "like-minded" allies, India, Japan and Australia, are resisting. None of them—not even the US—wishes to jeopardise its bilateral ties with China for the gains of the other three.

Trump's indiscriminate stress on fairness and reciprocity in trade with allies, and actions like ending the US's preferential trade treatment for India, will only succeed in making New Delhi feel more like-minded with Beijing, at least for a while.

In the South China Sea, although US allies such as Britain, France, Australia and Japan have sailed warships in the name of freedom of navigation, they are careful not to join the US Navy in sailing through the waters within 12 nautical miles of China's rocks and islands.

Today's global China can hardly be straitjacketed in America's Indo-Pacific strategy. The Trump administration's whole-of-government efforts to disrupt international rules for "America first" have made the US look more revisionist than any other country. According to a Gallup report in February, the median global approval rating of China's leadership across more than 130 countries and areas was 34 per cent, higher than the US's 31 per cent.

If one compares China's Belt and Road Initiative with America's Indo-Pacific strategy, it is interesting to note China is modest enough to describe its far-reaching infrastructure programme as an "initiative", while the US calls its much smaller vision for the Indo-Pacific a "strategy". The Belt and Road Initiative is open to all, but it is hard to imagine an Indo-Pacific strategy that accepts China.

When *Financial Times* columnist Martin Wolf writes of a "looming 100-year US-China conflict", perhaps he is thinking of the Hundred Years' War fought from 1337 to 1453 between England and France over succession to the French throne. He rightly characterises the China-US relationship as "manageable, albeit vexed", though it is rhetorical to suggest competition between the two powers will become "perpetual conflict".

An ageing China cannot overtake the US economy. And the competition won't necessarily last 100 years; a more likely time frame is 30 years, for two turning points can be expected in the first half of the 21st century. The first is around 2030–2035 when China, as widely anticipated, overtakes the US in terms of GDP. The second is around mid-century, when the People's Republic of China announces on the centennial of its founding that it has achieved its most cherished objective, "the great rejuvenation of the Chinese nation".

Each turning point should add to America's humility and help it realise it is not as exceptional and indispensable as it believes and has tried to make others believe. The US is but an equal member of the international community, like the rest of us.

This suggests the upcoming 10–15 years will be the most difficult time. Although the Trump administration said in its National Security Strategy report in 2017 that competition "does not always mean hostility", it actually mostly does.

Competition is never healthy, the only question is how to make it less ugly.

Currently, competition between the two countries ranges from trade to hi-tech. Although neither side wants a military conflict, America's much enhanced "freedom of navigation operations" in the South China Sea have increased the risk of miscalculation.

It is not clear if the adoption of the Indo-Pacific strategy signals the start of US retrenchment, at least militarily. If this is the case, the consequences will be felt around the world and people's perception of the US's inevitable decline will only deepen. Since the Obama administration, the US's strategic shift to the Asia-Pacific has made even the North Atlantic Treaty Organisation, the world's largest military alliance, feel neglected.

But if the most significant change in the US's Indo-Pacific strategy so far is the renaming of the US Pacific Command as the US Indo-Pacific Command, it sure looks like old wine in an old bottle with a new label.

NEUTRALITY IS KEY TO
ASEAN CENTRALITY

First published in *China Daily*, 24 March 2015

ASEAN Secretary General Le Luong Minh recently told *The Manila Times* that China's claim in the South China Sea based on the nine-dash-line was illegal, and that the happenings in the South China Sea were further complicating the situation and impeding the development of the ASEAN community. His remarks were immediately criticized by China's Foreign Ministry.

Le wears two hats, one as a senior Vietnamese diplomat and the other as ASEAN secretary general. It is not difficult to imagine what a Vietnamese diplomat might say about Vietnam's maritime dispute with China (especially to a newspaper in Manila, which too has a dispute with Beijing). But what if he made the remark as ASEAN secretary general? If his remark represents the views of ASEAN, then it should be seen as a new and dangerous move.

China and ASEAN relations are not bad. China and ASEAN signed the Treaty of Amity and Cooperation in Southeast Asia in 2003. The first decade of this century was hailed as a golden decade for the two sides, and China is now ASEAN's largest trading partner. But behind the glitter, there is the shadow of the South China Sea disputes. After all, China has disputes with four ASEAN member states.

So, when Le talks about the situation in the South China Sea and the ASEAN community, he apparently makes a link between the two. According to the 2002 China-ASEAN Declaration, the disputes in the South China Sea should be resolved by "sovereign states directly concerned", that is, China, Vietnam, the Philippines, Malaysia and Brunei. If the disputes are taken as an issue between China and ASEAN, the only conclusion would be that ASEAN is being hijacked by some countries, such as Vietnam and the Philippines which are at the forefront of challenging China.

The question is: Could ASEAN be hijacked? The answer: It is not impossible. The Philippines is trying to move the international maritime tribunal against China. When Manila launched such a surprise attack on Beijing, it didn't consult ASEAN. Although ASEAN knew fully well that such a move violates the 2002 China-ASEAN Declaration that "the parties concerned undertake to resolve their territorial and jurisdictional disputes through friendly consultations and negotiations", ASEAN chose to remain silent.

ASEAN is thriving and its influence has widened. It has announced that it would establish the ASEAN community by the end of 2015. Irrespective of the huge economic disparities among its members and the dissimilarity with the European Union, the process of integration is impressive. If indeed the art of survival of small nations is to maintain the right balance with major powers, then it makes sense for them to hang together to, at least, look big.

So far ASEAN has carefully maintained such a balance among regional powers. The strategy is to engage through the "ASEAN Way", which emphasizes comfort to all. No haste. No worry. I am only happy if you are merry. After two decades, such a strategy has worked. Major regional powers such as China, Russia, Japan, Australia and the United States all agree to ASEAN's centrality in regional security.

But ASEAN must exercise moderation. If balance is the key, then the key to balance is neutrality. And if ASEAN loses its neutrality, its centrality would be doomed. For ASEAN, neutrality means not only being impartial in its relations with major powers, but also being neutral in the disputes some of its members have with China, because this is what it has committed to. No matter how eagerly ASEAN wishes to conclude a Code of Conduct on the South China Sea with China, the precondition is that China has to have confidence in the Southeast Asian bloc.

It is noteworthy how the Chinese Foreign Ministry spokesman tried to differentiate Le from ASEAN when he said ASEAN is not owned by a particular country. This apparently means China doesn't wish to spoil its relations with ASEAN even after the ASEAN secretary general made the inappropriate remark.

NORTH KOREA'S SUPPORT FOR RUSSIA WON'T BE A GAME CHANGER IN UKRAINE

First published in *South China Morning Post*, 7 November 2024

It won't be long before the world finds out if Ukrainian officials were right in saying on Monday that their forces had fired at North Korean soldiers in combat for the first time since they were deployed by Russia to its western Kursk region. Despite denials from Pyongyang, US Secretary of State Antony Blinken said on October 31 that as many as 8,000 North Korean troops were in Russia's Kursk region and expected to enter combat.

Are North Korean troops a game changer in the grinding Russo-Ukrainian conflict? I think not. Russia has already gained the upper hand on the battlefield against the Ukrainians, who are weary, short of ammunition and outnumbered. So while the dispatch of North Korean troops may be useful, its significance would primarily be political.

Besides, such added strength from Pyongyang would not help Moscow claim a quick victory. It would, however, most certainly make the United States and Europe more determined to provide extra aid to Ukraine, which has been asking for heavy attack weapons to strike deeper into Russia.

On the European battlefield, the only beneficiary, it seems, is North Korea, a latecomer. First, the unprecedented public relations effort of sending its soldiers to faraway Europe is guaranteed to attract global attention. Isolated and sanctioned, North Korea sees itself as a nuclear power—what it wants most is to be treated as a nuclearised "normal" country. For that to happen, it needs to get the world to sit up so it can attempt to break international sanctions.

North Korea's periodic missile launches and recent declaration that South Korea was now a "hostile" state are in the same vein. Pyongyang's campaign is not to launch a suicidal attack against South Korea one day; it is to draw attention, especially from the US. Unlike Donald Trump, who spent time dealing with Pyongyang when he was president between 2017 and 2021, the Biden administration's attitude has been more one of strategic negligence.

Second, North Korea can benefit from much-needed supplies of food, fuel and other material from Russia even as its soldiers gain their first combat experience since the Korean War. The Korean People's Army, 1.28 million strong, can find out how effective their munitions and short-range ballistic missiles are on a battlefield. They will learn how to deal with drones and counter-attacks. North Korean soldiers will be combat-hardened.

So, the longer the war, the better it is for North Korean leader Kim Jong-un. Even if he has decided to send 12,000 troops to Russia, as alleged, it is still less than 1 per cent of North Korea's standing military. This would not tip the military balance on the Korean peninsula unfavourably for Pyongyang.

And, in return for a reportedly steady flow of munitions and soldiers to a most important ally, Kim is hoping for access to Russia's higher-end military technology, especially regarding satellites, missiles and submarines. As long as North Korean soldiers fight alongside Russian soldiers, Kim is counting on Russian President Vladimir Putin feeling obliged to give something back.

Meanwhile, it remains to be seen how the US administration will turn the screw on North Korea. The Yoon government in South Korea believes in ensuring peace through "overwhelming force" and will almost certainly feel it has to respond more forcefully to the North now, and possibly provide more economic and humanitarian support to Ukraine, even direct military assistance. Ironically, we could see the two Koreas fighting as proxies in Europe after years of detente on the peninsula.

China's attitude so far is a measured calmness. There is good reason for Beijing not to say too much when North Korea has flatly denied its involvement in the war in Ukraine. Beijing will not be happy to see the situation in Europe become more complex.

Arguing that Beijing is losing its influence over Pyongyang to Moscow is simplistic. However close Moscow and Pyongyang might become militarily, North Korea's economic dependence on China remains the foundation of its survival.

In fact, the presence of North Korean troops on a European battlefield will bolster China's influence over the Korean Peninsula as Beijing faces calls from Washington and European capitals to use its leverage on Pyongyang. Blinken last week said the US and China have had "a robust conversation" where China was urged to "use the influence that they have to work to curb these activities".

Much has been said about the alliance between the US, South Korea and Japan battling an axis represented by China, Russia and North Korea. This is bunkum. China, Russia and North Korea do not necessarily see the world through the same prism. North Korea will welcome a new cold war and Russia believes we are already in one—but China is opposed to a new cold war.

At first glance, North Korea's treaties with China in 1961 and Russia this year look similar when it comes to how one party should render military aid to the other when attacked. In reality, military interactions between Beijing and Pyongyang are scant. For instance, Chinese and Russian militaries have joint exercises practically every year but one would be hard-pressed to think of the last time Beijing and Pyongyang organised a joint military drill.

The treaty alliance between China and North Korea made over 60 years ago is only useful when Beijing wants it to be. Even if Russia and North Korea are happy to see the competition between China and the US intensify, as long as Beijing believes that its relationship with Washington is still manageable, the treaty will remain dormant, making a Beijing-Moscow-Pyongyang alliance impossible. On the grand chessboard, North Korea may look like a spoiler—but it is not capable of being a game changer.

CRISIS MANAGEMENT NEEDED BETWEEN CHINA AND JAPAN

First published in China-US Focus, 19 November 2014

The world collectively sighed with relief after President Xi Jinping and Prime Minister Shinzo Abe shook hands with solemn, even glum, expressions. The nerve-wracking ordeal that has rumbled on for the last two years seems over—at least for the time being.

Thanks to the "four points consensus," which owes its genesis in part to the clandestine visit of ex-Prime Minister Yasuo Fukuda, the two heads of state finally met and talked during APEC in Beijing. A wild guess is that both sides have reached a tacit understanding that Prime Minister Abe will not visit Yasukuni Shrine again during his tenure. Without directly mentioning the island dispute and history issue, the four points leave leeway for each side to interpret its own positions without compromising dignity to the other side. The good thing is, it signals a green light that is long overdue.

Sadly, one of the distinctive features of Sino-Japanese relations is vulnerability, especially compared to Sino-American relations that are characterized by more resilience. The impact of a crisis between China and the U.S.—be it U.S. arms sales to Taiwan, or U.S.-led bombardment of the Chinese Embassy in the former Yugoslavia—normally won't last for more than one year. But the relations between China and Japan have been frosty for over two years since Japan decided to "nationalize" the Diaoyu Islands. Whenever there is a problem in the Sino-U.S. relationship, there are many "firemen" from both sides who come to the rescue whereas in the Sino-Japanese relationship, a strong sense of hopelessness is often felt at all levels.

Such vulnerability is most obviously felt in the security field. The exchanges between the Chinese PLA and Japanese Self Defense Forces are always low profile and never in full swing. Whenever relations at government levels turn sour, military-to-military relations also come to a stop. In the last two years, the two militaries have had virtually no interaction, but sailors and pilots have had dangerous encounters at sea and in the air. Nobody can imagine what will ensue should a Chinese and Japanese military aircraft collide in the Air Defense Identification Zone (ADIZ), like what happened between a Chinese J-8 and an American EP-3 in 2001. An alarmist Japanese media has portrayed various scenarios of China and Japan going to war.

What is most needed between China and Japan today? The answer is not trade, but crisis management.

Crisis management starts with confidence building measures. In June 2012, the two militaries agreed to establish a maritime liaison mechanism. According to senior Japanese officials, all the details, including annual meetings at different levels and direct telephone links between captains of ships and pilots of aircraft were already discussed. However these details were abandoned because of the island dispute. The good news is that both governments have agreed to restart negotiations. Hopefully an agreement will come out soon.

Another stabilizer is the Code for Unplanned Encounters at Sea (CUES). In April 2014, twenty-one countries including China and Japan unanimously voted for CUES. The CUES provides various maritime procedures to avoid collisions with vessels in formation; maintain safe speeds and distance; and refrain from aerobatics and simulated attacks in the vicinity of ships encountered. Given that both Chinese and Japanese vessels are operating in the same waters off the disputed islands, it is critically important that the officers and sailors are fully aware of these rules and procedures. It is even necessary for them to conduct joint familiarization-oriented exercises on CUES, as the Chinese and the US navies did during RIMPAC 2014 exercise.

Crisis at sea is relatively easier to manage. The more dangerous area is in the air. China, Japan and the U.S. all have military aircraft that occasionally get too close to each other in the air. Due to geographic proximity, the ADIZs of China, Japan and the Republic of Korea overlap with one another. During President Obama's visit, China and the U.S. announced the conclusion of a memorandum on the rules of behavior for air and maritime encounters. Could China, Japan and the R.O.K. follow suit and conclude a similar agreement? This is not impossible, given that the Chinese military spokesman expressed in November 2013 that in the overlapping areas, China and Japan should coordinate and make joint efforts to maintain flight security. But this will not be possible if Japan still refuses to recognize the legitimacy of China's ADIZ.

How will the future look after President Xi shook hands with Prime Minister Abe? There is no clear answer. But China and Japan should steer the course clear of one thing: war. China and Japan will never fight again. This is the oath sworn and repeated by the leaders of the two countries. It should be remembered as a principle above all. It cannot afford to be an empty slogan.

DUTERTE'S GENIAL TONE ON THE SOUTH CHINA SEA IS JUST ONE OF MANY SIGNS OF WARMER SINO-ASEAN TIES

First published in *South China Morning Post*, 14 November 2016

Rodrigo Duterte is a godsend to China. The Philippine president's description of the international tribunal's verdict on maritime features in the South China Sea as "a piece of paper with four corners" could not sound more similar to former Chinese state councillor Dai Bingguo's early description of the verdict, as "a piece of waste paper".

For his first official visit abroad, Duterte chose Beijing, and reportedly harvested not only contracts worth US$9 billion in soft loans and US$15 billion in economic deals, but also an agreement from China to allow Filipinos to fish again near Huangyan Island, or Scarborough Shoal. What else can he achieve?

In a way, a man like Duterte was bound to emerge. His predecessor, Benigno Aquino, drove the Sino-Philippine relationship into a dead end. So, all Duterte needs to do is walk in the opposite direction.

Similar things are happening with some other claimants from Asean. Vietnam allowed three Chinese warships to visit Cam Ranh Bay in October. During his visit to Beijing in early November, Malaysian Prime Minister Najib Razak described the South China Sea issue as an issue among friends.

If that sounds diplomatic, his announcement that Malaysia would buy China-built littoral mission ships certainly speaks volumes about what Malaysia really thinks of China. No country would buy weapons from a potential enemy and, likewise, no country would sell weapons to a potential enemy.

Apparently, neither Malaysia nor China believes a military conflict between them is possible.

So, the pendulum is swinging back to the starting point – the 2002 joint declaration by China and the Association of Southeast Asian Nations on the Conduct of Parties in the South China Sea.

That obliges sovereign states directly concerned, that is, claimants, to resolve the South China Sea dispute through friendly consultations and negotiations. For China, Aquino's sudden and unilateral initiation of arbitration in 2013 was a clear breach of the China-Asean declaration.

China and countries in Southeast Asia are more than close neighbours. Today, China is Asean's largest trading partner and the 10-nation regional bloc is China's third-largest trading partner. Such ties, along with political, cultural and even military connections, are too important to be hijacked by any territorial disputes between China and four other claimants.

In fact most, if not all, Asean countries have territorial disputes of one kind or another with their neighbours. The Philippines has resolved the delimitation of the exclusive economic zone boundary in the Mindanao and Celebes seas with Indonesia following 20 years of negotiations. But it still has disputes with China, Malaysia and Vietnam. In the Asean

Charter, a whole chapter is dedicated to settlement of disputes among member states.

There has never been Asean solidarity against China. The only thing that can split China and Asean is a big "if"—that is, if the relationship between China and the US turns irreversibly hostile and Asean has to choose sides.

When American ships and aircraft conduct sailings and overflights in the South China Sea in the name of freedom of navigation, it also challenges the rights and interests of other littoral states. As a matter of policy, both Vietnam and Malaysia, like China, oppose foreign military activities in their exclusive economic zones.

So what will the South China Sea look like in the near future? The situation will most probably remain calm. Rather as if nothing has happened, neither China nor Asean will mention the arbitral verdict. Both have pledged to speed up negotiations on the code of conduct in the South China Sea which will be a follow-up to, and see further progress on, the joint declaration on the Conduct of Parties in the South China Sea. They have agreed to adopt a host of operational and communication procedures to avoid unplanned encounters by ships and aircraft in the South China Sea. A joint exercise on this is earmarked for next year. China has also expressed its readiness to set up a hotline with Asean.

The only question, however, is how the US Navy might continue its provocative sailings and overflights in the South China Sea under the Donald Trump administration. Making predictions is a dangerous business, but a safe bet is that, even if things continue as before, no littoral state or any of America's allies will join in, in spite of the lip service from some of them; and Chinese naval ships and aircraft will definitely follow.

The USS *Decatur's* sailing into waters around the Xisha, or Paracel, Islands on October 21 looks like a frustrated US eager to make a comeback amid China and the Philippines' recent rapprochement and the obvious decline in the US-Filipino relationship. In that case, it would be very easy for China to point out who the real troublemaker is in the South China Sea.

AVOIDING INCIDENTS AT SEA

First published in China-US Focus, 26 April 2014

At the 14th Western Pacific Naval Symposium held in Tsingtao on 22 April, 21 member states unanimously voted for a new edition of *The Code for Unplanned Encounters at Sea* (CUES).

First proposed by New Zealand in 1994, CUES offers safety procedures, a basic communications plan and maneuvering instructions when naval ships or naval aircraft of one state meet casually or unexpectedly with a naval ship or naval aircraft of another state. It provides procedures to avoid collision, such as: not getting too close to any vessels in formation; maintain safe speed and distance; avoid simulation of attacks by aiming guns, missiles, and fire control radars in the direction of vessels or aircraft encountered; and refrain from aerobatics and simulated attacks in the vicinity of ships encountered.

In the Western Pacific, unplanned encounters between naval ships and naval aircraft of different states are not rare at all, especially between Chinese ships and naval aircraft with those from the US and Japan. The US ships, aircraft and UAVs come to China's EEZ all the year round for close-in reconnaissance despite China's security concerns. When the Chinese naval flotilla navigates through the high seas in the Japanese straits to the western Pacific Ocean, the Japanese Maritime Self-Defense Force will almost certainly send ships to follow and will send aircraft to hover over the Chinese flotilla for surveillance and information gathering.

Such encounters without commonly accepted communications and procedures could be lethally dangerous. In March 2009, there was a standoff between Chinese ships and the USS *Impeccable*. In December 2013, a collision was narrowly avoided between the USS *Cowpens* and a Chinese amphibious landing ship trying to stop the US ship from getting too close to the Chinese aircraft carrier *Liaoning*. Worst of all, a Chinese J-8 jet fighter collided with a US EP-3 reconnaissance plane off Hainan Island in April 2001. These incidents invariably triggered immediate tit-for-tat accusations of the other side and in the last case, caused a free fall in bilateral relations.

In the Western Pacific, crisis management mechanisms as a whole are insufficient. The military hotline between China and the US is used only at top military levels. It is responsive rather than proactive. China and the US signed a Military Maritime Consultative Agreement as early as 1998, but the meetings are only held three times a year. In 2012, China and Japan failed to negotiate a maritime liaison mechanism as a result of the Japanese government's attempt to "nationalize" the disputed islands. The ASEAN countries and China issued a joint declaration on the Conduct of Parties in the South China Sea in 2002, but the principles are difficult to observe without a road map to follow through.

And this is why the CUES is so important. In the late 1960s, there were similar incidents between forces of the U.S. Navy and the Soviet Navy. Ships deliberately bumped one another, and both ships and aircraft made threatening movements against those of the other side. In March 1968 the United States proposed talks on preventing such incidents from becoming more serious. The *US-Soviet Incidents at Sea Agreement,* with many of the articles similar to those of the CUES, was signed during the Moscow summit meeting in 1972. In 1985, Secretary of the Navy John Lehman observed that the frequency of incidents was "way down from what it was in the 1960s and early 1970s."

The CUES is all the more significant in that it involves most of the Asian countries that have territorial disputes with one another at sea. It is an exaggeration to assert, as some people have argued, that currently there is a naval race in the western pacific, but it is true that the waters in the western pacific are getting more volatile with an increasing number of ships and aircraft from different nations. Unplanned encounters at sea could become more frequent.

The CUES is particularly important for China and the US. The two countries still have differences in interpreting international maritime law, such as the definition of freedom of navigation and the legal status of military ships in the EEZ of another country, but the two militaries have agreed to work towards establishing a notification mechanism for major military activities and setting-up of rules of behavior on military, air, and maritime activities. Before such agreements can finally be reached, if that is even possible, CUES will help reduce miscalculations and the chance of an incident at sea, and—in the event that one occurred—to prevent it from escalating.

The 2014 Tsingtao edition of the CUES is a win-win option for all, thanks to the joint efforts of 21 member states. This is a fine moment. Naval officers, mariners and airmen could relax and celebrate with a glass of Tsingtao beer.

3

SAFEGUARDING CHINA'S INTERESTS

THE FUTURE OF THE PLA

First published in *Foreign Policy*, 6 August 2019

In October 2017, at the 19th National Congress of the Communist Party, Chinese President Xi Jinping unveiled an ambitious road map for the future of the Chinese People's Liberation Army (PLA), the largest armed force in the world. According to his report, the PLA is to become mechanized by 2020, modernized by 2035, and world-class by the mid-21st century.

By some measures, the PLA already is one of the world's strongest militaries. Despite Western prohibitions on trading arms and military technology with China, the Chinese defense industry has been able to produce some of the world's most sophisticated weapons systems and platforms. According to a report by the International Institute for Strategic Studies, "since 2000, China has built more submarines, destroyers, frigates and corvettes than Japan, South Korea and India combined." China's first domestically designed aircraft carrier took a mere five years to be built. And when finished in 2020, the restructuring of the PLA, including downsizing by 300,000 service members, will make the 2 million-strong PLA leaner but mightier. Meanwhile, the application of artificial intelligence, which China vows to lead by 2030, will speed up the development of an "intelligent military."

How China uses its military strength matters, all the more so because it is widely expected to overtake the United States to become the largest economy within the next two decades. Yes, China still has territorial disputes with some countries, but a major power looks beyond its borders into the horizon. And a strong PLA will be more ready than ever to protect China's overseas interests and shoulder international obligations.

One doesn't need to see "Made in China" on the bottom of every product to know that China's interests are already global. As the world's largest trading nation and exporter, its overseas interests include, among other things, the safety and security of more than 1 million Chinese nationals working overseas, 140 million Chinese traveling abroad every year, some 40,000 Chinese enterprises around the globe, and overseas property and investment of $7 trillion. Needless to say, it is impossible to protect all these interests through military means, but a forward military presence is useful. For example, in February 2011, the Chinese frigate *Xuzhou* was sent from the Gulf of Aden into the waters off Libya to stand guard while 35,860 Chinese nationals and 2,103 foreign contract workers and citizens were evacuated as violence spread in that country.

Further, there is no better way for China to demonstrate its peaceful rise than by helping with global governance as a responsible power. Unlike in the past when Beijing talked about "establishing a fair and reasonable new international political and economic order," which was a thinly veiled dismissal of the current order, Chinese leaders now admit that the country benefits from the existing international order and vows to be a "builder of world peace, a contributor to global development, and a guardian of international order."

To that end, ever since the dawn of the 21st century, China has gradually given up some time-honored defense policies—such as prohibitions on joining military exercises with foreign countries, on stationing of troops overseas, and on establishing military bases overseas—to meet the changed situation. In 2002, China held a joint military drill with Kyrgyzstan. In 2017, China built a logistics supply station in Djibouti. Currently, 2,519 Chinese peacekeepers are working in the Democratic Republic of the Congo, Lebanon, Mali, South Sudan, and Sudan. The PLA Navy has been patrolling and escorting vessels in the Gulf of Aden and the Somali Basin for the last 10 years.

The PLA has also demonstrated openness through frequent visits, consultations and dialogues, joint military exercises, and humanitarian missions. In 2010, a PLA medical team of uniformed service members landed in earthquake-torn Haiti, a country with which China has no diplomatic ties, to help with search and rescue. From 2014 to 2015, around 500 military medical personnel were sent to Liberia and Sierra Leone to assist in fighting against Ebola. The PLA is also a regular participant in regional security-related forums, including the Shanghai Cooperation Organisation, the ASEAN Regional Forum, ADMM-Plus, and the Shangri-La Dialogue, to name just a few.

Wherever possible, the PLA has been trying to blend China's national interests with its international responsibilities. For example, the PLA Navy did not just protect Chinese ships transiting the Gulf of Aden and Somali Basin but also the ships of the U.N. World Food Program. Among the over 6,600 ships that the Chinese naval task forces have escorted since January 2009, over half of them were foreign ships. When three Chinese naval ships evacuated 613 Chinese nationals from war-torn Yemen, they also helped in withdrawing almost 280 foreigners from 15 countries.

China has demonstrated its potential in leading peacekeeping missions. For one, it is the largest troop-contributing country among the five permanent members of the U.N. Security Council and the second-largest financial contributor to peacekeeping. Beyond that, China could become a consistent source of so-called "enabling units"—the engineering, transport, communications, and aviation troops that the U.N. most needs—and also a consistent provider of equipment to many troop-contributing countries that can afford to buy only Chinese-made equipment.

In short, China has set a pattern for global security governance that places primacy on addressing nontraditional threats, such as piracy, terrorism, and natural disasters, and exercises restraint in the use of force and adherence to international cooperation. The U.N. mandates provide the PLA legitimacy as well as moral grounds for its operations. They also highlight the authority of China as one of the permanent members of the U.N. Security Council. In so doing, the PLA clearly draws a line in the sand, helping rather than policing the world.

The benefit of restraint in the use of force is obvious, especially for the protection of civilians in armed conflicts. According to the U.N., 65 million people were displaced from their homes in 2015. In the Middle East, the seemingly uninterrupted humanitarian disasters and exodus of refugees since the Iraq War in 2003 were in no small way spurred by outside invasions and military strikes. It is difficult to imagine that the PLA would be involved in such a debacle.

Rather, it will more likely engage in multilateral efforts that will bring it closer to its partners. The progress in Chinese-NATO military relations illustrates how common tasks can bind unlikely partners together. The relationship was once frosty. China saw NATO as a relic of the Cold War, and NATO's bombing of the Chinese Embassy in Belgrade in 1999, which the United States described as "mistaken," only made the relationship worse. But things started to change after a historic handshake between the PLA naval task force commander and a NATO commander in the waters off Somalia in 2009. This heralded the PLA and NATO's regular exchanges of visits since 2010. In 2015, the 21st Task Force of the PLA Navy and NATO's Combined Task Force 508 even had a joint drill in the Gulf of Aden.

Should China play a bigger role in global security governance, its leaders have to think carefully about how to deal with the United States. The Trump administration has labeled China as its primary strategic competitor. It remains to be seen how Chinese-U.S. relations might change over the next few years, but it is premature—even irresponsible—to conclude that the relationship is bound to become hostile. China's economic success could be attractive to other developing countries, but there is no indication that the Chinese government is trying to sell its success story as a way to spread its ideology and challenge the international order.

Can China and the United States leave behind their differences and make the world safer? If the two most powerful countries on Earth can manage not to sleepwalk into war, then the world is already much safer. Former U.S. President Barack Obama described China as "free riding" on the U.S.-backed global order. However wrong he was, his statement at least indicated that his administration wanted China to share some responsibility, say, in Afghanistan. So far, given U.S. regulations, the United States and China are most easily able to cooperate on humanitarian issues such as counterpiracy and disaster relief.

China today has two dilemmas: It doesn't harbor any ambition of policing the world, but it does have major overseas interests; China wishes to shoulder more international obligations, but the PLA has yet to build sufficient capabilities to fulfill them. As a result, Beijing's involvement in global security governance is selective, but it is incremental and most certainly irreversible.

Contrary to U.S. President Donald Trump's threat in 2017 to cut U.N. funding, China set up a 10-year China-U.N. peace and development fund of $1 billion in 2015.

When China celebrates the centenary of the founding of the People's Republic in 2049, it will presumably be prosperous, cosmopolitan, and enlightened. It will also be much more connected with the rest of the world and shouldering greater responsibility for the well-being of others. Chinese leaders used to say that China would fulfill its due international obligations in line with its national strength; since China's national strength is bound to grow, it can certainly contribute more to the world.

WHAT'S DRIVING CHINA'S PUSH TO BUILD UP ITS NAVAL POWER

First published in *The Straits Times*, 25 November 2021

What best represents China's military strength? The answer: its navy.

At the end of last year, the Chinese People's Liberation Army Navy had 360 battle ships, surpassing the United States Navy's 297 vessels. And that gap is expected to widen in the coming years by most estimates.

To paraphrase former Czech president Vaclav Havel, China's naval build-up has happened so rapidly that the world has not had time to be astonished. In the 1974 Battle of the Paracel Islands between the naval forces of China and South Vietnam, the four Chinese warships combined were dwarfed in size by the largest ship of the South Vietnamese navy.

Unlike the PLA Army, which fought to establish the People's Republic of China, and the PLA Air Force, which fought in the Korean War, the least war-tested PLA Navy now stands at the forefront, simply because today, all threats to China come from the sea.

Be it in the Taiwan Strait or in the South China Sea, the PLA Navy has to prepare for possible conflict with the US Navy. US President Joe Biden has said that US rivalry with China will take the form of "extreme competition" rather than conflict; the problem is, if competition is already extreme, it is probably like tiptoeing on a tightrope that is only one step away from conflict.

The US is said to maintain a policy of strategic ambiguity on Taiwan. But since the Trump administration, the US government has been salami-slicing away that ambiguity in diverse ways, including enhancing exchanges with Taipei, sending warships to sail provocatively through the Taiwan Strait and deploying its servicemen in Taiwan to help with military training.

It is not surprising then that Beijing is compelled to increase pressure on the island by sending more military aircraft to fly near Taiwan. In a meeting with US Secretary of State Antony Blinken on October 31, Chinese Foreign Minister Wang Yi warned the US not to pursue "a fake One China policy".

Should conflict erupt in the Taiwan Strait, China cannot afford to lose in a war defending its sovereignty. And it probably won't.

With Taiwan just 160km away from the mainland, the US military will find itself at an asymmetrical disadvantage from the start. It is questionable if its Asian allies will readily allow Americans to use their military bases to turn their homelands into battlefields.

In the South China Sea, the stronger the PLA Navy becomes, the less likely it will bear with American provocations on China's doorstep on a regular basis.

Unlike in the Cold War where there were clearly defined spheres of influence which allowed the two superpowers to deconflict, there are no buffer zones between the two navies in the South China Sea. Accidents and close calls have occurred, including a deadly collision of two military aircraft in 2001.

The so-called Hainan incident - which led to the death of a Chinese pilot and the detention of the crew of the American reconnaissance plane on the island - was resolved peacefully only after the US ambassador sent a letter in which he said "very sorry" two times.

The situation is far different now. The mutual distrust and lack of strategic consensus between Beijing and Washington leave hardly any room for "common-sense guardrails", in the words of President Biden during his recent virtual meeting with China's President Xi Jinping. De-escalation in a similar crisis will be far more challenging than in the past. The few confidence-building measures in place are only tactical arrangements which can hardly resolve strategic distrust.

Can US count on Aukus and Quad?

Both China and the US have vowed to avoid a new Cold War. But if the rivalry is set to intensify, can the US count on its alliances in the Indo-Pacific?

Admit it or not, Aukus, the trilateral security pact between Australia, the United Kingdom and the US, and the Quad, involving the US, India, Japan and Australia, are Washington's thinly veiled dual approaches in containing China.

The question is, how useful are they? If the first of Australia's eight nuclear-powered submarines under Aukus is not going to be delivered before 2040, the subs will not become serious game changers. Instead, they will haunt Canberra for decades to come. Australia has no nuclear industry. If these subs have to be maintained from time to time in another country, Australia's submarine capability cannot be sovereign.

The Quad could grow into anything other than a useful military coalition against China.

Fundamentally, are the dialogue partners prepared to sacrifice their bilateral ties, especially the huge economic interactions, with China, to go on a hostile footing?

Militarily, Australia, a Quad member, is already part of Aukus. Japan, while not an Aukus member, is supportive of it. Therefore India's attitude towards China is critical to the survival and growth of the Quad. But even if India is not happy with the PLA Navy's presence in the Indian Ocean, it can hardly protest because all the military operations of the PLA in the Indian Ocean are humanitarian in nature, be it counter-piracy or disaster relief. There is no likelihood of a military clash between the PLA Navy and the Indian Navy in the Indian Ocean like the one in the land border areas between the two armies in June last year.

Blue water navy for a global China

If it is only for resolving the Taiwan and South China Sea issues, the PLA Navy does not need so many ships. As about 90 per cent of global trade travels by sea, the security of the international sea lanes cannot be more crucial for China, the largest trading nation and the largest crude oil importer in the world. A global China calls for a blue water Chinese navy.

This is why since December 2008, China has been sending flotillas to patrol the waters off the Horn of Africa. Almost half of the merchant ships escorted by Chinese task forces are foreign ships, a demonstration of how China tries to combine its own interests with its international responsibilities. In the Gulf of Aden, China has been working in tandem with the North Atlantic Treaty Organisation, the European Union and the Combined Maritime Forces led by the US and other countries.

China aims to build a world-class military by 2049 when it celebrates its centenary. This is entirely possible as the PLA today is already seen by many as second only to the US military and there are still more than two decades to go. The question is how China might use its military that will one day be on par with the US military. Of course, a stronger PLA will be better positioned to protect China's sovereignty.

But unlike the US, China has no missionary zeal to intervene in the domestic affairs of others or to police the world. Despite speculation that China would establish a "string of pearls", that is, a series of overseas military bases across the Indian Ocean, China has so far built only a logistical supply base in Djibouti in 2017. It has no appetite to repeat the imperial overstretch that has, arguably, caused America's decline.

So, in a snapshot, how is one to view the PLA Navy?

Since 2010, *Peace Ark*, the hospital ship of the Chinese navy, has sailed around the world providing medical treatment to hundreds of thousands of people. This is in step with Admiral Zheng He's voyages in the Indian Ocean 600 years ago when his unrivalled fleet invoked more admiration than awe.

If China's biggest destroyer *Nanchang* represents the hard power of China, then *Peace Ark* sends another message: the heft of a great power lies in humility.

DEFENSE SPENDING REFLECTS CHINA'S OPTIMISM ABOUT REGIONAL SECURITY

First published in China-US Focus, 5 April 2016

China's announcement of a 7.8% military budget increase in 2016 surprised not only foreigners, but also Chinese. Many in China had anticipated a sharp increase even up to 20%, given the tension in the South China Sea and the assumed necessity for China to beef up further its military buildup.

The first explanation for the lowest budget growth since 2011 is that China still adheres to its principle that military development has to go in tandem with national economic development. The 6.9% GDP growth rate of 2015 was the lowest in the last 25 years, therefore the military budget for 2016 has to be readjusted. This reminds people of what Chinese leader Deng Xiaoping said to the PLA in 1985, that "we have to bear with the situation for a few years. The real modernization of the weaponry of the military is only possible when the nation's economy has laid a sound basis".

Another possible reason is the budget reflects the confidence of the Chinese government in the PLA and Chinese defense industry. The gap between the PLA and its Western counterparts is closing rather than widening, thanks to sustained R&D investment over the years and PLA's strenuous catch-up efforts. The two military parades in Tiananmen Square in 2009 and 2015 demonstrate how the PLA has advanced in a short period of six years. Simply put, a stronger PLA now can afford to have a smaller defense budget.

Most importantly, the budget speaks volumes of how Beijing views the region with optimism. Defense expenditure is the best indicator of a country's security assessment. China's lower budget reflects her belief that in spite of the spread of terrorism, exodus of refugees, tension on the Korean Peninsula and in the South China Sea, the world is not in a state of disorder, as is asserted in the western media.

The budget also underlines China's confidence in the Sino-American relationship. "Whoever becomes American president, the overall situation of the furtherance of the Sino-American relationship will not change", said Premier Li Keqiang recently in a press conference. Currently the US is doing salami-slicing intrusion into the Chinese islands and reefs in the name of freedom of navigation. But it will be irresponsible to conclude the US wants to challenge China even at the risk of a war. The budget reveals, almost inadvertently, that China doesn't believe a showdown with the US is inevitable.

Optimism matters, especially in hard times. China's peaceful rise so far is not only because of its successful management of crises, such as Taiwan ex-leader Chen Shui-bian's call for a referendum on independence in Taiwan, NATO's bombing of the Chinese embassy in Yugoslavia, and a Chinese aircraft's collision with American aircraft above China's EEZ, but also a result of correctly assessing the situation in the first place. Ever since China's reform began in the late 1970s, one thing remains unchanged, i.e., optimism in spite of the vicissitudes. China maintains that peace and development are still the major trends of the times. China no longer believes, as it did before, that a world war was inevitable.

China is getting closer to center stage in the world, and how China perceives the world matters all the more. If China believes its security environment has worsened to the degree it has to greatly increase its military budget, it will set its relationship with others in a dangerous situation. However if China remains confident and doesn't necessarily react to perceived threats with military means, it becomes a stabilizer in the region. Therefore it is critically important that China continues to believe in what it has said, that peace and development are still the major trends of the times; that its Period of Strategic Opportunity can last well beyond 2020; that the Sino-American relationship is not a relationship between two enemies.

China's 2016 defense budget raises eyebrows. However, it would be premature to conclude that this is a turning point that the Chinese military expenditure will irreversibly come down. PLA's J-20 fighter, Dongfeng-41 ICBM, jumbo airlifting plane and the second aircraft carrier in the pipeline, just to name a few, will not be small money spenders. The PLA's increased operations overseas are no less a consideration. The PLA's planned 300,000 personnel cut will also burn through a lot of money. Above all, China still has to sustain a high defense budget, even without a double-digit increase, to reach its prescribed goal of modernizing the PLA by mid-century. China can be sanguine about the future, but it has to prepare for the worst in case its optimism for the future is proven wrong.

HOW A 'VULNERABLE' CHINA CAN RESOLVE ITS INDIAN OCEAN SECURITY DILEMMA

First published in *South China Morning Post*, 29 December 2023

In response to the Houthis attacking ships in the Red Sea bound for Israel, the US recently announced Operation Prosperity Guardian, a security initiative that initially included more than 20 countries, such as Bahrain, Britain, Canada, France, Italy, the Netherlands, Norway, Seychelles and Spain.

But France, Italy and Spain have reportedly dropped out of the US-led coalition and many others decline to acknowledge their involvement. That Bahrain is the only Arab state offering public support speaks volumes about the Arab world's apathy towards the US—if not resentment of America's strong support for Israel's war on Hamas.

This does not look like the "broadest possible" coalition US Secretary of State Antony Blinken has called for. Unlike the counter-piracy initiative in the Gulf of Aden, none of America's Asian allies and partners appear to have turned up this time.

It is strange to hear the US call on Beijing to play "a constructive role in trying to prevent those attacks from taking place". China should have no such influence on the Houthis, a Yemeni militant group. Instead, should the Chinese naval flotilla operating in the Bab-el-Mandeb strait join the American-led operation, it would compromise China's position on the Israel-Hamas war and endanger Chinese ships.

If there are still Chinese merchant ships sailing through the Red Sea, the Chinese flotilla should sail northwards to protect them, of course. Chinese warships have previously sailed from the Gulf of Aden to evacuate Chinese nationals from war-torn Libya, Yemen and Sudan.

But should Chinese warships strike back against a Houthi attack on a Chinese vessel, China could be drawn into a conflict in a most volatile region. The Houthis have vowed to continue their Red Sea attacks until Israel stops fighting in Gaza.

So how can the People's Liberation Army (PLA) protect China's overseas interests without becoming embroiled in regional conflicts?

China is the world's top trader and most of the international trade goes by sea. About 12 per cent of global trade passes through the Red Sea with about 62 per cent of China's oil and 17 per cent of its natural gas imports going through the Malacca Strait and South China Sea.

Reuters journalist Greg Torode recently argued that the Indian Ocean could be Beijing's Achilles' heel in a Taiwan war because, apart from its Djibouti military base, China has no air cover from land or sea for Indian Ocean naval deployments. This brings to mind two myths about China's Indian Ocean strategy: the " string of pearls" and so-called Malacca dilemma.

The first, a 2004 hypothesis, assumed that China aimed to build a string of military bases and monitoring stations to support its naval outreach up to the Horn of Africa. The Malacca dilemma points to China's vulnerabilities should the US blockade the Malacca Strait in a war, cutting off China's trade flows.

But two decades later, the string of pearls is nowhere to be found. Instead, a Maritime Silk Road is linking Chinese ports to a string of commercial ports: Piraeus in Greece, Kyaukpyu in Myanmar, Gwadar in Pakistan and Colombo and Hambantota in Sri Lanka.

We can't know if the US would blockade the Malacca Strait but neither is there a guarantee of war in the Taiwan Strait. Beijing still talks about a peaceful reunification with Taiwan. A Malacca Strait blockade would cripple the economies of littoral states such as Thailand, Indonesia, Singapore and Malaysia. It would deal a heavy blow to Japan and South Korea, US allies that depend more heavily than China on the security of the strait.

Precisely because of the extreme importance of the Malacca Strait to China, a war triggered by an American blockade is unlikely to end there. If a war between China and the US involved the Indian Ocean, the conflict would have become uncontrollable— it would be a major war involving a lot of countries. The rest is up to everybody's imagination.

On the face of it, the PLA Navy, albeit the largest in the world, does indeed look vulnerable in the Indian Ocean. Building a military base in a foreign land requires the permission of the country involved. Even if some countries are happy to accommodate, how would they resist pressure from, say, the US or India that sees itself as the "net security provider" in the Indian Ocean?

But Beijing's so-called vulnerability may not be a disadvantage. The PLA's operations abroad are all humanitarian in nature, be it peacekeeping, vessel protection or disaster relief. So long as Beijing exclusively restricts its military operations to protecting its interests and providing humanitarian assistance when necessary, then China does not need a lot of military bases that are hugely costly and difficult to maintain.

Short of bases overseas, the Chinese navy has to maximise cooperation with other stakeholders. In countering piracy, although

China's flotillas work independently, they share information and coordinate with coalitions such as Nato, the Combined Maritime Forces, EU Operation Atalanta and other independent deployers.

In recent years, the PLA's naval vessels have conducted joint exercises with the Russian, Iranian and Pakistani navies in the Indian Ocean. Joint exercises have also been conducted with the United Arab Emirates and Saudi Arabia.

The best way to protect Chinese interests overseas is to blend them with the interests of others. Beijing does not need to look elsewhere for inspiration. Since 2008, Chinese flotillas have escorted some 7,200 ships transiting the Indian Ocean, including foreign ships. If the western Pacific Ocean is where China has to defend its sovereign rights, then the Indian Ocean looks more like a testing ground for what a stronger China might mean for others.

COUNTER-PIRACY IN THE GULF OF ADEN

IMPLICATIONS FOR PLA NAVY

First published in China-US Focus, 30 December 2013

Counter-piracy off the coast of Somalia is a story of success. Thanks to the concerted efforts of the international community, piracy is very much at bay. According to the Contact Group on Piracy off the Coast of Somalia (CGPCS), as of November 2013, 1,132 pirates have been detained and prosecuted in twenty countries. Only 50–52 hostages are still detained by the pirates. In the last year and a half, no successful hijacks were recorded since MV *Smyrni*, a Greek-registered tanker was hijacked on 12 May 2012.

So far 16 Chinese Task Forces have been sent non-stop to the Gulf of Aden since 26 December 2008 and each is composed of no less than three ships. These ships account for nearly half of the latest Chinese destroyers, frigates and replenishment ships from the three fleets of the PLA Navy. Such a strength and sustainability make the Chinese Task Force the largest among independent deployers. As of 22 December, 2013, the Chinese Task Forces have escorted 5,460 ships including 2,765 foreign ships. They have also escorted 7 ships of the World Food Program in cooperation with the EU CTF- 465.

Counter-piracy in the Gulf of Aden is a turning point for the PLA Navy. It is the first time that the PLA Navy has conducted military operations in the blue waters. It is also a familiarization with uncharted waters in the Indian Ocean which is getting increasingly important for China's maritime trade. With more and more state of the art ships including aircraft carriers anticipated to come into service, it will only be a given for the PLA Navy ships to cruise in the blue waters of the world's oceans.

Counter-piracy is also a learning curve for the PLA Navy and it is learning quickly. In spite of having the most sophisticated combat platforms and weapon systems among the three services, the PLA Navy, compared to the PLA Army and the PLA Air Force, has least experience in fighting a real war. Therefore interacting with 20 other navies with frequent exchanges of visits, day-to-day intelligence sharing, exchange of observers, joint exercises with Russia and U.S., coordination with other independent deployers and Task Forces of NATO, EU, CMF and maritime industrial organizations are critical and invaluable to the PLA Navy's capacity-building. These are not the things that the PLA Navy could learn just through friendly port calls that it did before.

Counter-piracy also indicates how in future the PLA Navy could join in safeguarding sea lanes of communications (SLOCs). Maritime trade accounts for 90% of world transport and the security of SLOCs are pivotal to maritime trade. Of 20,000–25,000 ships transiting the Gulf of Aden each year, 1,400–1,600 are Chinese ships. In quite a few cases, the U.S. Navy, the Turkish Navy and the Indian Navy helped rescue hijacked Chinese vessels in the Indian Ocean because the Chinese Task Force was simply too far away. The Chinese Task Forces reciprocated with assistance in kind. Among the ships escorted by the PLA Navy in the last five years, 50% are foreign ships. The Chinese Task Forces have also escorted foreign ships released by pirates to safe destinations and prevented more than 40 ships from pirate attacks.

Incidents of piracy off the coast of Somalia are at a historic low since 2006. But it could be reversible, too. Piracy is lucrative business. According to a report release by INTERPOL, UNODC and the World Bank at the 15th plenary session of CGPCS in Djibouti, $339–413 million are estimated to have been paid in ransom for 179 hijacked ships from April 2005 to December 2012. Given the on-going instability in Somalia, piracy is still attractive for young men who cannot find legitimate means for making a living. Worst of all, even children were found in piracy incidents. Without the presence of the international navy, pirates would certainly come back. In fact at least 6 attacks have been reported this year and the Royal Danish Navy ship HDMS *Esbern Snare* arrested 9 pirates between Kenya and the Seychelles coast on 10 November.

On 18 November 2013, the UN Security Council issued Resolution 2125, authorizing a further period of twelve months for states and regional organizations to cooperate with Somali authorities in the fight against piracy and armed robbery at sea off the coast of Somalia. This clearly indicates that the "war" is not over and a comprehensive and collective response from the international community including China is still needed. And there are new missions waiting for the PLA Navy, too. According to the Organization for the Prevention of Chemical Weapons (OPCW), the Chinese Task Force will enter the Mediterranean to join Russia in escorting chemical weapons of Syria to a US ship and monitor their destruction on the high seas. This is considered to be the first time that China, US and Russia have cooperated militarily after the Second World War.

China has some titles today such as "the second largest economy," "the largest exporter" and "the second largest importer." Given China's current situation, especially her connections with the rest of the world, it seems that history has tasked PLA Navy with more missions than PLA Army and PLA Air Force in the beginning of the 21st century. If indeed this is the case, the PLA Navy has a long way to go for its dual roles in the future: protecting China's ever-growing maritime interests and fulfilling China's increasing international responsibilities.

WHAT IS THE USE OF AN AIRCRAFT CARRIER FOR CHINA?

First published in China-US Focus, 26 May 2017

The April 26 launching of the first aircraft carrier designed and built in China is a big relief for all Chinese people. In less than four years, the Chinese shipbuilding industry has been able to produce the most sophisticated weapons platform so far found in the nation's military arsenal. Although the as-yet unmanned vessel looks like a copy of the *Liaoning* aircraft carrier, considerable improvements reportedly have been made. Most importantly, it has laid solid technological ground for China to produce upgraded aircraft carriers to come.

How useful is an aircraft carrier? For some, in today's irregular, asymmetric warfare climate, such a large vessel seems little more than a slow-moving target for precision-guided cruise missiles. But there are others who argue the vessel is hard to find and the multiple layers of sophisticated air and sea defenses are difficult to penetrate. Whatever the case, no existing aircraft carriers in any country have ever been attacked. Moreover, the US, the strongest military power with the largest number of aircraft carriers, is still building a *Gerald Ford*-class supercarrier.

At the dawn of the 21st century, a stronger China craves such prestige as befits the nation's status as both a global power and a maritime power. Having a domestically made aircraft carrier has the same cachet as having a Beijing Olympics and Nobel prizes. But it is more than sheer pride. China cannot forget the humiliation brought by the foreign invasions that came from the sea in the last Qing dynasty. Today, the risk of China being invaded on land is next to zero, but the nation's vulnerability is still felt at sea.

A carrier strike group led by submarines, flanked by destroyers and frigates and armed with fighters and helicopters would remind the Chinese of the heyday of Chinese sea power, when the fleet of "treasure boats" led by Admiral Zheng He was second to none. It demonstrates in no small way the progress the PLA has made in power projection, air superiority and long-distance strike capabilities. It will bring revolutionary changes to the chain of command and control. It is a turning point for the PLA Navy, which is starting to become a truly blue-water navy.

It needs a bit of imagination to think how the Chinese aircraft carriers could be used in a real combat situation. This is because China has enjoyed peace for nearly four decades. The first question raised by any American president during a crisis away from the homeland - "Where are my aircraft carriers?" - won't be equally applicable to the Chinese leadership. China has been the beneficiary of its own peaceful rise. By all means, China can be expected to continue to exercise caution and restraint, particularly when use of the aircraft carrier in an offensive attack has to be considered. It is difficult to imagine any scenario in which China would use such lethal and devastating force to help resolve, say, its territorial disputes with some competing ASEAN claimants in the South China Sea.

It remains to be seen how the US could still make as many "freedom of navigation" operations in China's EEZs if Chinese aircraft carriers become operational. Over the years China's protests against such American military activities have fallen on deaf ears. In 2013, the USS *Cowpens* tried to approach the *Liaoning* during the latter's sea trials and was intercepted by a Chinese naval ship in a narrow escape. With a fully operational Chinese carrier strike group around, US ships or aircraft intruding into Chinese EEZs will only feel more "inconvenienced", to say the least. Any American ships preparing to sail again into 12 nautical miles of China-controlled islands in the South China Sea would have to think twice.

For the Chinese navy, no international sea lane is more important than China's proposed Maritime Silk Road linking the Pacific Ocean with the Indian Ocean. Over 80% of Chinese energy imports go through the Strait of Malacca. The proposed China-Pakistan Economic Corridor and China-Bangladesh-Myanmar-India Economic Corridor, two mega-projects of the Maritime Silk Road, lie on the rim of the Indian Ocean. A workforce of over a million Chinese workers can be found in the littoral states. In 2011, a Chinese frigate stood guard near the Libyan coast when over 35,000 Chinese workers were being evacuated over two weeks. Should a situation like this occur again, a huge Chinese aircraft carrier standing by would not only create awe but also use its huge capacity to evacuate Chinese and foreigners.

Maritime trade accounts for 90% of world trade, therefore international "choke points" like the Strait of Hormuz, Strait of Bab-al-Mandeb and Strait of Malacca are critically important for China, the largest trading nation in the world. The PLA Navy harbors no ambitions to control these straits, but it doesn't want the straits to be controlled by others, either. So far the Chinese military has one supply station in Djibouti. An aircraft carrier, like a city afloat, could tremendously reduce the problem of not having enough logistical supply bases overseas.

The most-quoted teaching from ancient Chinese strategist Sun Tzu is "to subdue the enemy without using force". The question, now as then, is how such a desirable outcome can be achieved militarily if not diplomatically. For the Chinese navy, towering aircraft carriers with overwhelming military superiority and huge psychological effect are one of the best instruments ever found.

STATION LOOKS BEYOND
ANTI-PIRACY MISSION

First published in *China Daily*, 18 March 2016

China would not have thought of establishing a logistic supply station in Djibouti were it not for fighting piracy off the coast of Somalia. As the country contributing the largest force to the counter-piracy mission, China has had at least three ships in the Gulf of Aden at any given time since 2009. So far 65 ships from the People's Liberation Army Navy's 22 task forces have been deployed on counter-piracy missions, and they have escorted more than 6,100 ships, half of them foreign vessels.

These achievements have been made under stringent conditions, however. Since the PLA Navy vessels have no supply or maintenance stations overseas, they have to carry huge amounts of food and spare parts, prompting some Chinese Navy personnel to say the spare parts are more than enough to assemble a helicopter on board.

Piracy off the coast of Somalia has been largely curbed thanks to joint international efforts which includes, but is not limited to, military operations. But nobody can safely conclude piracy is no longer a threat.

The piracy threat at sea has its roots on land. Although a federal government is now in place in the Somali capital of Mogadishu, its control over the country remains miserably weak. A Western analyst has said, almost sarcastically, that the Somali government's control is restricted only to the airport and the presidential palace. And the United Nation has repeatedly warned piracy could stage a comeback if the political situation in Somalia remains unstable and the problem of high unemployment is unsolved.

Therefore, the counter-piracy mission is likely to continue, though under a more flexible arrangement. The North Atlantic Treaty Organization and the European Union have even publicly discussed discontinuing their counter-piracy missions by the end of 2016 but promised to maintain some kind of presence off the coast of Somalia if necessary. Every year about 1,600 Chinese vessels pass through the Gulf of Aden, and more ships carrying oil for China are likely to sail through the Strait of Hormuz. The security of sea lanes cannot be more critical for China, which relies on maritime transport for up to 90 percent of its foreign trade.

Militarily, Djibouti's advantage lies in its location, deep water ports and friendly attitude toward foreign troops. Djibouti is strategically located—at the entrance from the Indian Ocean to the Red Sea. It oversees the Bab al-Mandeb (or the Mandeb Strait), one of the busiest shipping lanes in the world. And the waters in the Port of Djibouti are deep enough for an aircraft carrier like France's *Charles de Gaulle* to dock. Moreover, the Djibouti government welcomes the presence of American, French, Japanese and Chinese troops on its soil.

Djibouti not only occupies a vantage point in the fight against piracy in the waters off the Horn of Africa. It is also a gateway for peacekeeping and humanitarian aid and disaster relief in Africa and the Middle East, two missions that are increasingly becoming part of the PLA's overseas operations. At present 2,787

Chinese peacekeepers are deployed in the Democratic Republic of Congo, Liberia, South Sudan, Sudan, Mali and Lebanon. A standby PLA force of 8,000 troops is being built. The PLA has also taken part in quite a few humanitarian aid and disaster relief operations along the rim of the Indian Ocean and other parts of Africa, from evacuating foreign citizens from war-torn Yemen to fighting the Ebola epidemic in Sierra Leone and Liberia.

In the long run, Djibouti could serve as a PLA station for regional capacity building. One of the ways China is helping global governance is by strengthening regional institutions such as the African Union. Beijing has also announced a $100-million military aid package for the AU to help establish the African Standby Force and the African Capacity for Immediate Response to Crisis.

The PLA's logistic support station can therefore serve more than counter-piracy missions. It could be a milestone in China's support for stabilizing Africa and the Middle East where China's greater role in regional security is more than welcome.

SAFEGUARDING CHINA'S OVERSEAS INTERESTS THROUGH MILITARY COOPERATION

First published in China-US Focus, 26 June 2015

In the recently published *China's Military Strategy* white paper, China's overseas interests are stressed like never before. Securing China's overseas interests is taken as one of the "strategic tasks" of China's armed forces, and the PLA vows that it will strengthen international security cooperation in areas crucially related to China's overseas interests.

What are China's overseas interests? Where are these crucial areas and cooperation with whom? The succinct white paper hasn't specified. As the largest trading nation and the second largest economy in the world, it is difficult to breakdown China's overseas interests. Today China's interests are not only global but in outer space too (a point people seldom think of).

As a rule of thumb, these overseas interests should include, but are not limited to, security of China's foreign trade of import and export; security of Chinese nationals and property overseas; security of Chinese investment and security of sea lanes, gas and oil pipelines that are critical to China's energy imports.

Additionally, great nations shoulder great responsibilities. As China grows in not only strength but also international political and economic influence, China's international responsibilities will grow together with its national interests.

China's overseas interests are endangered in the course of proliferation. Chinese workers have been hijacked in Sudan, Algeria, Nigeria, Ethiopia, Pakistan and Afghanistan and sometimes have even been killed. Before the war in Libya in 2011, the PLA helped evacuate 35,860 Chinese nationals within two weeks, but huge amounts of Chinese property and investment were left behind. Given the fact that 90% of world trade is maritime trade, China's concern over the security of sea lanes cannot be more justifiable. The oil and gas pipelines linking Kazakhstan, Turkmenistan, Uzbekistan, Russia and Myanmar with China could be easy targets of terrorist attack. China's One Belt, One Road initiative covers an "arc of instability" stretching from sub-Saharan Africa through North Africa, into the Middle East, the Balkans, the Caucasus, and South and Central Asia, to Southeast Asia.

China today has two dilemmas: China doesn't harbor any global security ambitions, but its interests are already global; China vows to be a responsible power, but the Chinese military hasn't all of the capabilities required to safeguard its national interests and fulfill its international responsibilities. Citing cooperation in areas crucially related to China's overseas interests, the white paper has actually admitted PLA's lack of capacity and experience. Such inability is reflected in some bitter lessons. For example, when Chinese ship *De Xinhai* was hijacked in the Indian Ocean in October, 2009, Chinese state media had to point out that the ship was 1,080 nautical miles away from the Chinese naval vessels in the Gulf of Aden, a hint that PLA naval vessels were simply too far away for an immediate rescue.

International cooperation is the only way out for the PLA working overseas. The white paper pledges that the PLA will "constantly explore new fields, new contents and new models of cooperation with other militaries" and "pushing ahead with pragmatic military cooperation".

Cooperation requires the PLA to share interoperability with other militaries. NATO, EU members and American allies use the same rules of engagement and communication systems while the PLA is hugely different in language, weaponry, communication systems and chain of command. This to some extent explains why over 6 years PLA naval vessels in the Gulf of Aden are still patrolling independently five nautical miles north of the International Recommended Transit Corridor where most international navies are working together. It is no surprise the white paper emphasizes "enhancing joint operational capabilities".

The first step of cooperation could be in military operations other than war (MOOTWs). Unlike wars led by the West in the name of "humanitarian intervention", these areas are not controversial. The PLA has been involved in MOOTWs for years. In humanitarian assistance and disaster relief, be it domestic or overseas, the PLA has demonstrated its capacity and experience.

Cooperation may take different forms. The Gulf of Guinea is one of the crucial sources of China's oil imports, but armed robbery at sea is rampant and one Chinese ship, *Yue Liang Wan*, was hijacked there. The PLA can provide more technical assistance, particularly to the navies which have boats and light frigates made in China. Currently seven out of nine of the PLA's peacekeeping operations are in Africa. China can continue its financial support to the peacekeeping troops under the umbrella of the African Union and join hands with the EU and the US to train African peacekeepers. The Chinese and the US military could cooperate in pandemic disease research such as Ebola in Africa. In the ASEAN Regional Forum and ASEAN Defense

Minister Meeting Plus framework, China can intensify its cooperation focusing on maritime security, counter-terrorism, de-mining, military medicine, disaster relief and peacekeeping.

Another important cooperation could be on security of sea lanes. Countering piracy in the Indian Ocean is a brilliant example of how international navies could work in tandem to secure sea lanes that are pivotal to international maritime trade. With 85% of Chinese oil imports going through the Strait of Malacca, the importance of the strait cannot be over-emphasized. The Chinese military could send liaison officers to join ReCAPP in Singapore, which monitors the piracy and armed robbery situation in Asia, and provide technical assistance to the countries that are currently involved in air and sea patrols of the strait.

THE STRING OF PEARLS AND THE MARITIME SILK ROAD

First published in China-US Focus, 11 February 2014

The phrase 'String of Pearls' was first used in 2005, in a report entitled "Energy Futures in Asia" provided to U.S. Defense Secretary Donald H Rumsfeld by defense contractor Booz Allen Hamilton. It alleged that China was adopting a "string of pearls" strategy of bases stretching from the Middle East to southern China. These "pearls" were naval bases or electronic eavesdropping posts built by the Chinese in Myanmar, Bangladesh, Pakistan and Sri Lanka. The purpose was to project its power overseas and protect its oil shipments.

Nine years have since elapsed. The phrase, or theory, still sticks in the international media and in some think tank reports.

These "bases" are found nowhere in the Indian Ocean. The most telling evidence is that the PLA Navy has been conducting counter-piracy operations in the Gulf of Aden for five years without any bases of their own. Jean-Paul Adam, the Seychelles Foreign Affairs Minister, announced in December 2011 that his country had invited China to set up a military base in his country, but the Chinese Ministry of Defense only responded that the Chinese side would "consider" replenishment or port calls in the Seychelles and other countries.

China has only two purposes in the Indian Ocean: economic gains and the security of Sea lines of Communication (SLOC). The first objective is achieved through commercial interactions with littoral states. For the second purpose, the Chinese Navy has, since the end of 2008, joined international military efforts in combating piracy in the waters off the coast of Somalia. In fact, the only thing justifiable in the "string of pearls" theory is that it underlines the growing importance, even then, of the Indian Ocean for China's ever-expanding national interests, especially in terms of energy imports. Nowadays China is securing its energy needs from all parts of the world, but the Middle East still prevails as the most important source. By the end of 2013, China had become the largest trader and the largest oil importer in the world. The Indian Ocean, and hence the security of SLOCs from Bab-el-Mandeb, Hormuz and the Malacca Strait, is thus vitally important for China.

Two countries are most important for China's freedom of navigation in the Indian Ocean: the U.S. and India. The U.S. is the only country that has the full capabilities to control the chokepoints in the Indian Ocean and cut off the SLOCs all the way to China, but it is unlikely to exercise such capabilities, unless, perhaps, in an all-out war with China. Even during the Cold War neither the U.S. nor the Soviet Union endeavored to cut off any SLOCs in the world. Besides, the SLOCs are life-lines for all states. Cutting off China's SLOCs will also affect U.S. allies of Japan, ROK and Australia. So long as Sino-American relations remain manageable, such a worst-case scenario is unlikely to occur.

The rivalry between the Elephant and Dragon is often hyped, but India would not challenge China unnecessarily. There is no dispute between China and India in the Indian Ocean. The Line of Actual Control along the Sino-Indian land border has by and large remained peaceful. Although there were a few standoffs, not a single bullet was fired across the border in over fifty years. The queer idea of China encircling India from the sea with the help of Pakistan only exists in the wildest imagination of some Indian "strategists".

Access, rather than bases, is what the Chinese Navy is really interested in the Indian Ocean. The unchartered waters of the Indian Ocean could be friendlier than the disputed waters in the Pacific. In the Pacific Ocean, China has territorial disputes with a number of countries, but this is not the case in the Indian Ocean. The security of SLOCs is thus in the interests of all other nations. The ongoing counter-piracy mission involves navies from over twenty countries. It could serve as a future model of cooperation of stake-holders in the Indian Ocean addressing common threats.

Interestingly the route of Chinese Task Forces departing the southern Chinese coast for fighting piracy in the Indian Ocean is not dissimilar from the Maritime Silk Road that Admiral Zheng He and his fleet embarked upon in 1405. Currently, the Chinese leadership is reinvigorating the Maritime Silk Road. China tabled a 3 billion Yuan China-ASEAN Maritime Cooperation Fund for the maritime economy, environment, fishery and salvage, and communications at sea. In October 2013, Chinese President Xi Jinping proposed to ASEAN that it would build the Maritime Silk Road of the 21st century. This coincides with Chinese Premier Li Keqiang's pledge to upgrade the Gold Decade (2000-2010) of China-ASEAN cooperation into a Diamond Decade. In the Indian Ocean, China is cooperating with littoral states in building the China-Pakistan Economic Corridor and China-India-Myanmar-Bangladesh Economic Corridor. These mega-projects, with heavy investment from China, will fundamentally change the political and economic landscape of the Indian Ocean and benefit all countries in the region. They will also help to mitigate security concerns in the Maritime Silk Road, ranging from territorial disputes in the South China Sea to transnational threats such as piracy, armed robbery and terrorism.

In the 15th century, Admiral Zheng He went on his seven voyages to the West Pacific and the Indian Ocean with the largest naval fleet in the world. These voyages were not aimed at conquest of peoples or of territory. Instead, they were visits to swap Chinese silk and porcelain for exotic souvenirs such as zebras and giraffes. Zheng He didn't venture to establish bases either. In so doing, he left a legacy that is intangible but invaluable for China today. It is an image of China that the Chinese people would like to project again in the 21st century as they did 600 years ago: a country standing tall in the center of world, strong yet benign, and friendly to all.

UNDERSTANDING CHINA'S MILITARY TRANSPARENCY

First published in China-US Focus, 18 July 2013

When China published her defense white paper "The Diversified Employment of China's Armed Forces" in April 2013, western critics lauded the efforts but pointed out that China didn't put much meat on the bone and that the paper is again short on details that people would like to see.

This raises a question: To what extent does a country need to be transparent militarily in order to build confidence with other countries?

The first answer is: It depends on whom you are dealing with. Transparency is based on trust. You are unlikely to make a 'confession" when you are not sure the listeners are your friends or, in the worst case, they could be your adversaries or even potential enemies. While the west holds that criteria such as the weapons systems, break-down of military expenditure, and listing of R&D efforts are essential for transparency, China stresses that there is no absolute transparency (as Prism whistleblower Edward Snowden seems to have proven. Otherwise why would the US monitor even his allies?) And, transparency only comes as a result of trust.

Transparency also has a lot to do with military strength. Normally under-developed countries hold more things as military secrets and the militarily strong ones are not shy of showing off their muscles. While the west believes that China today is strong enough not to be attacked by anyone, China is still concerned with a number of worst case scenarios where external forces could be involved in either China's internal affairs like the Taiwan issue, or maritime territorial disputes with other countries. China believes that there is still a gap between her strength and that of western powers. Her objective, as laid out in the defense white paper, is to achieve military modernization by mid-century.

Transparency is also dependent on strategic equilibrium. During the Cold War, strategic arms reduction talks took place between the US and the Soviet Union, only because both sides believed that their nuclear warheads were more than enough and that their strategic equilibrium would not be jeopardized even if they cut the excessive warheads. But China doesn't boast such a strategic equilibrium with, say, the US.

Then what explains China's efforts of publishing a white defense paper biennially since 1998? Such regularity is rare even among major powers. The answer is the growing confidence of China in her comprehensive national strength, including military strength. Recent years saw China's state media much more willing to unlock China's "military secrets", from the test flights of J-20 and J-31 stealth fighters, to success in ground-based mid-course anti-missile tests. The Chinese military has also stepped up PR efforts ranging from regular press briefings since 2008 to setting up an English MOD website in 2009. Foreign delegations are invited to observe exercises. Apart from the *Liaoning* aircraft carrier and nuclear submarines, China's military "warehouse" has basically all been open to foreign military visitors. With all this together, China wishes to project a comprehensive and positive image of a peace-loving country with a peaceful rise. Put in another way, the more confident China is about her military strength and the good intentions of others, the more transparent she will be.

Transparency is a western conception while 'keeping secrets' is part of the Chinese culture. Yes, culture can be cultivated. Today, even the most outspoken critics in the west would agree that Chinese society is much more liberal, and the Chinese military much more open than before. Therefore for the Chinese military to become more transparent, the west needs to convince China that their intentions are not ill and, above all, win trust from China.

CAN CHINA AND THE US AGREE ON FREEDOM OF NAVIGATION?

First published in China-US Focus, 22 July 2016

There can be no winner in the tug-of-war between China and the US over freedom of navigation. Both countries agree to this fundamental principle of international maritime law, but interpret it differently. China believes that American military activities, such as the close-in reconnaissance and surveillance by the US Navy in China's Exclusive Economic Zone (EEZ), infringe on China's security interests and therefore cannot be simply categorized as freedom of navigation. The US maintains that its military activities fall within the freedom of navigation and other internationally lawful uses of the sea. The increased sail and flight of American ships and aircraft in the South China Sea in the name of freedom of navigation just make the waters more troubled.

Such differences in interpretation are not surprising. Negotiations on the United Nations Convention on the Law of the Sea (UNCLOS) took nine years. The final text is an inclusion, but also a necessary compromise, of the interests of over 140 countries that are involved in the negotiations. Understandably controversies arise.

Could there be a way out? Theoretically one of the ways for China to establish equilibrium is to reciprocate with similar and frequent close-in surveillance and reconnaissance against the US territories, especially the continental USA. But China doesn't have such a military capability. More importantly, it doesn't harbor such a wish. Such an exchange of hostility in the name of freedom of navigation will only look like another Cold War.

Another way out is for China and the US to meet halfway. This stems first from an increasing need for China to enter other countries' territorial sea or EEZs. So far the Chinese Navy has entered the territorial sea of Somalia, Syria and Yemen and the EEZ of Libya in different UN-mandated missions and during evacuation of Chinese and foreign nationals. About one-third of international waters are EEZs. As a result of China's growing interests overseas and international obligations, the Chinese Navy will have to enter other countries' EEZs more often. The Chinese Navy will also conduct more passages through international sea lanes, even if they are in the territorial seas of other countries. Like the US, China may wish to have a wider global commerce at sea. Eventually it may prefer to have a more flexible view of freedom of navigation.

A compromise was already made in the 14th Western Pacific Naval Symposium (WPNS) in Tsingtao in 2014. Twenty-one member states unanimously agreed to adopt a new edition of *Code for Unplanned Encounters at Sea* (CUES). CUES offers safety procedures, a basic communications plan and maneuvering instructions when naval ships or naval aircraft of one state meet casually or unexpectedly with a naval ship or naval aircraft of another state. Previously China vetoed a draft that describes how naval vessels should avoid meeting each other unexpectedly in territorial waters. This is impossible, because Chinese law requires a foreign military ship to have approval of the Chinese government first before it is allowed to enter into Chinese territorial waters. In other words, there is no likelihood for a foreign military vessel to have an "unplanned encounter" with any Chinese naval vessels in China's territorial waters. At the 14th WPNS, all parties agreed not to mention "territorial sea" any more, therefore the new edition of CUES became a technical brochure without geographic limitation that could bring on political disagreement.

CUES is now being discussed at the Indian Ocean Naval Symposium (IONS) too, and is likely to be adopted as well. If agreed, 22 member states of the IONS will voluntarily observe the same procedures. The global common ground in both the Pacific and the Indian Oceans will become bigger for all countries including China.

If China needs to enter other countries' EEZs and territorial seas more often, it invites two questions: first, would China allow foreign military vessels to enter Chinese EEZs more easily? Secondly, would China revise its law one day to allow foreign military vessels to conduct innocent passages in its territorial waters without approval?

On the first question, although China is opposed to American surveillance and reconnaissance in its EEZ for security reasons, PRC Law on the EEZ and the Continental Shelf doesn't require notification of the Chinese government. On the second question, the fact is most of the countries in the world, especially the developed countries, don't require approval for foreign military vessels to conduct innocent passage in their territorial waters. Although China is still a developing country, it is also the second-largest economy in the world. If it is possible for China to accept a foreign military vessel's innocent passage without approval one day, accepting CUES that diminishes geographic limitation would look like the first step in that direction. The Rules of

Behavior (ROB) for Safety of Maritime and Air Encounter signed bilaterally between China and the US are in line with the rules of CUES. There is no specific geographic limitation either.

But one needs to bear in mind a major difference. Whenever Chinese naval vessels enter the territorial seas of other countries, usually the vessels would conduct transit passage rather than innocent passage in the international sea lanes. Transit passage doesn't need approval of the littoral states. Because of China's sensitivity to its own sovereignty, it wants to show full respect to the sovereignty of other nations. That is why China maintains that its naval vessels' passage through Tanaga Pass of the US and Tokara Strait of Japan is transit passage, even if innocent passage is allowed by American and Japanese law.

Currently there is no way for China and the US to agree on American military activities in China's EEZ, let alone in China's territorial seas. In China's view, such activities are not for peaceful purposes and represent a security risk. Quite a few dangerous encounters have happened. Both sides pointed fingers at each other. For China, such encounters are not "unplanned", because the US naval vessels have "planned" to come. The danger is if China believes such intrusion by the US is planned, then its willingness to abide by CUES or ROB can only diminish, and the danger of an incident or even conflict will grow. Although UNCLOS doesn't specifically restrict military activities by one country in the EEZ of another country, as claimed by the US, it doesn't justify them either, as claimed by China. However, "due regard for rights and duties of the coastal states" and "for peaceful purposes" are clearly stated which touch a chord with the Chinese side.

The US is challenging China in the South China Sea on an issue in which it claims to have no position. The US certainly enjoys freedom of navigation in the South China Sea, but its sailing within 12 nautical miles of China-controlled islands and reefs can only be a provocation in that these waters are not internationally recognized sea lanes. Harping on the legitimacy of such passages is a misinterpretation, if not abuse, of freedom of navigation, to say the least.

Although the award of the South China Sea arbitration is in favor of the Philippines, it is hardly a game-changer given China's declared position of non-acceptance. If the US takes advantage of the verdict and increases its military activities in the South China Sea, it will only irk China all the more. Even if China doesn't respond militarily, it will surely cost Sino-US cooperation elsewhere.

Sino-US cooperation on freedom of navigation is possible when it is not at the cost of the security of the other side. Rather than in the vicinity of their territories, it could start elsewhere around the globe. The cooperation between China and the US in the Gulf of Aden and Somali Basin is a good example: it is counter-piracy, it is also maintenance of sea lines of communication, and perseverance of freedom of navigation.

WAR IN THE TAIWAN STRAIT? IT'S THE SOUTH CHINA SEA, STUPID

First published in *South China Morning Post*, 25 January 2023

For those watching the war in Ukraine and worrying that a similar conflict might occur in the Taiwan Strait, my response is simple: it's the South China Sea, stupid.

With tensions in the Taiwan Strait rising, the South China Sea issue has seemingly died down. This is not the case. On December 21, a Chinese fighter jet and a US surveillance plane flew within metres of each other over the South China Sea. Both sides released video clips and pointed fingers at each other.

The South China Sea is far more dangerous than the Taiwan Strait. A war in the Taiwan Strait between China and the US, if it is likely at all, is very unlikely to be triggered by an accident like we have seen in the South China Sea.

The Taiwan issue is so flammable, every word from Beijing and Washington would be scrutinised. US President Joe Biden's "gaffes" on defending Taiwan were quickly walked back by his aides, who insisted that the White House had not changed its one-China policy.

What if another fatal collision occurred in the air, like the one in 2001? For over two decades, bilateral talks on risk reduction between the two militaries have been just tit-for-tat, focusing on safety versus security.

The Chinese side points out that the United States' reconnaissance is detrimental to China's security while the US wishes to discuss ways to ensure safe encounters. The Americans ask Chinese ships and aircraft to keep a safe distance and the Chinese say, "You are certainly safe if you don't come at all."

What is happening today is very much like what happened during the Cold War. In the early decades of the Cold War, more than 100 American and Soviet pilots died as a result of air clashes. This led to the 1972 US-Soviet Incident at Sea agreement.

China and the US have similar agreements to reduce tension. But, in both cases, the agreements didn't fully play their roles in risk reduction.

To avoid an accident, the eventual solution lies in an equilibrium of military strength. The real lesson from the Cold War is not the two superpowers establishing a litany of confidence-building measures to avoid accidents but that, because of the balance of power, both were willing to sit down to talk.

While the US and the Soviet Union were enemies of almost equal strength, China and the US are competitors with a military gap that is quickly closing. China has vowed to speed up building the People's Liberation Army into a world-class military by mid century.

The question is: what could happen before that? Short of an equilibrium, this might turn out to be the most dangerous time.

A few suggestions are already on the table. First, China could send ships on reciprocal surveillance and reconnaissance missions in American waters. Historically, Chinese ships did sail sporadically in the waters off Guam, Hawaii and the Aleutian Islands.

But how can the PLA Navy do that routinely along the American coast without a forward military presence such as bases? And why should it do that at all if China's focus is on maintaining its legitimate rights and interests in the Western Pacific?

Second, China could amend its maritime law. Most countries in the world, including the US, allow innocent passage of foreign vessels in their territorial waters. Will China allow innocent passage in its own territorial waters one day? And if China does, would the US give up its freedom of navigation operations?

This is what happened after the 1988 Black Sea bumping incident in which two Soviet frigates were ordered to push an American cruiser and a destroyer out of Soviet territorial waters. In 1989, the US and USSR issued a joint statement agreeing that all ships, including warships, enjoy the right of innocent passage through the territorial seas of another. The decades-old rivalry at sea came to an end.

The easiest thing to do is to resume the military-to-military dialogues that China cancelled in the wake of former US House speaker Nancy Pelosi's visit to Taiwan. But it should not be business as usual.

The two navies have been talking to each other since 1998 and have done at least three exercises aiming for good seamanship. What is sorely needed are exercises to ensure good airmanship in an air-to-air encounter. Given the speed of today's aircraft, it is extremely difficult to disengage in proximity.

According to the China-US memorandum on rules of behaviour for safety of air and maritime encounters, the pilots of both sides are responsible for operating with professional airmanship and paying due regard to the safety of the other side's aircraft.

The two militaries should explore building confidence in new fields where the gaps are not huge. In a track II dialogue I attended, experts from both sides concurred that strategic stability, which normally refers to US-Soviet nuclear equilibrium, won't be applicable to China-US relations.

Instead, China-US strategic stability has to include new fields such as outer space, cyber and artificial intelligence. Talks could start at the track II level first. The ongoing talks between the Center for International Security and Strategy at Tsinghua University and the Brookings Institution on mitigating the risks of artificial intelligence in the military domain are a bold step in the right direction.

That the Cold War turned out to be a long peace is not sheer luck, but the result of the two superpowers being hell-bent on preventing a hot war. Similarly, the real challenge for China and the US now is not to avoid a new Cold War, but avoiding conflict most likely triggered by an accident. The latest incident in the South China Sea tells us that peace has to be earned.

CHINA'S RED LINES ON TAIWAN ARE CLEAR, WHATEVER THE US SAYS ABOUT ITS POLICY OF STRATEGIC AMBIGUITY

First published in *South China Morning Post*, 22 June 2022

Will the United States come to defend Taiwan militarily in a war across the Taiwan Strait? This million-dollar question so far has two answers from the same administration—yes, according to US President Joe Biden when he was asked in Tokyo in late May; not necessarily, according to White House aides who quickly walked back his comment and said America's "one China" policy had not changed.

This question becomes all the more interesting if one compares Biden's attitudes towards Moscow and Beijing. Ever since the beginning of the war in Ukraine, Biden has consistently said US troops would not directly engage in this conflict.

If Biden is determined to avoid direct conflict with Russia, why is he so adamant to provoke a potential war with China? The People's Liberation Army, the largest armed force in the world, would be no less formidable than the Russian military.

The PLA Navy has three aircraft carriers—compared with Russia's one aircraft carrier that has been undergoing repairs for years—and even more ships than the US Navy. On June 17, China unveiled its third aircraft carrier, the *Fujian*, a locally designed carrier equipped with an electromagnetic catapult for launching aircraft.

According to China's anti-secession law, China would only resort to non-peaceful means in its attempt to reunify with the island under three circumstances: if Taiwan declared independence; if a major incident occurred leading to Taiwan's secession from China; or if all the possible avenues for a peaceful reunification have been completely exhausted.

The probability of the Taiwanese authorities declaring independence is next to impossible, since it would most certainly invite a military response from across the strait. But in Beijing's eyes, Washington has never ceased in creating "incidents" to impede the mainland's efforts for a peaceful unification.

The Pentagon has sent more warships sailing through the Taiwan Strait in recent years—30 since the start of 2020. Last year, *The Wall Street Journal* reported that a US special-operations unit and a contingent of marines have been secretly operating in Taiwan to train military forces there.

Beijing has good reason to suspect Washington is only paying lip service to its "one China" pledge. If the competition between China and the US is to be "extreme", as Biden described, and if indeed China is "the only country with both the intent to reshape the international order and, increasingly, the economic, diplomatic, military, and technological power to do it", as Secretary of State Antony Blinken asserted, won't the US make use of Taiwan as a convenient pawn in the grand chessboard of the Indo-Pacific?

The conflict in Ukraine provides lessons to learn for the PLA. The Russian military's biggest error was underestimating its enemy in the beginning. This was clear in its attacks on multiple fronts without adequate troops, sufficient supplies and logistics support, and a clear line of command.

So, if China is indeed a greater long-term threat than Russia, as the Biden administration has concluded, shouldn't Washington try to avoid a conflict with China, especially as it would be fought in a faraway battlefield where the US has fewer allies while Beijing has all the advantages of fighting on home turf?

Perhaps the reason is, unlike Moscow that has threatened Nato with nuclear attacks, Beijing vows it would never be the first to use nuclear weapons in any circumstances.

If Russia's nuclear stockpile—the world's largest—had played a decisive role in deterring US involvement, Beijing might have to reconsider its "small and effective" nuclear arsenal. Theoretically, a no-first-use policy requires a large nuclear arsenal to enable an effective retaliatory second strike after surviving the enemy's first strike.

In spite of Biden's reiteration afterwards of US adherence to the "one China" policy, his apparent gaffe—the third in nine months— would seem to signal a burgeoning US policy of "strategic clarity", a shift from its decades-old policy of "strategic ambiguity".

Supporters of strategic ambiguity believe such a policy would deter China while not emboldening those in Taiwan who favour independence. Supporters of strategic clarity, however, argue that such vagueness is already inadequate to deter a possible attack by mainland China.

Notwithstanding China's determination for reunification and the PLA sending its aircraft to fly near Taiwan as a warning, there is no indication that the mainland is accelerating its plan to take over Taiwan because of the war in Ukraine.

China's 2022 defence budget, announced after the eruption of the conflict, was kept within 2 per cent of GDP, as it has been in recent years. It speaks volumes of China's assessment of the security environment and its confidence about eventual reunification with Taiwan.

Such mistakes are unlikely to be made by the PLA. The Taiwan Relations Act does not explicitly oblige American forces to come to the island's defence. But you can be sure the PLA would be prepared for such a fight, involving not just American troops but all its allies in the region.

In other words, neither America's strategic ambiguity nor strategic clarity could hold back the PLA's military build-up. At the recent Shangri-La Dialogue, Chinese defence minister Wei Fenghe vowed to "fight to the very end" to stop Taiwanese secession.

The Taiwan issue is one of China's core interests. That means the PLA cannot afford to lose in a war fighting for China's sovereignty. Once a war starts, a stalemate as we are seeing in Ukraine is highly unlikely, and a ceasefire would be out of the question.

Biden likes to quote his father in saying the only conflict worse than an intended one is an unintended one. The problem is, in the Taiwan Strait, there won't be any unintended conflicts.

HOW NANCY PELOSI CHANGED THE TAIWAN STRAIT STATUS QUO IN BEIJING'S FAVOUR

First published in *South China Morning Post*, 11 August 2022

History is not always written by the victors. It is equally written by the losers. US House Speaker Nancy Pelosi's visit to Taiwan is a typical example of how a self-centred egoist has gone out for wool and come home shorn.

Pelosi, one of the US's highest-ranking legislators and second in line to the presidency, has gained little more than some limelight before her retirement. Her Taiwan visit was widely considered unnecessarily provocative. Even *The Washington Post*, which published her op-ed explaining why she would make the trip, published an editorial that can hardly be misunderstood: "The damage from Pelosi's unwise Taiwan visit must be contained".

Beijing's response was carefully calibrated yet exceptionally strong. It didn't attempt to obstruct Pelosi's flight, as some had speculated, but in the wake of her arrival in Taipei on August 2, Beijing announced that it would conduct air and sea drills in six areas around the island that would effectively seal off Taiwan for three consecutive days.

Two target zones were placed inside Taiwan's "territorial waters" and dozens of fighter planes were flown across the median line in the Taiwan Strait, as a show of disregard for that boundary. For the first time, missiles were fired over the island.

With these measures, the People's Liberation Army has proven it could coordinate operations to impose a full blockade should it ever choose to. It has progressed from the much smaller missile firing exercises conducted during the 1995-1996 Taiwan Strait crisis. Those exercises were meant to send a warning to then Taiwanese "president" Lee Teng-hui after his visit to the US.

But, unlike in 1996 when one American aircraft carrier sailed through the strait and another manoeuvred close by, this time, the USS Ronald Reagan cautiously kept away from the entrance to the Taiwan Strait.

How might the Biden administration reflect on all this? China and the US have been pointing fingers at each other for changing the status quo in the Taiwan Strait. This time, Pelosi has changed the status quo, ironically, in China's favour.

This is very much like the situation in 2012 when the Japanese government announced that it was going to nationalise the Diaoyu Islands which China claims as part of its territory. A furious Chinese government sent vessels into the archipelago's contiguous zone. Today, Chinese coastguard ships sail regularly there, despite Japan's protests, to demonstrate Beijing's sovereign claim.

Whether such exercises around Taiwan become more common in the future depends on Taipei and Washington, not Beijing. Taiwan's authorities, led by the separatist Tsai Ing-wen, can hardly have a real change of heart, even as the cost of their opposition to reunification with the mainland continues to grow.

The real question is how this unprecedented move by the mainland might change the mentality of the Taiwanese people, especially in their next election. China still has strategic patience. After all, it is in Beijing's interests to achieve peaceful reunification with Taiwan. But China's patience is not infinite. According to its Anti-Secession Law, it may resort to non-peaceful means to achieve reunification if it concludes that all possibilities for peaceful reunification have been completely exhausted.

For peace to prevail in the Taiwan Strait, then, the key is to let China believe peaceful reunification is still possible. Over the years, both Beijing and Washington have maintained a policy of strategic ambiguity, albeit for different reasons. China talked about its "red line", but didn't explain what it would do explicitly to safeguard it. Now, thanks to the unremitting efforts of the PLA to build its strength, Beijing has been able to show for the first time that it has not only the will but the capability to protect its core interests.

Today, America's strategic ambiguity—not clarifying explicitly if it would come to Taiwan's defence if the island was attacked—looks more like a fig leaf to hide the reality that it might lose in a direct confrontation with the PLA in the strait, where China has all the advantages of fighting on its home turf.

Neither China nor the US wants a war, but there is no guarantee they can avoid one. For China, America's one-China policy is already hollowed out. Although the two countries have a few confidence-building mechanisms, they are essentially a litany of technical rules aiming to avoid an accident, say, in the South China Sea.

The problem is, a clash between Chinese and US militaries in the Taiwan Strait can hardly be accidental. The Biden administration has talked about the need to establish "guardrails", but if China concludes that such guardrails are America's way of preventing its use of force as a last resort for reunification, they won't be established in the first place.

On August 5, China's Foreign Ministry made clear its displeasure at the US with a series of measures ranging from the cancellation of all defence consultations to the suspension of climate change talks. This second-wave response shows that, for Beijing, everything can come to a stop for the Taiwan issue.

Looking down the road, we will probably see a chain reaction: the United States will speed up arms sales and expand training and personnel exchanges to turn Taiwan into a "porcupine"; a more confident and capable China will then respond more forcefully. As a result, Taiwan's room to manoeuvre will shrink further. It is hard to tell what the endgame is, but two things are certain: Taiwan cannot move away and time is on the side of mainland China.

TO AVERT WAR ACROSS THE TAIWAN STRAIT, THE US MUST REINVIGORATE THE ONE-CHINA POLICY

First published in *South China Morning Post*, 26 September 2022

With China-US relations in free fall, the bare minimum needed for both powers to coexist is not to increase trust, but to avert a conflict in the Taiwan Strait, something that looks increasingly likely.

Since the Trump administration, a vicious circle of action and reaction has spiralled. It culminated in August when US House Speaker Nancy Pelosi visited Taiwan despite China's warnings. The response of the People's Liberation Army was an unprecedented military exercise in six areas around Taiwan that effectively sealed off the island for three days.

How to avoid a conflict that neither side wants? Simple: let China believe that a peaceful reunification with Taiwan is still possible. This will mean the Taiwanese authorities coming back to the one-China principle and the US reinvigorating the one-China policy it claims to have maintained.

This won't be easy. In 1992, the mainland and Taiwan's ruling Kuomintang agreed that there was only one China, although they differed in their definitions. But the Taiwanese authorities, led by Tsai Ing-wen, asserted that Taiwan had never accepted the 1992 consensus. Beijing's worry is that, should the stalemate continue, a Taiwan led by separatist authorities could remain de facto independent for good.

The US insists it respects the one-China principle but sells arms to Taiwan worth tens of billions of dollars. President Joe Biden has more than once said the US would defend Taiwan in an attack from the mainland.

Most recently, the bipartisan Taiwan Policy Act proposes to recognise Taiwan as a "major non-Nato ally". Amid growing tensions, Beijing has to suspect that Washington is developing what Henry Kissinger called "something of a 'two-China' solution".

Washington has to search its soul to answer two questions. First, is Taiwan really America's asset if it risks dragging the US into a war with a peer competitor? And, if the US doesn't wish to confront Russia in Ukraine for fear of a third world war, why would it risk confronting China? Repeated American war gaming has shown that the US might lose in a direct confrontation with China's military in the Taiwan Strait.

Or is it because China has a much smaller nuclear arsenal than Russia's and has a "no first use" nuclear policy? Nukes aside, China's military strength should be no less formidable than Russia's.

The PLA is the largest armed force in the world. Its military budget is more than triple Russia's. It even has more naval ships than the US. If Beijing concludes that it is Russia's next-to-none nuclear stockpile that is deterring the US from intervention, then expanding China's own nuclear stockpile needs only a change of mind.

Beijing and Washington have a few tactical agreements on avoiding accidents at sea or in the air. The problem is, a conflict in the Taiwan Strait can hardly be accidental. If Beijing believes any suggestions on "guardrails" are simply American guile to handicap China's reunification efforts, these guardrails will not be established.

Much has been said about how the US could turn Taiwan into a "porcupine" by enhancing its self-defence capabilities. But a few more sea mines, armed drones and anti-ship missiles are hardly game-changing.

Today's PLA is much more confident and capable of guarding China's "red lines" than at its last missile exercises in the strait in 1995-1996. A Taiwan Strait that is only 180 kms wide can only feel narrower for the PLA in the future.

Beijing still has strategic patience and that is a chance for Washington. Quite a few Western capitals suspect the war in Ukraine will encourage Beijing to take over Taiwan soon. There is no indication of that.

The best example of Beijing's patience is the military budget announced after the war in Ukraine began. It remains below 2 per cent of gross domestic product, a level it has maintained for decades. China has never announced a timetable for reunification. After all, what is the use of an island that is shattered?

It is in America's interests to invigorate rather than hollow out the one-China policy. Given its extensive connection with both sides, it could have a unique role to play as an honest broker. As the first step, Washington should encourage the Taiwanese authorities to accept the one-China consensus.

The one-China pledge made by then-leader Ma Ying-jeou gave Taiwan tremendous benefits, including a tacit agreement from the mainland not to shake up Taiwan's relationship with a handful of countries that diplomatically recognise Taiwan. The sooner Taiwan has a conversation with the mainland, the more it stands to gain. Only in this way can Beijing believe there is still peace to maintain in the strait.

Second, the US needs to exercise more self-discipline. Even if Biden and the Pentagon didn't like Pelosi's visit, it still happened.

Beijing is not so naive as to believe that Biden couldn't make a phone call to stop the trip.

Visits to Taiwan by American officials, which are likely to increase, are merely symbolic. But they will invite a steady and substantive Chinese response. Taiwan will feel the ever-harder pinch even as the prospect of a China-US conflict looms larger.

One lesson from the Cold War is that even enemies can find ways to avoid a military conflict. China and the US are not enemies yet. In a cold war where both face mutually assured destruction, the best thing that two competitors can achieve is mutually assured coexistence. War doesn't have to be inevitable, but prevention requires earnest effort.

US SHOULD NOT ALLOW TAIWAN ISSUE TO HURT ITS ALL-IMPORTANT RELATIONSHIP WITH CHINA

First published in *South China Morning Post*, 12 January 2017

It is like opening Pandora's box right in front of Beijing: on December 23, outgoing US President Barack Obama signed into law the National Defence Authorisation Act for Fiscal Year 2017. Section 1284 of the act authorises the Secretary of Defence to carry out a programme of exchanges between the United States and Taiwan involving senior military officers and top officials. This allows generals or flag officers of the US military on active duty, as well as Pentagon officials higher than the level of assistant defence secretary, to visit Taiwan.

Such a move is far more consequential than Tsai Ing-wen's phone call to President-elect Donald Trump. The call, the first of its kind since 1979, is viewed by Beijing as a violation of the "one China" policy. The permitted US-Taiwan military exchanges, juxtaposed with American arms sales authorised by the Taiwan Relations Act, may well become another persistent irritant that will haunt China-US relations in years to come.

The exchanges, allowing threat analysis, force planning, logistical support, intelligence collection and analysis, present a sharp contrast to the authorisation act for the fiscal year 2000, which restricts the US military's exchanges with the Chinese military in 12 similar but more sophisticated operational areas, such as force projection operations, advanced combined-arms and joint combat operations and advanced logistical operations. In fact, if the 2000 act is implemented to the letter, there won't be any significant exchanges between the Chinese and the US military except in humanitarian areas. Capitol Hill fears the exchanges might help enhance the People's Liberation Army's capabilities and "create a national security risk" for the US.

Trump likes to say that he is unpredictable, but US-Taiwan relations are predictable. The stronger China becomes, the less the US can play the Taiwan issue as a wild card. Today, China is an indispensable partner for the US in addressing major global issues, including counterterrorism, climate change and the North Korean nuclear issue. America's relationship with China far outweighs its ties with Taiwan. The last thing the US wants is to become involved in a war triggered by Taiwan's move for independence.

Taiwan's security doesn't lie in its military exchanges with America. Rather, it depends on how much trust mainland China places in the Taiwanese leader. The Taiwan-US military exchanges, seen against the growing strength of the mainland military forces, are only symbolic in nature. Yes, the phone call between Tsai and Trump might be a "breakthrough" for Taiwan, but it couldn't be more expensive. In December last year, the government of São Tomé and Príncipe decided to cease its recognition of Taiwan, and instead recognise the People's Republic of China. This is widely taken as Beijing's warning to Tsai who, unlike her predecessor, still dodges acknowledging the "one China" policy by shrouding it in calculated ambiguity.

If the latest US act won't help the Taiwanese government as much as it wishes, the 2000 act has proved to be no strict barrier to military relations between China and the US. The reason is simple: the US military cannot afford not to have exchanges with the PLA. Without exchanges such as mutual visits, policy talks and joint training, the US military won't be able to monitor and engage an ever stronger PLA. Without mutual understanding, the danger of miscalculations, as proved in a series of incidents including the deadly J-8/EP-3 collision in 2001, will also grow.

This is why the Pentagon sometimes "violated" the act, as claimed by some congressmen, to invite the PLA to attend the US-led Rim of the Pacific, and Cobra Gold, exercises. The two militaries also held joint exercises to counter piracy, as well as in humanitarian assistance and disaster relief. During the G20 Summit in Hangzhou, China and the US announced that they would work together to build capacity for peacekeeping activities in African countries. The two militaries have started to discuss counterterrorism efforts. It remains to be seen whether they can one day join hands in combating international terrorist organisations such as Islamic State.

The 2017 act raises a dilemma for Trump. If he chooses to ignore it, Congress will push him from behind; if he chooses to honour it, it will definitely sour relations with China. So far, China's response towards him has been calm but measured. But Beijing has made it crystal clear that cooperation with the US "would be out of the question" if Trump were to forsake America's long-standing position that Taiwan is part of "one China".

It won't be long before Trump comes to realise, while tiptoeing on the tightrope of the Taiwan issue, that maintaining balance is a delicate art for the performer.

RULING A CHANCE FOR TSAI TO
BREAK IMPASSE

First published in *China Daily*, 29 July 2016

The arbitral tribunal's ruling that Taiping Island, 0.51 square kilometer in area and the largest island in the South China Sea, is a "rock" rather than an "island" sparked public outcries in Taiwan. Sixty-two percent of the people wished Taiwan leader Tsai Ing-wen could visit the island to demonstrate Taiwan's defiance of the ruling.

The South China Sea issue was not Tsai's priority. So far she has eschewed China's historic rights in the South China Sea and the implications of the nine-dash line so as to distance herself from the position of the Chinese mainland. But overwhelming public resentment against the ruling gave her no choice but to denounce it as "totally unacceptable".

Tsai's first priority, realistically, is the economy, which depends heavily on the mainland. The poor performance by her predecessor Ma Ying-jeou on the economic front explains why Taiwan residents selected her—for a change. Her second priority is to break the cross-Straits impasse. The mainland insists that exchanges are possible only if she accepts the 1992 Consensus on one China. So far her attitude has been one of studied ambiguity.

Here is the chance. The protest in Taiwan over the ruling, in fact, resonates with that of the mainland. She could use this to respond positively to public opinion across the Straits. The only price to pay is the pressure from the United States and Japan, neither of which wants her to stress China's historic rights in the South China Sea, let alone join hands with the mainland on the sovereignty issue. But Tsai could still frame her move by citing the obvious loophole in the ruling and the overwhelming public opinion. This is a price she can afford.

She could, in the first place, heed public opinion to visit Taiping Island. Her predecessors Chiang Ching-Kuo, Chen Shui-bian and Ma Ying-jeou did so while in office. The one who didn't is Lee Teng-hui. She could show that she is no less determined on China's sovereignty. And she could make a difference. If she visits two months after taking office, it will be impressive. Ma visited the island only toward the end of his tenure. Apparently he didn't need to bother about US disapproval any more.

Tsai could make the position of Taiwan on the South China Sea clearer. A day after the ruling, she stood on the frigate *Di Hua* and said: "Now is the time for us to demonstrate our resolve to safeguard the country's interests." But her remarks that the frigate's upcoming patrol "carries special significance as new changes just occurred yesterday (July 12) in the South China Sea" sound more like a concealed analogy.

In contrast, Ma made it crystal clear on Taiping Island that the sovereignty of Nansha, Xisha, Zhongsha, Dongsha islands and their surrounding waters is beyond doubt Chinese. Ma also elaborated how islands in the South China Sea had been included in the coastal defense system since 1721 during the Qing Dynasty and how, legally speaking, the island was not a rock at all.

Also, Tsai could strengthen the defense of Taiping Island, organize more frigate patrols and even drills in the South China Sea. She could even take the boldest step—allow scholars from the mainland to use the archives on the South China Sea in Taiwan. Most of the archives were shipped to Taiwan when the Kuomintang withdrew from the mainland. Historians and legal experts across the Straits could hold workshops or seminars making use of the documents. She could also allow low sensitivity cooperation on, say, fishing and salvage operations with the mainland in the South China Sea. None of these steps have been taken by her predecessors. So she could make history.

A SHOT AT CROSS-STRAIT DIPLOMACY

CAN TSAI ING-WEN TURN THE MISSILE MISFIRE CRISIS INTO AN OPPORTUNITY?

First published in *South China Morning Post*, 16 August 2016

It cannot be more ironic: over the years, the Taiwanese authorities have labelled the tactical missiles of the mainland as the biggest threat, but on July 1, an anti-ship missile was misfired by the Taiwanese navy in the direction of the mainland, killing a Taiwanese fisherman and wounding three in a fishing boat.

Appalled Taiwanese media hyped up how the mainland could have retaliated with showers of missiles, if the stray one had hit anywhere on the other side of the Taiwan Strait.

This shows how precarious peace can be across the strait. Compared with situations around the Diaoyu Islands and in the South China Sea, few would describe the Taiwan Strait as dangerous. During the meeting between Xi Jinping and Ma Ying-jeou in Singapore, Ma declared that the strait was more peaceful than at any time since 1949. However, the stray missile reveals how, in life, the seemingly impossible can suddenly become possible in a dangerous way. The fact is that, of all the wars in history, almost a third were triggered by accidents that were misread.

The Taiwan Strait is more volatile after Tsai Ing-wen became Taiwanese leader on May 20. There are no more cross-strait exchanges. Beijing maintains that such exchanges can only be conducted under the "one China" principle which Ma accepted, but Tsai has so far dodged. Thus, the Taiwanese authorities could reportedly only inform the mainland about the missile misfire via a fax and a mobile phone text message.

This is in sharp contrast with the military hotlines China has established with Russia, the US, South Korea and Vietnam. There is even a video link between the Chinese and the US military. And, in spite of the Diaoyu dispute, China and Japan are negotiating a maritime and air liaison mechanism.

The mainland is distrustful of Tsai, with good reason. Her "green camp", the Democratic Progressive Party, is pro-independence. She was one of the chief drafters of the "special state-to-state relations doctrine" of former Taiwanese leader Lee Teng-hui, which describes the mainland and Taiwan as special but equal states across the strait. Her remarks on the 1992 Consensus on "one China" at her inauguration ceremony were shrouded in studied ambiguity, which the mainland has refused to buy.

Tsai's challenge is to make a quick U-turn while pretending she is still the same person. Time is not on her side, not now or in the future.

If indeed the first 100 days in office serve as a good indicator of a leader's capability, her quick fall in public opinion in the first two months makes her a lame duck in the beginning. The economy, her first priority, is a shambles. Worse still, it depends largely on the mainland. She has few bargaining chips. The mainland's resumption of diplomatic ties with Gambia before she officially took office is a reminder of how Taiwan's diplomatic ties could crumble, if Beijing were to give a nod to those countries ready to switch ties from Taipei to Beijing.

She has to whitewash her "green" colour, from now. Here is the chance. Beijing is adamant that secession means war, but it doesn't want a war, either. That is why since 2004, the mainland, while maintaining its "one China" policy, has been calling for establishing a cross-strait military mechanism for mutual trust. The misfired missile is proof of Beijing's insight. Tsai could use the grave mistake on the Taiwanese side to respond to the mainland initiative, starting with a sincere apology and a responsible explanation.

She could go further, and turn the crisis into an opportunity. During Ma's tenure, his ruling Kuomintang had an on-off but generally positive attitude towards Beijing's proposal. During his meeting with Xi in Singapore, Ma raised some security-related points such as lowering the level of hostility, resolving disputes in a peaceful manner and setting up a hotline for emergencies. These points accord, by and large, with the mainland's initiative. Tsai should have no difficulty accepting them. She could elaborate further on the Taiwanese proposals and, more importantly, draw up a road map for future cross-strait talks.

However, if this is difficult at this stage, she could take a bottom-up approach and allow for non-governmental exchanges first. At the 2013 Cross-Strait Peace Forum in Shanghai, 120 mainland and Taiwanese experts and academics concluded it was necessary to have contact and exchanges between the militaries across the strait. This could start in less-sensitive areas such as humanitarian aid and disaster relief, and then spill over into other more sophisticated spheres.

According to Ma, Taiwan and the mainland have 23,000 sq km of overlapping air defence identification zones. The People's Liberation Army has been carrying out more and more drills in the Western Pacific. The militaries on either side of the strait need to discuss how to reduce the risk of conflict. So far, both sides have a tacit agreement for military ships and aircraft not to trespass over the intermediate line in the Taiwan Strait. In the South China Sea, Taiwan-controlled Taiping Island is situated among mainland-controlled Yongshu, Meiji and Zhubi reefs. Could the two sides sign and adopt the same procedures as in the "Code for Unplanned Encounters at Sea" that China signed with 20 other countries in 2014 to avoid accidents?

Finally, is it possible one day to have a Xi-Tsai meeting? Such a possibility looks remote now. But, in politics, everything is possible.

4

SHOULDERING CHINA'S INTERNATIONAL RESPONSIBILITIES

HOW CHINA CAN IMPROVE
UN PEACEKEEPING

THE RIGHT WAY FOR BEIJING TO STEP UP

First published in *Foreign Affairs*, 15 November 2017. Reprinted by permission of *Foreign Affairs*. Copyright (2017) by the Council on Foreign Relations, Inc. www.ForeignAffairs.com

The world's need for peacekeeping has never been higher. Conflicts have displaced more than 65 million people and are affecting the lives of a record number of others. Yet today, the United Nations' peacekeeping programs are shrinking, rather than expanding: its peacekeeping mission in Côte d'Ivoire ended in June, its mission in Liberia will end next year, and its 14 other peacekeeping programs are under review by the UN Security Council.

China can help. It is the biggest contributor of peacekeeping troops among the five permanent members of the UN Security Council and the second-biggest financial contributor to the UN's peacekeeping programs. Since September 2015, when Chinese President Xi Jinping pledged to increase China's peacekeeping efforts in a speech at the UN, it has stepped up further. Some

1,100 foreign peacekeepers have already been trained in Beijing, and China plans to train 900 more by 2020. This August, the first contingent of Chinese helicopters arrived in Darfur, a war-torn region in western Sudan. And in September, China registered a peacekeeping standby force of 8,000 troops that the UN can draw on in times of need. Eight hundred fifty of those soldiers will join the UN's so-called Vanguard Brigade—a rapid-response group that will quickly deploy to conflict zones during crises. (In my role in China's Ministry of National Defense, I manage the PLA's multilateral cooperation programs, including those related to peacekeeping.)

By providing the UN with high-quality equipment and manpower, working to make peacekeepers' mandates more achievable, and helping to train the forces and maintain some of the Chinese-made equipment of troop-contributing countries, China could do more to improve UN peacekeeping. Cooperating with the United States to develop the peacekeeping capacities of some African states, meanwhile, would help improve the Chinese-U.S. relationship and contribute to Africa's stability.

Why China Should Step Up

China has good reason to beef up its peacekeeping commitments. Supporting global governance provides what the country needs most: an image as a responsible nation on a peaceful rise. What is more, two of peacekeeping's guiding principles—impartiality and the "nonuse of force except in self-defense and defense of mandate," as the UN puts it—resonate with China's foreign policy and military ethos. Whereas the former aligns with China's commitment to avoid interfering in the domestic affairs of other states, the latter recalls the classical Chinese strategist Sun Tzu's axiom that it is best to subdue one's adversaries without violence. And thanks to its deep resources and major interests in global stability, China has the potential to become a peacekeeping leader.

Because the United States seems likely to scale back its own role at the UN, China's commitments will be especially important in the years ahead. U.S. President Donald Trump's call for a $1 billion cut to the United States' peacekeeping contributions would deal a blow to the world body. That does not mean that China will replace the United States as the UN's biggest donor. But by supporting peacekeeping further, Beijing can make a difference.

Doing so effectively requires improving not just the quantity but also the quality of UN peacekeeping. First, China could become a consistent source of so-called enabling units—the special forces, engineering, transport, communications, and aviation troops that are essential to peacekeepers' success. It could also provide more female peacekeepers, who tend to have an easier time working with female civilians, especially in Muslim communities. So far, around 800 Chinese women have served on UN peacekeeping missions, and 60 foreign female peacekeepers have been trained in China.

China and other governments should also try to move peacekeeping missions away from so-called Christmas-tree mandates, or lists of responsibilities that are so extensive that the UN has trouble meeting them. When UN peacekeeping began in 1948, peacekeepers' only job was to observe a ceasefire between Israel and its Arab neighbors. Since then, the demands on peacekeepers have grown. The UN's mission in the Central African Republic, for instance, tasks peacekeepers with 11 different responsibilities, from protecting civilians and facilitating humanitarian assistance to supporting justice and the rule of law. The UN should streamline those oversized mandates. It should also do more to improve the intelligence and logistical operations it carries out to support peacekeepers. This could help prevent losses like those suffered by UN troops in Mali and South Sudan in 2016, when three Chinese peacekeepers were killed.

Improving UN peacekeeping requires working not just with the world body but also with other countries. Many of the developing states that are involved in peacekeeping buy Chinese military equipment, partly because it tends to be cheaper than similar products made elsewhere. There are a few ways that this process could become smoother. In 2007, for example, Nepal bought a number of Chinese armored personnel carriers. Instead of shipping them to Nepal, the Nepalese military sent them directly to the Golan Heights, where a number of Nepalese peacekeepers are based; the UN paid for the shipping costs. These types of arrangements can make delivering equipment to peacekeepers cheaper.

Train and Maintain

Much of China's military assistance goes to Africa, which is also the site of most of the UN's peacekeeping missions. If African states agree, China could devote more of its own military assistance programs to peacekeeping on the continent. Its delivery of military assistance in support of Burundian and Ugandan peacekeepers in Somalia in 2008 set a good precedent. At a conference in Tokyo in August, Chinese officials raised the possibility of setting up a facility in Africa where China could train more African peacekeepers, either on its own or together with troop-contributing African governments. This would be cheaper than training African peacekeepers in China. Beijing could also help maintain African peacekeepers' Chinese-made equipment.

As for the African Union, its independent peacekeeping missions tend to be undermanned, undertrained, and underresourced. Since 2010, China has supported the AU's efforts; in 2015, it pledged to give the AU $100 million to help it establish a standby force and to improve its ability to respond to crises. China and the AU are working together to use that assistance to help AU peacekeepers get better at projecting force and surviving in the field. Next, China should join the European Union and the United States in their own efforts to improve the peacekeeping capacities of African states. In Mali, Chinese commanders supporting the UN's peacekeeping mission and EU commanders working on their own training program for Malian troops already meet regularly. They could now explore cooperation between EU Battlegroups (battalion sized forces to which various EU countries contribute) and the Chinese peacekeeping standby force, as some European officials have suggested. Troops from both forces, for instance, could deploy on short notice in response to UN requests.

The Chinese-U.S. relationship is sometimes characterized by competition, but that is less the case in Africa, especially when it comes to military issues. More collaboration between the two countries on peacekeeping would contribute to stability on the continent, improving the world's most important bilateral relationship at the same time. At the G20 Summit in Hangzhou in 2016 and during Trump's recent visit to China, the two countries pledged to achieve just that. Such Chinese-U.S. cooperation could make the world less dangerous and convince more people that Chinese-U.S. relations, however complicated, are not hostile. If Beijing and Washington jointly support peacekeepers in African states—for example, by assisting them with training and equipment—Africans, Americans, and Chinese would all win.

CHINA CAN USE ITS LEVERAGE WITH RUSSIA TO PREVENT A NUCLEAR WAR

First published in *Financial Times*, 27 October 2022

Will Putin use nuclear weapons in Ukraine? This billion-dollar question matters not only to Kyiv and Europe, but also to China. So far Beijing has trodden a careful line between Russia, its strategic partner, and Ukraine, which is a significant trading partner. During September's Samarkand summit, Vladimir Putin thanked China for its "balanced position" on the Ukraine conflict.

But if Moscow decides to use tactical nuclear weapons against Ukraine, China can hardly maintain such a position anymore. A joint declaration between Beijing and Kyiv in December 2013 agreed that China will not use or threaten to use nuclear weapons against Ukraine and, more importantly, will provide security assurances in the event of any such threat by a third party.

Putin's intensifying rhetoric is therefore raising the stakes for Beijing. He said last month he would be ready to defend the "territorial integrity" of Russia "by all means." If his military is struggling on the battlefield—which it is in areas such as Kharkiv, where Ukrainian forces are retaking lost territory—

then the likelihood of Russia deploying tactical nuclear missiles only increases.

China has so far refrained from providing any military assistance to Russia. But given Beijing's huge influence on Moscow, it is uniquely positioned to do more to prevent a nuclear conflict.

First, Beijing should tell Moscow to honour the five nuclear powers' joint statement in January that "nuclear war cannot be won and must never be fought". Russia has the largest nuclear arsenal in the world and threatening Ukraine—which chose to give up its nuclear weapons—has already tarnished its reputation. It would be all the more appalling if Putin followed through on his threat against Ukrainian citizens, who he had previously described as "practically one people" with Russians.

Second, Beijing should make clear to the Kremlin that using nuclear weapons on the battlefield would put China in a very difficult situation. Beijing has maintained a policy of "no first use" of nuclear weapons for more than half a century. While other defence policies have changed, this has held firm and China prides itself on having nuclear strategies which are the most stable, sustainable and predictable among nuclear powers.

The last thing Beijing wants now is a sour relationship with European capitals. At a time when the US is ramping up its competition with China, it is particularly important that Europe does not always take America's side. Putin has admitted that Beijing had "questions and concerns" about Russia's invasion— but if he uses nuclear weapons, then Beijing's response will go far beyond questions and concerns. Could China remain neutral in the event of international protests against Moscow? And could Beijing abstain from a UN Security Council vote condemning Russia for its actions?

Finally, Beijing could play a significant role in brokering a deal between Russia and Nato. For example, Nato could promise to halt any further expansion in exchange for Moscow agreeing to not to use nuclear weapons. Such a compromise would save face on both sides. During the 1962 Cuban missile crisis, US President John F. Kennedy and Soviet leader Nikita Khrushchev reached a similar agreement: the Soviets would dismantle their ballistic missiles in Cuba in exchange for a US pledge not to invade Cuba again. Secretly, America also agreed to dismantle all of the Jupiter medium-range ballistic missiles which had been stationed in Turkey for possible use against Russia.

Since Moscow's primary concern has been Nato expansion, Putin might find this option worth considering. It would be worth thinking about for Nato too. The alliance's expansion in the face of the Kremlin's warnings has helped push Europe to the brink of a nuclear conflict. Putin is right to conclude this is a war between Russia and the west rather than between Russia and Ukraine. As a goodwill gesture, Nato could pledge not to use nuclear weapons first against Russia or within Moscow's sphere of influence.

In a 2018 documentary, Putin asked, "Why do we need a world without Russia in it?" The answer should be, "But where is Russia without the world?" If Putin now opens a nuclear Pandora's box that was kept closed even during the Cold War, it would be a moment of infinite stupidity. China can help the world by simply telling Putin: don't use nuclear weapons, Mr President.

IN UKRAINE AND GAZA, CHINA'S GREAT POWER COMES WITH GREAT RESPONSIBILITY

First published in *South China Morning Post*, 9 August 2024

History is mostly made up of the mundane but remembered for the remarkable. For historians of Chinese diplomacy, China's success in restoring diplomatic ties between arch-rivals Iran and Saudi Arabia might well be remembered as a turning point. The signing of the Beijing Declaration for unity by 14 Palestinian factions should have raised eyebrows further—in a most volatile region, China has succeeded in herding the cats, at least for a while.

Can China build on these to become a global peacemaker? The precondition to being a peacemaker is being trusted for neutrality or, more precisely, impartiality. The neutrality of great powers is not normally very reliable because, given the realism of international relations, self-interest could drive them to alter the distribution of world power in their favour. That is why when it comes to honest brokers, people often think of middle powers such as Norway, Switzerland and Sweden.

But China stands out. Unlike Britain or France, it has no historic burden of being a coloniser. Unlike Russia, which would use force to maintain its spheres of influence, China needs no such spheres as its influence, especially in the global economy, is ubiquitous. And unlike the United States, China has shown no missionary zeal to police the world through hegemony or alliance. All of China's military operations overseas in recent decades, whether in peacekeeping, counterpiracy or disaster relief, have been invariably humanitarian in nature.

If China has waded into deeper waters in the Middle East, then in Ukraine, Beijing has tried its best to strike a balance in a war between two of its friends.

It has almost never voted against or vetoed any of the UN resolutions condemning Russia, but rather only abstained. While the US-led Nato has provided full military support to Ukraine, Beijing has provided no military aid or weapons to Moscow. True, China's trade with Russia has helped it skirt Western sanctions, but the trade went on before the war and none of it violates international rules or regimes. Last year, Ukraine's largest trading partner remained China, with a trade revenue of around US$12.9 billion.

It remains to be seen how China's 12-point peace plan and its six-point joint proposal with Brazil might work. After all, China is not the only country that has tabled a peace plan, and all peace plans rest on the precondition of a ceasefire.

But none is in sight. Russia must gain full control of the four annexed regions in Eastern Ukraine to be able to declare victory while a Ukraine fully supported by the West has every reason not to relinquish territory.

Still, no war can last forever. As Ukrainian forces lose ground and the US gears up for a presidential election that could fundamentally change Western support for Ukraine, Kyiv may find it imperative to reach out to Beijing.

During his first trip to China since Russia invaded Ukraine in February 2022, Ukrainian Foreign Minister Dmytro Kuleba said "a just peace" in Ukraine is in China's strategic interests and that Beijing's role as "a global force for peace" is important.

Beijing can help in at least three ways. First, it can facilitate a ceasefire dialogue between Moscow and Kyiv. Russia was not invited to the peace summit held in Switzerland in June and China did not attend. Now Ukrainian President Volodymyr Zelensky is calling for a second peace summit to be held in a Global South country, and suggested that Russia could be invited. Could that Global South country be China? Should the warring parties agree, Beijing could well be the willing host.

On August 12, a Chinese Foreign Ministry spokesman answered a question on the entry of Ukrainian troops into Russian territory. China called on all sides to abide by the 'three principles' for cooling down the situation.

Second, China could, with other major powers, help provide a collective security guarantee for an armistice, the most likely scenario so far after a ceasefire. Without such a guarantee, Ukraine can never be sure that Russia will remain content with what it has annexed, and Russia would worry about the annexed lands becoming another Afghanistan with Ukrainian fighters in the role of the 1980s mujahideen.

Other questions are bound to crop up. If Ukraine has to give up some of its territory, where will the new border be drawn? Will the contested territory be put under an international trusteeship with proper referendums so residents can state their preferences? Will peacekeeping forces be allowed to monitor ceasefire lines?

None of these issues can be bilaterally resolved by Moscow and Kyiv. They demand United Nations involvement and a large dose of US-China cooperation. If Russia listened to anyone, it would be China. The onus on the US, then, is to secure Ukrainian cooperation.

Third, China is in a better position than any other country to help with post-war rehabilitative reconstruction, be it in Ukraine or Gaza. In March last year, the World Bank estimated the cost of the reconstruction and restoration of Ukraine's infrastructure at US$411 billion, more than double its 2023 gross domestic product. According to the UN, reconstructing Gaza will need US$40–50 billion at least, with rebuilding lost homes alone taking a minimum of 16 years.

While who will pay for reconstruction in Ukraine and Gaza remains an open question, China's capabilities in infrastructure-building, which are second to none, can most certainly help.

It is intriguing to see how Beijing is starting to have a say in Europe and the Middle East where it has traditionally pursued economic gains and downplayed any security role. When China started reforms in the late 1970s, it was "crossing the river by feeling the stones". It is now wading into the ocean and there is no seabed it can touch nor can it turn back. Being a responsible global power comes at a price.

CAN CHINA AND THE U.S. COOPERATE MILITARILY IN AFRICA?

First published in China-US Focus, 20 August 2014

The recently concluded US-Africa Leaders Summit is seen as a "catch up with China" campaign. When President Obama said that "we don't look to Africa simply for its natural resources ... We don't simply want to extract minerals from the ground for our growth", he didn't mention China by name, but everybody can see easily that he was chewing some sour grapes.

With less than half of China's $210 billion trade volume with Africa last year, economically the US has clearly lost ground. Then what about in the security arena which is truly the US focus? Militarily, is the US more influential than China on the African continent?

On the face of it, the US influence seems greater. The US military involvements are so variegated that they range from changing Gaddafi's regime, combating militant Islamism to counter-piracy and prevention and treatment of HIV/AIDS. Some of these operations didn't go without controversies. A simple truth is that 7 years after the setup of AFRICOM in

Stuttgart, Germany, the US has yet to find an African country that volunteers to accept AFRICOM on its territory.

Chinese military influence in Africa doesn't look as salient as its trading, but it is deep-rooted. In fact except a very few countries that don't have diplomatic relations with China, there exist strong and extensive military links between China and the African countries, characterized with visits, military assistance, arms trade, and personnel training both in China and in Africa.

It started with China supporting the independence movement by training thousands of "freedom fighters" against colonial rule from the 1950s. Among the most distinguished people trained by the Chinese are President Laurent Kabila and President Joseph Kabila of DRC, President Sam Nujoma of Namibia, President Isaias Afewerki of Eritrea, President Robert Mugabe of Zimbabwe, President Samora M Machel and President Joaquim Chissano of Mozambique. In fact, PLA training is so wide-ranging that wherever you go in Africa, you can easily meet military officers trained in China.

China is the largest exporter and the largest trader in the world. It has extensive national interests overseas, and it is ready to shoulder more international obligations as a responsible power. China's security needs in Africa include the security of Chinese citizens, property, investment and strategic lines of communications in both the Indian Ocean and the Atlantic Ocean.

Unlike the US, China doesn't have military bases abroad. So far Chinese military involvement in Africa is essentially or almost deliberately humanitarian in nature. PLA assisted African countries in disaster relief and de-mining. PLA Navy's hospital ship visited the Somali Basin twice and provided free medical treatment to the local people. And the military operations of PLA on the continent are just peacekeeping.

Do China and the US have the same security interests in Africa? The answer is yes, except in the case of "humanitarian intervention". So far China has refrained from using any force overseas. In December 2013, the international media hyped up about China sending "combat troops" to Mali for the first time in history. But the troops are merely meant to protect the UN peacekeepers. Even in counter-piracy in the Gulf of Aden, the Chinese Navy is more deterrent than aggressive towards the pirates. China would not take part in any military operations unauthorized by the UN. In 2013, Premier Li Keqiang announced that China would support the African people in resolving African issues by African means.

China and the US could cooperate in Africa, primarily in three areas:

Peacekeeping. Of the current ten peacekeeping missions of PLA in the world, eight are in Africa. China is the largest troop contributor among five permanent members of the UN Security Council while the US is the largest fund contributor. The US has also contributed significantly in peacekeeping training of African soldiers. Not only can the two militaries exchange experience in troop deployment, rules of engagement, security awareness and logistic support, but they can also provide support and training to peacekeepers of the African Union who are considered less effective due to lack of funds, equipment and expertise.

Counter-piracy. Right now piracy is kept at bay in the Gulf of Aden and Somali basin thanks to the joint efforts by the international navies including China and the US. The problem now is the Gulf of Guinea where piracy and armed robbery are rampant. The Gulf of Guinea is a vital source of oil imports for China. Chinese merchant vessel *Yue Liangwan* was hijacked there. From late May to mid-June, 2014, the 16th Task Force of PLA Navy had bilateral exercises with Cameron, Nigeria and Namibia, the first time that the Chinese navy appears off the west coast of

Africa. Equally the US, French and British navies have patrols in the gulf. They could have joint exercises with the Chinese navy and the littoral states in these waters to demonstrate their collective resolve and enhance their interoperabilities.

Capacity building. The Chinese and the US military can help a lot in the capacity building of African countries. In May 2014, Premier Li Keqiang declared that China will provide assistance to African standby forces and quick response forces, support collective security mechanisms in Africa, cooperate with African countries in training, intelligence sharing and joint exercises and strengthen their capabilities in peacekeeping, counterterrorism and counter-piracy. Given that the US military is making almost similar efforts in these areas, they could collaborate, coordinate and synchronize their efforts. The Chinese and the US militaries used to have a bilateral program on preventing pandemic disease. The outbreak of Ebola in Africa looks like a perfect new ground for cooperation again.

AFRICA IS A TEST LAB FOR HOW CHINA APPROACHES INTERNATIONAL SECURITY AND PEACEKEEPING

NON-INTERFERENCE BUT NOT INDIFFERENCE

First published in *South China Morning Post*, 8 August 2019

The 1st China-Africa Peace and Security Forum in Beijing in July was impressive. Of all 54 African countries, except Swaziland which has no diplomatic relations with the People's Republic, 50 African countries and the African Union sent high-powered delegations including 15 defense ministers and chiefs of defense forces to attend the week long forum.

China's ubiquitous economic activities in Africa are known to all. But fewer people know China's military involvement on the continent has been decades old. From the late 1950s to 1970s, the PLA trained thousands of African "freedom fighters" who played a decisive role in fighting against colonialist rulers for national independence. Among them are seven African presidents such as President Laurent Kabila of DRC, President Sam Nujoma of Namibia, President Isaias Afewerki of Eritrea.

A global China today has to answer this question—how to protect China's ever-growing overseas interests and shoulder her international obligations that are incumbent upon a major power? These interests are particularly vulnerable in the Middle East and in Africa, and there are good and bad lessons to learn. In 2015, Beijing was caught totally unprepared having to withdraw 35,860 Chinese nationals from Libya when violence spread. All the investments and properties were abandoned. But the PLA Navy's counter-piracy operation in the Gulf of Aden since the end of 2008 is a success story. So far the Chinese flotillas have escorted over 6,600 Chinese and foreign ships.

Africa is a lab to test China's outlook for global security governance. Beijing's "five-no" policies towards Africa, i.e., no interference in ways of development; no interference in domestic affairs, no forcing China's will upon African countries, no assistance with political conditions attached and no pursuit of selfish political interests in investments and financing towards Africa, could almost be applied anywhere else around the world. However the west grumbles over such policies for having no "principles" on human rights and democracy, they could at least prove that China really has no intentions to sell her ideology abroad.

All types of PLA overseas involvement, be it peacekeeping, counter-piracy, non-combatant evacuation or disaster relief, could be found in Africa. In dealing almost exclusively with such non-traditional threats, the PLA has given a clue to its modus operandi overseas —helping rather than policing the world. Both China and the US have bases in Djibouti. But China's is only a logistic supply station for counter-piracy and peacekeeping while America's Camp Lemonnier is, according to *The Economist*, "the most important base for drone operations outside the war zone of Afghanistan", with drones conducting missions in Yemen and Somalia.

The biggest challenge for UN peacekeeping in Africa is how to balance, if not reconcile, the principle of non-interference in the domestic affairs of a sovereign state and the responsibility to protect civilians. Non-interference is enshrined in the UN Charter while protection of civilians is now at the heart of UN peacekeeping. For those who vowed "never again" to see another Rwandan Genocide, their cry cannot be louder: What is the use of peacekeeping if civilians cannot be protected? But what if a host-state government changes its consent when its interests conflict with peacekeeping activities such as supporting the implementation of a peace agreement on which the government wishes to renege? And in extreme cases, what if the perpetrator harming civilians happens to be the government itself? The UN has no ready answers to these questions. The African Union purports to have the right to intervene in its member states in "grave circumstances", namely, war crimes, genocide and crimes against humanity, but it is not easy to decide upon or implement, given the practical, legal and procedural problems.

Such a situation could be particularly challenging for the Chinese government which takes non-interference as the core of its foreign policies but wishes to be taken as "non-indifferent". Beijing didn't sign the Kigali Principles on the Protection of Civilians, but China's support for protection of civilians as a permanent member of UNSC is reflected in Security Council resolutions which have gradually placed protection of civilians as top priority of peacekeeping since 1999. Besides, out of 8,000 standby peacekeeping troops that China has established, 850 of those soldiers are already registered with the UN's Vanguard Brigade. They have to be deployed within 60 days to new trouble-spots primarily for the purpose of protecting civilians.

China has neither colonies nor sphere of influence in Africa, therefore it can actually provide more help with clean hands without being misinterpreted. But the best way to enhance security in Africa is to support Africans in resolving African issues by African means. This explains why ever since 2010, China has been stepping up military assistance to the AU to support collective security mechanisms in Africa. Cooperation is found in training, intelligence sharing and joint exercises. In 2015, President Xi Jinping announced in UN Headquarters to provide $100 million to the AU to support African standby forces and quick response forces.

The forum, being called the 1st China-Africa Peace and Security Forum, indicates it is not a one off. Rather, it is a new start for Chinese and Africans to join hands again to change the continent's security landscape for the better.

SAUDI-IRAN DEAL IS A STEPPING STONE FOR CHINA IN ITS GLOBAL ROLE AS HONEST BROKER

First published in *South China Morning Post*, 29 March 2023

China's success as a mediator between Iran and Saudi Arabia is more than a milestone. It is also a stepping stone leading to higher expectations: can China help similarly elsewhere?

In the Middle East, where it is sometimes said that the enemy of my enemy is not necessarily my friend, there are enough troubles for Beijing to address. Being the only major power that befriends everybody thanks to its policy of non-alliance and non-interference, China can probably further help with another more pressing problem—the Iranian nuclear issue.

According to the Pentagon, Tehran's nuclear development has been remarkable; it can now produce enough material for a nuclear bomb in 12 days.

The Trump administration withdrew from a nuclear pact in 2018 and negotiations between the Biden administration and Iran on restarting the nuclear deal have stalled. Perhaps Beijing, one of the negotiators of the deal struck in 2015, can first persuade

Tehran behind closed doors—like it did with the Saudi-Iran deal—not to cross the threshold of making a nuclear bomb, before bringing together like-minded stakeholders, including Washington, to renegotiate a new deal with Tehran.

The situation is much more complicated in Ukraine where China's two friends have been at each other's throats. No one knows how long the war will last except that it will last.

The challenge is to find the foundations for a peace agreement—whether it involves Russia's unconditional withdrawal from Ukraine or territorial negotiations and concessions.

Presumably Russia would want to be able to claim at least some victory. Otherwise, Russian President Vladimir Putin would find it hard to explain why he launched the war at all.

Ukraine's President Volodymyr Zelensky said in February that victory is inevitable if allies keep their promises. That means there is indeed a risk of the allies not keeping their promises if this war turns out to be a war of attrition.

Perhaps the end game is an armistice akin to that between North and South Korea, which no one likes. The difference, though, is that Russia is much more powerful than Ukraine, and therefore the border, wherever it might be, would be much more difficult to secure.

It is hard to tell what a new security architecture in Europe might look like. But there would have to be negotiations between Russia and Nato.

The core question is how to address Russia's sense of insecurity. Nato is right to say it hasn't forced countries to join the security alliance, but it is Nato's unrelenting expansion since the end of the Cold War that has backfired.

If Moscow believes Nato's expansion constitutes an existential threat to Russia that it has to use force to push back, then the more popular Nato is, the more insecure Europe will become. It is ludicrous for the most powerful military alliance on Earth, which includes some of the world's strongest nations, to describe itself as a self-defence organisation.

Like in the Middle East, China is the only major power that can play a constructive role in Russo-Ukrainian war. All other major powers have already sided with Ukraine. Beijing is not allied with Moscow, and still friendly with Kyiv. China has Russia's trust even though it has not provided any military support.

And Beijing's role as an honest broker is likely to be welcomed by Kyiv. During then Ukrainian president Viktor Yanukovych's visit to Beijing in December 2013, China declared that it would not use or threaten to use nuclear weapons against Ukraine and would provide security assurances against any such threat by a third party.

Beijing's 12-point peace plan announced at the one-year anniversary of the war is a huge step forward from its carefully balanced position since the outbreak of the conflict. It includes some core concepts that few can challenge, such as the need for all parties to respect sovereignty, exercise rationality and restraint, and prioritise the effective protection of civilians.

But there is no guarantee the peace plan will succeed when both sides have shown no inclination to stop fighting. In 2022, Zelensky even signed a decree banning any negotiation with Putin. The recent arrest warrant for Putin issued by the International Criminal Court will make any chance of a ceasefire slimmer.

Washington is strongly opposed to a ceasefire too, saying that this will only freeze Russia's gains on the ground.

In spite of Russia's announcement of deploying tactical nuclear weapons in Belarus, thanks to Beijing, the possibility of Europeans' worst fear—that the war will spill over into a nuclear war—being realised has been considerably reduced.

In his meetings with German Chancellor Olaf Scholz and US President Joe Biden, President Xi has made it crystal clear that no nuclear weapons could be used in Europe. Therefore,

SHOULD THE WORLD FEAR CHINA?

Putin's reiteration in the joint statement with Xi this month that a nuclear war cannot be won and must never be fought should be a huge relief to everyone.

It remains to be seen what Beijing might do next, but it is clear that it has a long to-do list. Apparently in an ever-divided world, people look to China to be a stabiliser as well as an honest broker.

When China kicked off its reform over four decades ago, Chinese leader Deng Xiaoping famously said China needed to cross the river by feeling the stones on the riverbed. Now a global China has entered the ocean. It cannot feel the seabed, but there is no turning back.

ISRAEL-GAZA WAR

WHAT CHINA CAN AND SHOULD DO FOR PEACE IN THE MIDDLE EAST

First published in *South China Morning Post*, 1 November 2023

What is the difference between the Russia-Ukraine conflict and the Israel-Hamas conflict? The answer is: no one knows when the former will end, while no one knows when the latter will begin again even if it ends.

Can China help win peace in the Middle East? The question is asked because of the obvious limitations of the other major powers at the moment.

Russia has considerable influence in the Middle East, but given that it is fighting a war of its own, with Iran believed to be one of its arms suppliers, it has little hope of winning Israel's trust. The EU is deeply polarized and powerless in the face of pro-Palestine Muslim protests across the continent and beyond. The US, being Israel's staunch ally, has historically provided unconditional support to Israel in all conflicts.

That leaves China. After brokering a historic rapprochement between once-estranged Saudi Arabia and Iran, a more ambitious Beijing had been trying to initiate peace talks between the Israelis and Palestinians even before the latest conflict erupted.

Chinese support for the Palestinian cause goes back to the days of Mao Zedong. At the same time, China has developed robust economic ties with Israel starting from the 1980s. Tel Aviv has said it was disappointed that Beijing did not denounce Hamas directly in the wake of the October 7 attacks. But, as foreign ministry spokeswoman Mao Ning put it, Beijing considers itself a friend to both Israel and Palestine.

Since the latest outbreak of violence, Beijing has made phone calls, provided humanitarian aid and sent an envoy to the region. But the best thing China can do—short of stopping Israeli retaliation, a mission impossible even for the UN—is help avert a regional conflagration.

This is possible. Middle Eastern countries have moved closer to China in recent years. In the recent expansion of the China-centered BRICS grouping, four Middle Eastern countries—Egypt, Iran, the UAE and Saudi Arabia—joined.

Especially helpful now is if China could use its sway with Iran, a long-term supporter of Hezbollah, to prevent the militant group from opening a war front in Israel's north. Hezbollah is a more serious threat to Israel than Hamas because of its vast arsenal of missiles and thousands of experienced fighters.

Another area where China could contribute is in peacekeeping. Israel is unlikely to eliminate Hamas with its war, and an Israeli occupation will surely backfire. This means peacekeeping could be needed one day.

Israel has in the past rejected Palestinian calls for peacekeepers in Gaza and the occupied West Bank, but it may have to reconsider this.

The first UN peacekeeping mission was in fact set up to monitor the truce agreement in the 1948 Arab-Israeli war. Today, peacekeepers are authorised to do much more than observe a ceasefire. They can help protect civilians, maintain civil order, repatriate refugees and rebuild basic services. China, which is already the largest provider of peacekeeping troops among the permanent members of the UN Security Council, is well placed to lead this peacekeeping effort.

Much has been said about how Beijing might fill the vacuum left by Washington in the Middle East. This is misleading. Even if Washington wants to leave, it cannot extricate itself, as can be seen in the current conflict.

Instead, Beijing and Washington have common interests in a stable and peaceful Middle East. Neither side has any reason to oppose efforts by the other to foster peace. Notably, both share similar views on the two most important issues in the region—a two-state solution for the Israeli-Palestinian conflict, and preventing the Iranians from developing nuclear weapons.

As Gaza grapples with the worst violence in 50 years, the two-state solution first proposed in a 1974 UN resolution looks like utopia now. Therefore, Beijing and Washington should join hands in diplomacy, adopting the two-state solution as the paramount principle guiding any road map forward.

Without a political solution, the Israelis will always live in fear. And the latest violence has brought home why the Palestinians deserve a homeland.

Beijing and Washington must also work together to find a solution to the Iranian nuclear impasse. The Gaza war will exacerbate Iran's concerns over its own security, and may make it more determined to develop nuclear weapons.

On this issue, China's biggest advantage is Tehran's trust. China has been the only major power to give Iran an economic lifeline in the face of US sanctions. China should make it clear to Iran that even if it is entitled to the peaceful use of nuclear energy, Iran must not develop nuclear bombs under its guise.

This distinction must be made. Despite its solid relations with Russia, for example, China also made it crystal clear it would not tolerate the use of nuclear weapons.

Thus Beijing should tell Tehran that even if Iran were to succeed in developing a nuclear bomb, it would not enhance its security. Instead, Iran might suffer a pre-emptive military strike by Israel, or Israel and the US together. It would most certainly invite severe UN sanctions, which China, despite being Iran's largest trading partner, has to honour.

A nuclear-armed Iran might trigger a chain reaction of other regional powers, such as Saudi Arabia and Turkey, developing nuclear weapons. Like a nuclearised North Korea, Iran would never become a "normal country".

In a region where my enemy's enemy is not necessarily my friend, China's traditional neutrality makes sense. But China is also the only major power that is friendly with the regional players. This is a huge asset. Beijing should make the best of it to make the Middle East safer.

WHY THE UN—NOT ISRAEL—SHOULD OVERSEE PEACEKEEPING AND SECURITY IN GAZA

First published in *South China Morning Post*, 11 November 2023

The outcome of Israel's sweeping invasion of Gaza is not hard to foresee. Israel's military strength is overwhelmingly superior to that of Hamas. But Hamas can hardly be wiped "off the face of the Earth", as Israeli Defence Minister Yoav Gallant has vowed. The question is, amid mounting civilian deaths, what to do even after a ceasefire?

There is no panacea to what former American president Barack Obama recently described as "century-old stuff that's coming to the fore".

As the Israeli military campaign against Hamas entered its second month, Prime Minister Benjamin Netanyahu said: "Israel will, for an indefinite period ... have the overall security responsibility" in Gaza once the fighting is over.

But Israeli troops can ill afford to stay indefinitely in Gaza where, to resentful Palestinians, they are but occupying invaders. Even the White House has told Israel that reoccupying Gaza is "not the right thing to do".

The Palestinian Authority that has maintained relative cooperation with the Israeli government might be the most suitable candidate for taking over, but it could be reluctant too. A war that destroys Hamas would also seriously discredit the Palestinian Authority.

With the probability of a two-state solution even more remote, how can it convince Palestinians that cooperation with Israel is still necessary?

According to Bloomberg, the US and Israel have discussed three options: the first is to grant temporary oversight of Gaza to countries from the region, backed by troops from the United States, Britain, Germany and France.

The second is a peacekeeping force, modelled on the Multinational Force and Observers (MFO) group that operates on and around the Sinai Peninsula between Egypt and Israel. The third would be temporary governance of the strip under a UN umbrella.

None of these options looks perfect. On the first option, the White House has ruled out stationing US troops in Gaza. Despite being the largest financial contributor to global peacekeeping, the US has never really sent out large numbers of troops for such missions.

Even if it changes its mind, such a multilateral force from countries that have so far supported, albeit not wholeheartedly, Israel's no-ceasefire determination, simply won't be trusted by the Palestinians in the first place.

On the second option, the MFO group overseeing peace between Egypt and Israel has proven highly effective and successful. But this is because both countries hold a strong desire for durable and lasting peace.

It is far from certain that any Arab nation, say Egypt or Saudi Arabia, or even a group of Arab countries, would wish to bear the brunt of stabilising a war-torn area engulfed by misery and hatred.

The third option ushers in new light, in spite of inherent problems. Establishing a peacekeeping mission requires the consent of the parties involved. But who are the parties in this conflict? Israel will surely not allow Hamas to be one.

Following the Oslo I Accord in 1993, the Palestinian Authority and Israel conditionally recognised each other's right to govern specific areas. Can Israel accept the Palestinian Authority as the other party, even if it implies a greater degree of sovereignty and statehood?

The other thing is how Israel might trust the UN, with which it has long-troubled relations. Israeli opposition leader Benny Gantz labelled UN Secretary General Antonio Guterres a "terror apologist" after Guterres argued that the October 7 attacks by Hamas " did not happen in a vacuum". And Hamas is likely to see any peacekeeping mission as just another type of occupation and respond with violence.

Still, this option looks the most practical. The UN has seldom succeeded in stopping a war, but its peacekeeping operations have experience with cleaning up the mess. The legitimacy of UN Security Council mandates is second to none. With the consent of the parties—hopefully worked out through diplomacy—the UN Security Council would presumably have no problem in agreeing to establish a mission in one of the world's most fragile and volatile regions.

The Middle East is the incubator of peacekeeping. The first UN peacekeeping mission started with the Arab-Israel ceasefire in 1948. Today, the UN has more than 10,000 peacekeepers along Israel's border regions, with operations in Lebanon and Syria.

Both missions monitor the ceasefire between Israel and its two neighbours, from patrolling the "Blue Line" along Lebanon's southern frontier, to monitoring such areas as Mount Hermon in the Golan Heights, which Israel annexed from Syria.

The UN has more than enough troops to deploy. Despite growing tensions and conflicts in recent years, peacekeeping around the globe is shrinking. As a result, there are only 12 missions and about 90,000 personnel, down from the 125,000 UN peacekeepers deployed across 16 missions in 2015.

The most useful peacekeepers that could be sent to a would-be Gaza mission would be the UN's "vanguard brigade" of 4,000 rapidly deployable troops, selected from member states. They can be dispatched within 60 days to trouble spots with protection of civilians as their first priority. Given the huge loss of life in Gaza, one can easily imagine how such peacekeeping troops are badly needed over there.

But however useful peacekeeping may be, it is but an ad hoc measure pending a final political solution. After the October 7 Hamas attacks, Israeli President Isaac Herzog said that "tragedy is part of Israeli life". To end the tragedy, Israel needs to think about how and when the Palestinians can have their own homeland one day.

LESSONS FROM GENERAL
SOLEIMANI'S DEATH

First published in China-US Focus, 3 February 2020

Few people outside Iran, including me, know much about the Achaemenid, Sassanian or Safavid dynasties, the high point of the Persian Empire. But when President Trump warned that 52 Iranian cultural sites would be "hit very fast and hard" if Tehran retaliated for the killing of General Qasem Soleimani, I felt as if he was threatening to bombard the sites in the Arabian Nights, the bedtime stories we grew up with.

Such a threat by an American president is almost as appalling as the killing of General Soleimani itself, especially if it indicates how a superpower might behave without regard for international law in the days to come.

The Taliban deliberately bombarded the Bamiyan Buddha in Afghanistan in 2001, a group affiliated with al-Qaida destroyed ancient religious monuments in Timbuktu, Mali, in 2012 (which the International Criminal Court took on as a unique criminal case), and ISIS fighters destroyed significant parts of the ancient Syrian city of Palmyra in 2015.

Has America's moral high ground fallen to such a level as appears only at the end of Hollywood blockbusters?

A couple of years ago, I heard two questions that I thought were most interesting at an international conference: If China's ascent and America's decline are inevitable, could China create an international order that the Chinese are happy with but foreigners could also live in? And if the abuse of force by the United States has brought on world catastrophes, how can China make a difference?

China today looks like a magician wearing three hats at the same time—a socialist country with Chinese characteristics, a developing country with GDP per capita of $10,000 and the second-largest economy in the world. This could be confusing, understandably.

The first hat is easiest to explain. If miracles have color, it must be red. No country has benefited more from globalization than China in the last 40 years since it decided to reform and open up to the world. This explains why, as a socialist country, Beijing has vowed to safeguard the current international order, which to a great extent was designed by the West after World War II. Further, China has become a champion of multilateralism. It has demonstrated potential for leadership on issues of global concern ranging from multi-polarity to climate change and the development of artificial intelligence.

The confusion is increased when the second and third hats are put together. How to balance the seemingly contradictory roles of a developing country and the second-largest economy in the world? China has said that it would make contributions to the world in line with its actual national strength. This is usually taken to mean that China's contributions will be limited to that of a developing country, but this is the wrong conclusion. Since China's national strength is bound to grow, it can certainly contribute more to the world, especially because it is widely assumed that in 10 to 15 years China will surpass the United States to become the largest economy in the world.

If China's ascent and America's decline are indeed inevitable, China should resist the temptation to fill in the "vacuums" left by America. These vacuums could easily turn out to be traps, particularly in the Middle East. Nowhere else on Earth has seen so many conflicts, proxy wars and major power rivalries. China's non-interference may not be what the warring parties or nations there need the most, but its impartiality is trusted by all parties in the Middle East precisely because they believe China is not allied with any one of them.

So far, China's operations overseas, such as peacekeeping, counter-piracy and disaster relief, have been mainly humanitarian in nature. This is not a coincidence. For Beijing, the aim is helping rather than policing the world. It is hard to imagine any circumstance in which the PLA would use its drones to assassinate a foreign leader, let alone in a third country.

Beijing's contribution to global security is not necessarily what it has done but equally what it surely won't do to the world. This is not just because non-intervention in the affairs of other nations is enshrined in the UN charter. It is underlined in China's foreign policy.

If the world were a jungle of trees, perhaps it would be better to let a devastated region recover naturally, as with Mother Nature, given that external interference is often a force of destruction rather than construction. For example, the United States has been fighting in Afghanistan for 18 years. More than 2,300 of its troops have died and more than 20,000 wounded in the longest war in American history. Yet, Afghanistan is no safer than it was 18 years ago, and there is no foreseeable peace in sight. By comparison, since 1990 the PLA has sent around 40,000 peacekeepers on 24 UN peacekeeping missions around the world, but only 13 of them have died.

What does an ideal world order look like to the Chinese? Unlike Pax Britannia in the 19th century and Pax Americana in the 20th century, the 21st century will not be shrouded in Pax Sinica, as some people have assumed. Despite the awesome buildup of the PLA, the Chinese military won't catch up with the Americans until at least midcentury, if at all. Nowadays, amid accelerating globalization and persuasive technological advances, no single civilization can dominate the world. Every culture is a hybrid. Yes, the world will have more Chinese elements, but China will be equally colored with more international hues.

Some scholars in China talk about an ancient Chinese vision of world order—"humane authority," or *wangdao*. This is fine if the word represents China as an enlightened and benevolent power willing to fulfill other countries' security and economic needs, but it is wrong if it suggests that China does all this as a hegemon in exchange for deference.

What might be closest to humane authority is the authority of the UN. Despite problems such as bureaucracy and low efficiency, which are criticized from time to time, the largest intergovernmental organization in the world represents the international community better than any other organization and therefore should be strengthened rather than weakened. In this regard, China has rightly increased its financial contribution to the UN and the number of standby peacekeepers.

Thank goodness Trump's threat has proved hollow, but the price Washington paid for General Soleimani's death will be more than Tehran's retaliatory missile attacks at American bases in Iraq. The genie is out of the bottle.

NONINTERFERENCE AND ASSISTANCE BEST FOR MIDDLE EAST

First published in *China Daily*, 28 May 2016

At the Xiangshan Forum in Beijing last year, an ex-journalist of Al Jazeera asked me why China couldn't fill the power vacuum in the Middle East. China can be accepted by all parties, he said, because "unlike Western powers, China's hands are clean".

He is not alone in saying something like that.

Today, China's stake in the Middle East goes far beyond oil imports, and covers infrastructure, trade and investment, nuclear energy, satellite launches, and aerospace cooperation, among other things. But one only needs to look at Syria to know there is no such thing as a power vacuum in the Middle East. Instead chaos spreads unabated. It only brings in more rivalry, both from within and from outside. True, China's hands are clean. But would they still be clean if China became involved militarily?

The best China can offer to the region is noninterference plus necessary assistance. Nowhere else on earth has seen so much bloodshed, tears and homeless people as the Middle East. This is not only because of the ethnic and religious strife, but also a result of proxy wars before, during and after the Cold War.

China's noninterference may not be what the warring parties or nations need most, but it makes Beijing acceptable to bitter enemies such as the Arab states and Israel. In fact, China's strongest point is that all parties believe China is not allied with anyone of them. Therefore, China can be trusted to be neutral and impartial.

Having said this, China can assist. Contrary to what some people have suggested, China doesn't have a "unique" role or special interest in the security of the Middle East. Its role as an honest mediator in the Middle East is very much like the role it has played in the Six-Party Talks on denuclearization of the Korean Peninsula, that is, to facilitate dialogue which hopefully leads to a resolution.

The success of the nuclear deal between Iran and the six powers, which included China, is a brilliant example of how China's consistent proposal of dialogue and negotiation rather than sanctions or use of force has eventually prevailed.

At present, China is only involved militarily in the Middle East in peacekeeping operations and evacuating people from war-torn countries. More than 400 Chinese peacekeepers are deployed in Lebanon. Given the situation in Syria, it is widely believed an international peacekeeping force might be needed one day.

In this regard, some of China's 8,000-strong standby peacekeeping force could be deployed in Syria to monitor a ceasefire and supervise an armistice agreement.

In 2011 and 2015, Chinese naval ships helped evacuate both Chinese and foreign nationals from war-torn Libya and Yemen. In March, China and the United Kingdom held a Non-Combatant Evacuation Table Top Exercise in Nanjing. The scenario was based upon their respective experiences of evacuating their nationals from the Middle East.

This was the first joint effort by two permanent members of the UN Security Council to address a highly possible scenario in future. It represented a refreshing new model of cooperation among major powers.

The Middle East is often described as a touchstone for the major powers. However if that means major powers' involvement, or more often, intervention, is unavoidable or even justifiable, it is simply wrong. China needs to beware that such a "vacuum" doesn't turn out to be a trap.

CAUGHT BETWEEN RUSSIA AND THE WEST, CHINA IS TREADING A TIGHTROPE ON UKRAINE

First published in *Financial Times*, 25 January 2023

Will the war in Ukraine spill over into a third world war? The short answer is: not unless China lends military support to Russia. Over the past year, Beijing—despite not being involved in this faraway conflict—was nevertheless asked which side it would take, whether it would become a mediator between Russia and the West, and whether it might launch an attack on Taiwan.

This is the price China pays for being a global power. Caught between Russia, its strategic partner, and Ukraine, which counts China as its largest trading partner, Beijing is treading a tightrope. While stressing the importance of sovereignty, China has gently criticized Russia's invasion of Ukraine. But it has also emphasized that regional security cannot be strengthened by expanding a military bloc, an explicit rebuke to NATO and its most powerful member, the US.

This position is frowned upon in Western capitals as "pro-Russia neutrality". Beijing and Moscow's "unlimited" friendship has alarmed the West. But imagine for a moment: if two countries vow to develop their friendship, then how could they place limits on it? Russia is China's largest neighbor and vice versa. For peaceful coexistence, this relationship must be amicable.

Two of Beijing's contributions have been particularly under-appreciated. First, not adding fuel to the fire. This war has served to prove that however close China and Russia might be, this is not an alliance. If Beijing takes Moscow's side in the conflict, then we are already in the dawn of the third world war. This would make the situation far worse than the Cold War era, in which the US and the USSR avoided any direct confrontation.

Second, China's stance against the use of nuclear weapons in Europe has reduced the prospect of a nuclear war, if not entirely ruled it out. No one knows whether Russian president Vladimir Putin was bluffing about using nuclear weapons. But Chinese president Xi Jinping's public remarks about no use of nuclear weapons should have been heard in Moscow.

Looking ahead, escalation of this conflict unfortunately looks inevitable. At last month's Munich Security Conference, I heard applause whenever Ukrainian president Volodymyr Zelenskyy or British prime minister Rishi Sunak talked about the need to send more military assistance to Ukraine. Having provided tanks, the West is now talking about sending aircraft. But Russia, even without deploying its nuclear stockpile (which is larger than those of the US, Britain, and France combined), cannot lose completely.

This is where China has a role to play. US secretary of state Antony Blinken has suggested that Beijing is considering providing lethal weapons support to Russia. This is impossible. If China sends weaponry of any kind, it won't go unnoticed. And if Beijing has refused to send any such support to Moscow in the past 12 months, then why should it change its mind now, especially when it has urged a peaceful resolution to the conflict?

Beijing will most likely continue to be neutral. Unlike a small country that risks being unwillingly swept up in the conflict, a strong China can afford to stand its ground. It is also not alone. Most countries in the global south, notably India and South Africa, are similarly unwilling to pick a side.

But Beijing is becoming more constructive. China's position paper, released on the anniversary of the Russian invasion, is a case in point. This called for all parties to exercise rationality and restraint, as well as to prioritize the effective protection of civilians. Critics may argue that the paper's call for a resumption of peace talks and an end to unilateral sanctions stops short of being a tangible road map. Of course, there is no guarantee that the proposal would succeed, but no war can last forever.

It remains to be seen whether China will perform the same role that it has done in the past—as a de facto leader in the six-party talks on denuclearization on the Korean peninsula, or a participant in the Iranian nuclear negotiations. But Beijing has a unique advantage. If Russia will listen to anyone, it would most probably be China. Beijing is not only talking to Moscow, though—the Chinese Ministry of Defense recently announced it had sent a delegation for talks with NATO.

The war in Ukraine has nothing to do with China. But the longer it drags on, the more people will look to Beijing as a broker. During the current raging conflict, peaceful settlement may look like a pipe dream. But make no mistake: China's role is looming ever larger.

WHY CHINA IS REFUSING TO CHOOSE
BETWEEN RUSSIA AND UKRAINE

First published in *South China Morning Post*, 16 March 2022

We are stepping into a world with two cold wars to come. In Europe, where the war is raging on, panicking Europeans are already preparing for another cold war. The prospect of a "Russky Mir" (Russian world) has revived a "brain-dead" Nato.

Germany, a country most reluctant to embark on military build-up, has reversed decades of hesitancy and poured 100 billion euros (US$109.8 billion) into its defence budget. This makes "European strategic autonomy", so far a slogan French President Emmanuel Macron has been championing, look more probable down the road. The only question is whether it will add strength to the transatlantic alliance or weaken it.

In Asia, the cold war that dawned with US president Donald Trump's "great power competition" was intensified by Joe Biden's "extreme competition" with China. Biden had hoped to put Russia policy on a "stable and predictable" footing to focus on China, which is the US's top priority. But the war in Europe further hollows out the US president's Indo-Pacific strategy, which already has too many purposes without adequate tools.

If the key to small nations' survival is making the right choice, then the art of living for a major power is to strike a balance. This is not "a moment of choice for China", as Australia's Prime Minister Scott Morrison asserted.

Should China ditch Russia and walk into the Western camp, it won't even reap the benefit of expediency. China will lose a strategic partner, and it is only a matter of how quickly the US will take on China again.

This explains why Beijing has expressed understanding of Russia's "legitimate concerns" over Nato's expansion while underlining that the sovereignty and territorial integrity of all countries must be respected. It is also continuing to provide humanitarian aid to Ukraine.

In tough times, China doesn't need to look elsewhere for inspiration. It only needs to stand firm on some of its time-tested principles, which could also be illuminating for others.

First, no-first-use of nuclear weapons. The Russian armed forces outgun and outnumber the Ukrainian forces, which have no nuclear weapons. Therefore, one wonders why Russian President Vladimir Putin needs to put his nuclear forces on high alert if this is not a strategy to "escalate to de-escalate".

This strategy risks encouraging would-be nuclear weapon states and is definitely a heavy blow to non-proliferation. But it could become an opportune moment too, for China and the US to demonstrate their responsible attitude through discussions on no-first-use of nuclear weapons, a position China has held since it detonated a nuclear device in 1964.

Biden's position that the "sole purpose" of the American arsenal "should be deterring—and if necessary, retaliating against—a nuclear attack" is not far from that of China. In mid-December 2021, nearly 700 scientists and engineers, including 21 Nobel laureates, asked Biden to cut the US nuclear arsenal by a third, and to declare that the United States would never be the first to use nuclear weapons in a conflict.

Second, non-alliance. The war in Ukraine again raises the West's worst fears of the prospect of a China-Russia alliance. Such an alliance is impossible. Both China and Russia call for multipolarity, but for different reasons.

No country has benefited as much from globalisation as China, which has a strong stake in safeguarding the international order. Despite differences and even tensions sometimes, China has deep ties with the West, including the US, that neither wish to sever.

In comparison, Russia resents the existing international order and sees itself as a victim. Putin called the break-up of the Soviet Union "the greatest geopolitical catastrophe of the 20th century".

As long as China doesn't harbour the desire for global military expansion which requires allies, it doesn't need an alliance. All the military operations of the People's Liberation Army overseas are humanitarian in nature. Its primary security concern lies in the Western Pacific, where the military balance between the PLA and the US military is closing.

One thing that was crystal clear before the Russian-Ukraine war, and which remains clear today, is that neither the US nor the 30-member-strong Nato, which includes three nuclear powers, dares to confront Russia head on.

China's military strength is presumably no less formidable than Russia's, apart from a nuclear arsenal that China chooses to keep small. The PLA is the largest armed force in the world in terms of active personnel. Its military budget, although less than 2 per cent of gross domestic product, is three times bigger than Russia's. It has two aircraft carriers, with more in the pipeline, while Russia has just one.

Third, no pursuit of spheres of influence. The war in Ukraine is a clash between Russia and Nato over spheres of influence. Perhaps no region looks more like China's sphere of influence than East Asia, but it isn't. North Korea won't give up its nuclear weapons as China and the whole world wish, quite a few countries are American allies, and in the South China Sea, China has disputes with a few claimants.

The "Indo-Pacific Strategy of the United States", released in February, claims that "[China] is combining its economic, diplomatic, military and technological might as it pursues a sphere of influence in the Indo-Pacific".

This cannot be more wrong. "Influence" and "sphere of influence" are two different things. Today, China's influence, especially in the economic field, is already felt worldwide. Therefore, it doesn't need to establish spheres of influence anywhere that are costly and difficult to maintain.

The war in Ukraine, however disruptive, won't stop the global political and economic shifts towards Asia with China at the centre. China is now the eye of the storm. Therefore, it should be the stabiliser. The benefit of making no choice is avoiding a bad choice.

THE U.S. AND CHINA CAN LEAD THE WAY ON NUCLEAR THREAT REDUCTION

First published in *Foreign Policy*, 20 August 2024

Since the end of the Cold War, the role of nuclear weapons has only grown. Nuclear arsenals are being strengthened around the world, with many nuclear states continuing to modernize their arsenals. In June, outgoing NATO Secretary-General Jens Stoltenberg said that the alliance was in talks to deploy more nuclear weapons, taking them out of storage and placing them on standby. Robert C. O'Brien, a former national security advisor to former U.S. President Donald Trump, has urged him to conduct nuclear tests if he wins a new term, arguing that it would help the United States "maintain technical and numerical superiority to the combined Chinese and Russian nuclear stockpiles."

There are two bleak conclusions about nuclear diplomacy in this age. First, it will be impossible to ban such weapons anytime soon. Since its passage in 2017, no nuclear-armed states have signed the United Nations Treaty on the Prohibition of Nuclear Weapons, some of them instead contending that it will distract attention from other disarmament and nonproliferation initiatives.

It is also very hard, if not impossible, to convince these states to reduce their nuclear stockpiles amid ever-intensifying geopolitical and military competition. On the contrary, in February 2023, Russia announced that it was suspending its participation in the 2010 Treaty on Measures for the Further Reduction and Limitation of Strategic Offensive Arms (New START)—the last remaining nuclear arms control treaty limiting Russian and U.S. strategic nuclear forces.

In response, the United States has also suspended the sharing and publication of treaty data. In November, Russia went a step further and withdrew its ratification of the Comprehensive Nuclear Test Ban Treaty (CTBT), citing "an imbalance" with the United States, which has failed to ratify the treaty since it opened for signature in 1996.

Amid such a situation, it is impossible for Beijing to stand by idly. The Stockholm International Peace Research Institute estimates that the size of China's nuclear arsenal has increased from 410 warheads in January 2023 to 500 in January 2024, and it is expected to continue to grow. For the first time, China may also now be deploying a small number of warheads on missiles during peacetime. According to the U.S. Defense Department, China is likely to increase its nuclear warheads to 1,500 by 2035.

Given this reality, perhaps the most promising near-term way to guard against nuclear risks is not by limiting the number of nuclear weapons but by controlling the policies that govern their use. In this regard, a pledge by nuclear-armed states of "no first use" of nuclear weapons looks to be the most realistic approach in reducing the escalation of nuclear threats.

In theory, no first use refers to a policy by which a nuclear-armed power formally refrains from the use of nuclear weapons or other weapons of mass destruction in warfare, except in the case of doing so as a second strike in retaliation for an attack by an enemy power using weapons of mass destruction.

Of the five nuclear states that have signed on to the Treaty on the Nonproliferation of Nuclear Weapons (NPT)—China, France, Russia, the United Kingdom, and the United States—only China has ever declared a no-first-use policy. On Oct. 16, 1964, when China successfully detonated its first atomic bomb, the country immediately declared that it would not be the first to use nuclear weapons at any time and under any circumstances, and unconditionally committed itself not to use or threaten to use nuclear weapons against nonnuclear states or in nuclear-weapon-free zones.

India, which is not a party to the NPT, made a similar pledge in 1998, but stipulated that the promise extended only to states that did not have nuclear weapons and were not aligned with a nuclear-armed state.

American scholars, however, have long doubted the validity of China's pledge and debated whether Beijing might use or threaten to use nuclear weapons in a worst-case scenario, such as during a conflict over Taiwan. Some observers in the United States believe that if China's leaders decide to attack Taiwan, there is nothing that anyone can do to change their minds if conventional means fail to achieve success.

Such arguments are not really tenable. An ever-stronger China is now in a better position to honor its decades-old policy than ever before. Although China has not ruled out the possibility of using nonpeaceful means for what it refers to as "reunification" in specific circumstances, Beijing has never mentioned use of nuclear weapons against the people of Taiwan, whom the mainland refers to as "compatriots." In semiofficial nuclear arms talks held in Shanghai in March, the Chinese delegation told the U.S. side that they were absolutely convinced that China would be able to prevail in a conventional fight over Taiwan without using nuclear weapons.

All nuclear powers could afford to adopt a formal no-first-use policy—taking the moral high ground without reducing their capabilities for retaliation.

Though it has never adopted a no-first-use policy itself, the United States' nuclear posture is actually more similar to China's than it seems. In its 2022 Nuclear Posture Review, the Biden administration declared that it would only consider the use of nuclear weapons "in extreme circumstances to defend the vital interests of the United States or its allies and partners." But it is hard to imagine which interests are so vital that they might require Washington to use nuclear weapons as a first measure to defend them.

To be sure, it is important for the United States to assure its allies that it will follow through on its deterrent promises. It is equally hard to imagine who would venture to launch a nuclear strike on a U.S. ally, knowing the dire potential consequences.

The United Kingdom's nuclear deterrent, meanwhile, is operationally independent. But in terms of its nuclear policy, the British government has made it clear that "we would consider using our nuclear weapons only in extreme circumstances of self-defence, including the defence of our NATO allies." France, meanwhile adheres to a principle of "strict sufficiency."

The real challenge, then, is getting Russia to commit to a no-first-use policy. The Soviet Union adopted a formal policy of no first use in 1982. But after its dissolution, the Russian Federation reversed this approach in 1993, likely to mitigate the comparative weakness of the Russian Armed Forces in the post-Soviet era.

In Article 4 of an executive order on nuclear deterrence published in 2020, Russian President Vladimir Putin declared that "in the event of a military conflict, this Policy provides for the prevention of an escalation of military actions and their termination on conditions that are acceptable for the Russian

Federation and/or its allies." This has been interpreted by some international nuclear observers as describing nonnuclear scenarios in which Russia might use such weapons.

From the start of the full-scale Russian invasion of Ukraine in 2022, there has been a concern that Russia might explode a tactical nuclear bomb somewhere to send a warning to Ukraine and NATO. Although Putin has never explicitly threatened the use of nuclear weapons, he has repeatedly hinted at Russia's willingness to use them and said at the May 9 Victory Day parade in Moscow that "our strategic forces are always in a state of combat readiness." And in May, Russia carried out tactical nuclear weapon drills close to the Ukrainian border.

This strategy has been dubbed "escalate to de-escalate" by some observers, which indicates early escalations, such as threats to use nuclear weapons (even in a limited fashion), followed by demands for immediate war termination. The goal of such a strategy is not to completely disable or defeat the enemy, but rather to compel the adversary to decide to quickly end the conflict on terms set by the escalating state.

Like it or not, Russia's escalate to de-escalate strategy has partially worked in the war in Ukraine, limiting NATO's direct involvement and prompting the United States to put limits on what Ukraine can do with the weapons that it supplies.

So why should Russia consider adopting a no-first-use policy instead?

The escalate to de-escalate method depends on fear and bluffing. If a nuclear-armed state really launches an attack against another nuclear power, it cannot control the scale of the retaliation by its adversaries. A tit for tat risks becoming a full-blown nuclear war that no one wants. Russia has effectively limited itself in Ukraine when it comes to nuclear weapons exactly because their usage would likely prompt the very thing that Moscow fears most—NATO involvement.

The actual usage of a tactical nuclear bomb could prompt that involvement. So—to avoid mutual destruction—Moscow has to make its utmost effort to deter NATO from joining the war.

A dual-track approach may be the best bet for the adoption of a formal no-first-use policy.

In Europe, NATO can start with a unilateral no-first-use pledge against Russia as a gesture of goodwill. Even if such an offer isn't immediately reciprocated by Russia, it might begin to thaw tensions.

As a second—and crucial—step, NATO could pledge to halt any further expansion of its alliance in exchange for Moscow adopting a no-first-use policy. This would be a difficult pill for the alliance to swallow. But after Sweden's and Finland's entry earlier this year, there are only three aspiring countries on the waiting list: the barely significant Bosnia and Herzegovina as well as Georgia and Ukraine, which have deeply problematic ongoing conflicts with Russia that NATO is sensitive about.

The path forward would likely be smoother if it went through Asia. Both Russia and China have already agreed to no first use against each other. China and the United States could reach a similar agreement, thus de-escalating potential conflicts involving U.S. allies—such as the Philippines and Japan—as well as the dangers that could be provoked through accidental collisions in the sea or air. A U.S.-led example might then make it easier to bring the Europeans on board.

This may seem far-fetched in the current geopolitical climate, but there is precedent for it. When India and Pakistan tested nuclear devices in May 1998, they incurred swift condemnation from the U.N. Security Council, which called for both countries to sign both the NPT and the Comprehensive Nuclear Test Ban Treaty. In a rare show of solidarity, China and the United States made a joint declaration in June 1998 agreeing to de-target their nuclear weapons against each other.

This was largely a symbolic and unverifiable step. But it was not only a defusing of tensions, but also good to see nuclear states at least partially honoring the vision of nuclear disarmament laid out in Article VI of the NPT. And this China-U.S. joint statement eventually led to another joint statement among the five nuclear-armed permanent Security Council states in May 2000, which affirmed that their nuclear weapons are not targeted at each other or at any other states.

No first use is a big step forward from nontargeting. It's not out of bounds to imagine that, with enough diplomatic capital, a similar but more important pledge of no first use could be made today. In fact, in January 2022—only a month before Russia's invasion of Ukraine—these five nuclear powers agreed in a joint statement that "a nuclear war cannot be won and must never be fought."

What is more significant is that during Chinese President Xi Jinping's visit to Moscow last year, China and Russia reiterated this commitment, even amid Russia's ongoing war.

If, indeed, a nuclear war cannot be won, then what is stopping these nuclear powers from making a no-first-use pledge? Nuclear weapons didn't help the United States in its wars in Vietnam, Iraq, and Afghanistan—or the Russians in Ukraine. A commitment of no first use by the nuclear-armed states would give people hope that a nuclear-free world, however distant, is still possible one day.

IT'S ABSURD TO ASK CHINA TO DISARM

First published in *The Wall Street Journal*, 31 July 2019

The Chinese government sent Vice Premier Liu He to the U.S. in April with a brief to settle the tariff war between Beijing and Washington. But during an Oval Office news conference to address the progress of trade negotiations, President Trump abruptly changed the subject: "Between Russia and China and us, we're all making hundreds of billions of dollars' worth of weapons, including nuclear, which is ridiculous." Mr. Trump has since ordered his administration to prepare a push for new arms-control agreements with Russia and China.

If Mr. Liu was surprised by the pivot from trade to arms control, he wasn't alone. To Chinese ears, Mr. Trump's claims make no sense. Between them, the U.S. and Russia possess 90% of the world's nuclear weapons. China has fewer nuclear warheads (290) than France (300), according to the Stockholm International Peace Research Institute.

No wonder China's Ministry of National Defense essentially laughed at the idea of a three-way deal on arms control involving the U.S. and Russia. For such an agreement to work, either the U.S. and Russia would need to bring their nuclear arsenals down to China's level, or China would need to increase the size of its arsenal drastically. Neither scenario is realistic.

At the moment, the Trump administration is building up U.S. nuclear capability, developing low-yield warheads for submarine-launched ballistic missiles and tactical nukes for use in battlefield situations. Russian President Vladimir Putin announced in March 2018 that Moscow is developing a nuclear-powered cruise missile with "unlimited range and unlimited ability to maneuver."

Since China has pledged no first use of nuclear weapons and only seeks a small and effective deterrent force, it has to keep a larger arsenal of ground-based intermediate-range missiles for strategic equilibrium with other nuclear powers. In other words, if China reduces the number of its ground-based intermediate-range missiles, most of which are subject to the Intermediate-Range Nuclear Forces Treaty, it has to increase its nuclear-strike capabilities massively. Which is the "lesser evil" for the West?

China is no stranger to nuclear disarmament. In 1994 China presented a draft of a no-first-use policy to France, Russia, the U.S. and the U.K.—the four other countries in the nuclear club at the time. After India and Pakistan conducted nuclear tests in 1998, China and the U.S. agreed to point their nuclear missiles away from one another. Other nuclear powers followed suit in 2000.

Do we really need another ineffective nuclear-disarmament treaty, as Mr. Trump suggested? The Treaty on the Non-Proliferation of Nuclear Weapons only recognizes the nuclear powers that conducted tests before January 1967. It hasn't prevented India, Israel and Pakistan—not to mention North Korea—from becoming de facto nuclear states. The 2017 Treaty on the Prohibition of Nuclear Weapons understandably reflects frustration over "the slow pace of nuclear disarmament," but it probably won't come into effect. So far only 23 nations have ratified the treaty, which requires 50 to come into force. Ironically, Japan refuses to join. The only country to have suffered a nuclear attack claims to see no use in the treaty.

Washington and Moscow need to take the lead on this issue and reduce the size of their nuclear arsenals if they want to live in a world with fewer weapons. The prospect of this happening appears remote. The U.S. is set to withdraw from the INF treaty on August 2. North Korea refuses to make even superficial concessions without the promise of an economic payoff, and if Iran decides to go for a bomb, Saudi Arabia will follow. Dominoes in Egypt and Turkey would likely fall after that.

The number of nuclear warheads in the world has fallen from about 65,000 at the peak of the Cold War in the mid-1960s to 13,865 at the start of 2019. That's progress but it didn't happen by accident. It required brave leaders to make smart decisions.

NATO AND THE WEST MUST HEED RUSSIA'S WARNINGS TO AVOID NUCLEAR HOLOCAUST

First published in *South China Morning Post*, 26 May 2022

Russia is repeatedly dropping escalatory hints about possibly using nuclear weapons. It might be bluffing, but what if it is not? Unlike the atomic bombing of Hiroshima and Nagasaki that sealed the surrender of Japan in World War II, if Russia opens another nuclear Pandora's box, everyone can imagine the rest.

Put yourself in Russian President Vladimir Putin's shoes for a moment. You are convinced this is a proxy war between the United States, its Western allies and Russian forces in Ukraine. Military weaponry of all sorts from Europe is pouring into Ukraine. US intelligence support reportedly helped lead to the sinking of the *Moskva*—the flagship of Russia's Black Sea Fleet—and the battlefield deaths of several Russian generals.

Unlike US president John F. Kennedy, who was bold yet careful enough to reach agreement with Soviet leader Nikita Khrushchev on removing Soviet missiles from Cuba in exchange for the US promising not to invade Cuba in 1962, current US

President Joe Biden has been provocative. He has called Putin a war criminal and said "this man cannot remain in power".

We are closer to a nuclear war now than we were during the Cold War. No one can tell when or where Putin might use nuclear weapons. But if he feels he must rely on nuclear weapons as a game-changer in a grinding war in which Russian troops have so far fought poorly, the likelihood he will use them will continue to simply grow.

As Stephen Walt of Harvard University wrote in *Foreign Policy* this month, Putin has a track record of following through on his warnings. This is seen in Russia's war in Georgia in 2008, its annexation of Crimea in 2014 and, of course, the current conflict in Ukraine.

If Putin believes he is chosen to be St George who slew the dragon—a symbol that is part of Russia's coat of arms—the weapon he will use is not a long spear but a nuclear missile, of which Russia has more than anyone. The targets might be one or two European countries rather than Ukraine, which, home to what Putin called "one people", is also close to Russia.

With no prospect of even a ceasefire in sight, the challenge is how to reduce tensions. As a first step, Nato could unilaterally pledge not to be the first to use nuclear weapons against Russia in any circumstances. It is unlikely that Russia will reciprocate now, but this would be a goodwill gesture and talks could start from there.

Nato can afford to make such an offer as it would not compromise its deterrent capabilities. It is hard to imagine why the 30-member transatlantic alliance with unmatched conventional forces would need to use nuclear weapons first against one adversary.

According to the Pentagon, the US "would only consider the use of nuclear weapons in extreme circumstances to defend the vital interests of the United States or its allies and partners". This is already close to a "no first use" policy.

As a second step, Nato could pledge to halt any further expansion in exchange for a Russian promise not to use nuclear weapons first. Moscow might find this proposal worth considering since its stated primary concern has been Nato's eastward expansion.

The alliance—which could grow to 32 members if Finland and Sweden join—is already a juggernaut. All military alliances are like leeches that live on "threats". However, if Nato has to expand because of the threat from a single nation, that says more about its incompetence than its strength.

Nato could easily argue it is not that it wants to expand but that countries fearful of Russia want to join. There is some truth to that, but it is still not justifiable. The more popular Nato becomes, the more insecure Europe will be.

Take Finland's application for Nato membership, for example. Finnish President Sauli Niinisto told Putin how Russia's invasion of Ukraine had altered the security environment for Finland, but the security environment is not security itself.

Does Finland have to break with eight decades of neutrality that has created a stable and pragmatic relationship between Moscow and Helsinki? This move would more than double the length of the alliance's border with Russia and risk adding to Moscow's feelings of insecurity.

The third step is to negotiate new security arrangements in Europe, including but not limited to a security guarantee for Ukraine. This might include a pledge not to deploy nuclear weapons in Russia's periphery, which Moscow sees as its sphere of influence, but the key is to negotiate a new conventional armed forces treaty.

The Conventional Armed Forces in Europe Treaty, signed in 1990, eliminated the Soviet Union's quantitative advantage in conventional weapons in Europe. It set equal limits on the number of tanks, armoured combat vehicles, heavy artillery, combat aircraft and attack helicopters that Nato and the Warsaw Pact could deploy between the Atlantic Ocean and the Ural Mountains.

The new treaty should set a limit on Nato's quantitative advantage in conventional weapons in Europe given the apparent disparity between Russia and Nato today. As a condition, Nato could ask Russia to reduce its nuclear stockpile, which is bigger than that of the US, France and Britain combined.

The war in Ukraine stems from Nato's neglect of Russia's warnings against its expansion. If Nato also neglects Russia's warnings that it could use nuclear weapons, a nuclear war that leads to a global disaster the world managed to avoid during the Cold War would be a testimony to infinite human stupidity.

5

THE FUTURE OF THE INTERNATIONAL ORDER

THE WAR IN UKRAINE WILL ACCELERATE THE GEOPOLITICAL SHIFT FROM WEST TO EAST

First published in *The Economist*, 9 May 2022

If the enemy of my enemy is my friend, is the enemy of my friend also my enemy? Not necessarily. Or so China's thinking goes when it comes to the raging Russian-Ukrainian war. On the one hand China is Russia's strategic partner. On the other, China is the largest trading partner of Ukraine. Beijing therefore tries painstakingly to strike a balance in its responses to the war between two of its friends. It expresses understanding of Russia's "legitimate concerns" over NATO's expansion, while underlining that "the sovereignty and territorial integrity of all countries must be respected".

Such carefully calibrated neutrality may not be what the warring parties really want, but it is acceptable to both. If China joins the West in condemning Russia, it will be much applauded in Washington and most European capitals. But it will lose Russia's partnership. And it is only a matter of time before America takes on China again. The Biden administration's policy towards my country is "extreme competition" that stops just short of war.

Obviously, the conflict in Ukraine has done tremendous damage to Chinese interests, including its Belt and Road initiative in Europe. But Beijing sympathises with Moscow's claim that the root cause of the conflict is NATO's inexorable expansion eastward after the fall of the Soviet Union. All Russian leaders since Mikhail Gorbachev have warned of the consequences of such expansion. Russia feels that it cannot allow its Ukrainian brethren to leave *Russkiy mir*—the Russian world—to join another camp. If NATO looks like Frankenstein's monster to Russia, with new additions here and there, Vladimir Putin probably believes he must slay the creature.

The future of Europe is not hard to fathom. Mr Putin's all-out war against Ukraine has failed. Precisely because of that, he will fight until he can declare some sort of "victory". Presumably this will involve Ukraine's acceptance that Crimea is part of Russia, its promise not to join NATO and the independence of the two "republics" of Donetsk and Luhansk. The challenge is whether Russian troops are able to control Donbas after occupying it.

A protracted war looks probable, if not inevitable. The situation bears similarities to the one in Afghanistan during Russia's war there in the 1980s. An American-led alliance sent endless weapons to the mujahideen who managed to bog down and exhaust the invading Soviet soldiers.

Thanks to the crisis, a brain-dead NATO has revived. In February Germany's chancellor, Olaf Scholz, created a special €100bn ($105bn) fund for defence and announced that his country would spend 2% of its GDP on defence every year—a NATO guideline. It will beef up the alliance and bolster the idea of European "strategic autonomy" (little more than a French slogan until now).

The irony is that the more popular NATO becomes, the more insecure Europe will be. If Finland joins NATO, as looks likely, the alliance's troops would be a stone's throw from St Petersburg.

The Kremlin has warned that such a move would end the "non-nuclear status of the Baltic Sea". This could be a bluff. But who knows? If NATO's worst fear is that Russia might launch a tactical nuclear attack, then why keep poking Mr Putin in the eye? Europe's security, now as in the past, can only be achieved with Russia's co-operation.

In recent months speculation abounded that Beijing and Moscow's "unlimited" partnership—announced during Mr Putin's visit to China in February for the Winter Olympics—might usher in a military alliance. But the war in Ukraine has inadvertently proved that Beijing and Moscow's rapprochement is not an alliance. China didn't provide military assistance to Russia. Instead it provided humanitarian aid and money to Ukraine twice, including food and sleeping bags, and has pledged to continue to "play a constructive role".

One reason behind the Sino-Russian non-alliance is that it allows a comfortable flexibility between two partners. And in spite of the fact that China and Russia both call for a multipolar world, a non-alliance suits them because they see such a world differently. Mr Putin's Russia is nostalgic for the heyday of the Soviet empire. (He lamented its demise as "the greatest geopolitical catastrophe" of the 20th century.) Russia sees itself as a victim of the existing international order. By contrast China is the largest beneficiary of the rules and regulations of global commerce and finance made by the West after the second world war. China has a huge stake in safeguarding the existing international order. This is why, despite ideological differences and even tensions sometimes, China has at least maintained robust economic ties with the West. Neither side wishes to sever them.

How America can focus simultaneously on two theatres—the Indo-Pacific and war in Europe—remains to be seen. Joe Biden had hoped to put Russia policy on a "stable and predictable" footing in order to focus on America's Indo-Pacific strategy. The war in Ukraine undoubtedly will distract America's attention and syphon away resources. It will further hollow out Mr Biden's Indo-Pacific strategy, which already has too many aims, too few tools and not enough supporters. The question is for how long Mr Biden will allow Ukraine to remain a distraction. In a region where China is the largest trading partner of most countries, even America's greatest allies wouldn't wish to sacrifice their relationship with China for the benefit of America.

Is the Russia-Ukraine war a turning point that heralds new global disorder? Rumor has it that when China's Premier Zhou Enlai was asked what he thought of the French Revolution of 1789, he supposedly said that it was too early to tell. But perhaps it isn't too early to say that the war in Ukraine will accelerate the geopolitical and economic shift from the West to the East. China standing in the centre matters all the more, and it should stand firm as a stabiliser.

CHINA IS RESHAPING
INTERNATIONAL ORDER

First published in *Financial Times*, 16 September 2018

No country looms larger on the horizon of the 21st century than China. Having benefited hugely from globalisation, China does not stand in truculent opposition to the current international system. Although it has resisted pressure to embrace western democracy, it is precisely the openness of the international order that has enabled the country's rise over the past four decades.

During that time China committed itself to a vast and close study of the west, focusing particularly on advanced technology and the principles and practices of modern management. What it learnt not only changed the country, but has also changed the world.

The best lens through which to view modern China is the Belt and Road Initiative. No matter how grandiose the scheme appears, it stems from China's own experience in the early stage of reform—better roads lead to better lives. Given that China is still a country with people who live below the poverty line, its vast infrastructure building projects in developing countries are understandable.

347

The initiative is neither charity nor a debt trap—China has to prioritise the return on investment. Those countries that criticise the Belt and Road Initiative overlook developing countries' real need for foreign investment, while remaining reluctant investors themselves.

Some analysts have announced the end of "the democratic century". They note that within five years the share of global income held by countries considered "not free"—such as China, Russia and Saudi Arabia—will surpass the share held by western democracies.

This is not going unnoticed—reporting produced today by state-funded news channels, including Qatar's Al Jazeera, China's CCTV, and Russia's RT, regularly finds millions of American viewers. One possible conclusion is that the road to prosperity no longer runs only through liberal democracy.

Yet China's rise does not mean that Beijing intends to foist its ideology and social system on others. Nor does it intend to impose a dominant new model for the "international order". China is extending the reach of its soft power and promoting Chinese culture and language through its Confucius Institutes. This is no different to the work long done by the UK's British Council or France's Alliance Française.

In any event the phrase "liberal international order" is a western oversimplification of the complex era it seeks to describe. It fails to capture the realities of the Cold War, the dissolution of the Soviet bloc and the emergence of the Non-Aligned Movement.

History shows us that although empires and great powers have been dominant for long periods, the world has never been unipolar. The international order is a hybrid of different coexisting political systems, security architectures and civilisations. No one set of values suits everyone and despite political scientist Francis Fukuyama's assertions, history has not ended.

What is different, however, is how interdependent the world is today. This is why US president Donald Trump's determination to wage a global trade war, in particular against China, is misguided. Threatened US tariffs on $200bn of Chinese exports would affect some American imports. In addition, these exports amount to less than 10 per cent of Chinese exports. Nevertheless, Beijing would not hesitate to retaliate. When the dust settles, the US will not emerge unscathed.

Perhaps the most significant global change is the dramatic decline in violence. As the cognitive psychologist Steven Pinker has pointed out, we are living in the most peaceable era in our species' history. At the same time, the global economic pie is being divided up in new ways and the east's share—led by China and India—is increasing rapidly. There is a great deal at stake.

This change could herald the beginning of a grand reconciliation and a new equilibrium of power in the international order. But, if the US should find the changes intolerable, and responds accordingly, these could also be very dangerous times.

NO MORE A VICTIM

CHINA MUST LEAVE ITS PAST BEHIND AND EMBRACE ITS STRENGTH

First published in *South China Morning Post*, 5 July 2021

Much has been said about the so-called "Wolf Warrior" diplomacy. Rhetoric aside, the real question is about Chinese victimhood over the "century of humiliation" that started from the Opium War in 1840. When Deng Xiaoping met Mikhail Gorbachev in Beijing in 1989, he reportedly talked for quite some time about how China was maltreated by imperial Russia in history before he said "let's put an end to the past and face the future". In other words, he wasn't able to talk about the future without talking about the past first.

Victimhood is ubiquitous. I once saw how a senior Finnish official suddenly got agitated simply because someone in the room mentioned "Finlandization". And victimhood can be a card too. The best player is Donald Trump—"Come to think of it, who gets attacked more than me?" The president-elect misled the majority of American voters to believe the strongest nation on earth was in "carnage" and he was the man to "Make

America Great Again". Once in the Oval Office, he lashed out at adversaries and allies alike as if the US was a victim of the whole world.

When Mao Zedong declared that "the Chinese people have stood up" in 1949, the "century of humiliation" should have ended. Such a short stretch in history won't even necessarily overshadow the Qing dynasty. The High Qing era was a period of sustained peace, economic prosperity, territorial expansion and population growth. The Qing dynasty was essential to the subsequent formation of the concept of the Chinese nation.

Rather than a victim, China today is the envy of the world. The center of international gravity is shifting toward East Asia. At some point in the early 2030s, China will surpass the US as the largest economy in the world. If in modern times the Japanese invasion had made Chinese victimized the most, in 2020, Chinese consumers spent $7.3 trillion, greater than the entire GDP of the Japanese economy.

A few years ago, I heard what I thought was the most intriguing question at an international conference: If China doesn't like American hegemony, then what will an ideal world order look like—one that the Chinese love most, but foreigners would also find acceptable?

A straight answer is that there won't be such an order. Unlike Pax Britannica in 19th century and Pax Americana in 20th century, the 21st century won't necessarily be Pax Sinica. Yes, China's economic influence is already felt world-wide. In Africa and most of the regions in Southeast Asia, Beijing's influence is even greater than that of Washington. But when China realizes its second "centennial goal" of becoming a "strong, democratic, civilized, harmonious and modern socialist country" in 2049, the centenary of the founding of the People's Republic of China, the US is still wealthier than China measured by GDP per capita. A "world-class" Chinese military might look neck and neck with the US military, but is not necessarily stronger than it. It is more likely that China and the US are evenly matched.

Then what can China contribute to a better world? First, unlike Washington that wishes to bring its form of liberty to all, Beijing without missionary zeal prefers to assist rather than police the world. Its caution in use of force, as demonstrated in her peaceful rise over four decades, would most certainly make the world less volatile. Compared to the US military that is involved in one war after another, the PLA has restricted all its military operations overseas to humanitarian operations.

Second, Beijing can share her experience in alleviating poverty with other developing countries where more than 700 million people are still living in extreme poverty. And who can be more qualified than China in this regard? In 2013, one in every three counties in China, 832 counties in total, was labeled "poverty-stricken". In November, 2020, China announced that it had eliminated absolute poverty nationwide.

China's Belt & Road Initiative, too, will help in shaping the world economic landscape for the better. Ironically, the initiative, being criticized for years by the west, now has a western copycat - the Build Back Better World (B3W), a new global infrastructure initiative that President Biden and G7 partners agreed to launch to help narrow the $40+trillion infrastructure need in the developing world. Imitation is the sincerest form of flattery, especially when it comes from the most developed countries. If this is the competition between China and the US, then the world can indeed benefit from such "healthy" competition.

How China will look like in mid-century needs a bit of imagination. Presumably it will maintain some pleasant features of the Tang Dynasty that the Chinese are most proud of, that is, diversity and tolerance. Tang China was prosperous, multiethnic and cosmopolitan. It was home to "foreign" religions ranging from Buddhism, Nestorianism, Zoroastrianism and Islam to

Manichaeism. It sets a good example of how a great power that is next to none can be confident but humble, and loved rather than feared.

ARE WE ALREADY IN A NEW COLD WAR?

First published in The Ambassador Partnership, May 2023

The enthusiasm of international relations pundits for talking about whether we have entered into another cold war is not surprising. It is like guessing the sex of a baby to be born. One has a 50% chance of being right. Not bad at all! The problem is that we shall only be able to conclude it's a cold war when the prospect of an all-out war has eventually disappeared.

Predicting the future is a difficult business. But, presumably, three things will shape how the first half of the 21st century looks: the war in Ukraine, China-US competition in the Indo-Pacific and the rise of the "Rest" in contrast to the decline of the West in a changing world order.

Although no one knows how long the war in the heartland of Europe will last, no war lasts forever. The worst outcome would be for President Putin to decide to use a tactical nuclear weapon as a game-changer, while the best outcome would be an armistice, which no one likes. Ukraine can only fight on with the seamless and endless support of the West; this is not a sure thing if the war turns out to be one of attrition. Russia has failed to make obvious gains, but it can sustain the war given its advantages in manpower, military industry and an economy that is not substantively crippled by the war.

It seems probable that a new "Berlin Wall" will eventually appear in Ukraine. This will change Europe's security architecture. Europe will have to live with a Russia that is much weakened but far more dangerous. It will be more dangerous precisely because it is much weakened, but still has the largest nuclear arsenal in the world.

The war in Ukraine will most certainly accelerate geopolitical and geoeconomic shifts from the West to the East. The Biden administration had hoped to put Russia policy on a "stable and predictable" footing in order to focus on China, which it perceives as a long-term threat. But the war has undoubtedly distracted America's attention and syphoned off resources.

Cynically speaking, if there is consensus—the only consensus—between Beijing and Washington to avoid a conflict, then probably we are already in a new cold war. What makes this new cold war different, though, is that this is a rivalry between two giants, rather than two blocs. Washington could not lead an anti-China alliance and Beijing could not lead the Global South against America. All countries will deal with China and the US carefully, with pragmatism, making choices on specific issues, rather than blindly picking sides.

Much has been said about Taiwan becoming the next Ukraine. But a war in the Taiwan Strait is not inevitable so long as Beijing believes peaceful reunification is still possible. So far, Beijing has not lost patience. This is reflected in its defense budget which is still lower than 2 percent of its GDP, as it has been for decades. It is also reflected in the PLA's second military exercise around Taiwan, in April. Unlike the first one, which involved live firing of weapons, after US House Speaker Nancy Pelosi's 2022 visit to Taiwan, Beijing's April response was more calculated and measured, with only simulated attacks.

Whatever the outcome of the Ukraine war, two trends are likely to continue: the shrinking influence of the West and the further rise of the Rest. According to a Freedom House poll the western democracies have been in steady decline for 17 years. In contrast, countries are queuing to join the Shanghai Cooperation Agreement and the BRICS. Talk of trading with local currencies instead of American dollars is getting louder.

Should the world be afraid of China? This is the first question I was asked by *Die Zeit* in a recent interview. If the same question is asked of someone from a Global South country, I guess the answer, like mine, will be "no". The major difference between Chinese and western involvement in the Global South is that China acts and delivers without moralizing. If there is a competition to win over third parties, the US-led West is very much losing to China, especially in Africa and Latin America.

At the Munich Security Conference this year, China and Russia were put on one side and the West on the other side, to mark a democracy-autocracy cleavage. Such a simplistic black and white picture is not how the world looks. Even if both Beijing and Moscow talk about a multipolar world, their world views are subtly different. Beijing is the largest beneficiary of the globalization that depends on the existing international order; Moscow resents that order and considers itself a victim of it. As its relations with Washington grow steadily worse, Beijing has at least maintained a plausible relationship with the West; this appears to be impossible for Moscow now.

But when China and the West talk about the international order, are they talking about the same thing? The prevailing idea in the West is that the international order after World War II is a West-led "liberal international order". This is narcissism. Although many rules, regimes and even institutions such as the IMF, the World Bank and GATT/WTO were designed and built by the West after World War II, they are primarily found in the economic field and cannot define a whole system. The international order should include, among other features, different religions, cultures, customs, national identities and social systems. And it must address globalization, climate change, pandemics and nuclear proliferation, to name but a few.

It remains to be seen whether China can surpass the United States to become the largest economy in the world by 2030. This won't matter much economically in that any difference will be marginal. But it will have a psychological impact. The world will perceive a new dawn to have arrived. This will not be a Pax Sinica. Rather, it will be a return to common sense: nations rise and fall. The only "city upon a hill" is the empty temple of the Parthenon.

BRIC BY BRIC, THE BUILDING OF A NEW 'HOME' FOR THE GLOBAL SOUTH

First published in *The Straits Times*, 12 September 2023

The best example of a shift in the international order is not the outbreak of an improbable war in the heartland of Europe, but the rapid expansion of BRICS from a clutch of five nations (Brazil, Russia, India, China and South Africa) in 2010 to a grouping of 11 in August 2023. This is despite the fact that one of its members, Russia, is involved in that war.

The inclusion of six more countries—Argentina, Egypt, Ethiopia, Iran, Saudi Arabia and the United Arab Emirates (UAE)—means that BRICS has more than doubled in size in just over a decade, out-stripping the pace of growth of any other international grouping.

What to make of this surge of interest in BRICS? Related to this, as it grows and evolves, what challenges will this motley group of nations face?

Origin-wise it began as "BRIC"—a catchy term coined in 2001 by a Goldman Sachs economist to draw investors' attention to the growth potential of Brazil, Russia, India and China. In 2009, the group held its first leaders' summit, and a year later, a new letter was appended to the acronym with the entry of South Africa in to the club.

BRICS' enlargement is a reflection of the interest of Global South nations in jointly carving out a new path in a world less in the grip of Western domination. A key concern is the global economy's risky reliance on the American dollar.

As Brazil's President Luiz Inacio Lula da Silva remarked in a speech earlier in 2023: "Every night I ask myself why all countries have to base their trade on the dollar." For many analysts, too, the freezing of Russian central bank reserves by the United States in 2022 in response to the conflict in Ukraine was a chilling demonstration of unchecked American power.

While concerns about the West are a shared concern, some critics such as *The Financial Times* have argued that BRICS is basically a "fan club" for Beijing, and other BRICS nations risk becoming satellites of China.

That assertion is misleading. New members Saudi Arabia and UAE are American allies. Brazil and India have both been forging closer ties with the West.

Furthermore, in spite of their common call for multipolarity, China and Russia do not necessarily share the same world views.

Russia, nostalgic for past glories, sees itself as a victim of the international order and resents it. China, on the other hand, has been the largest beneficiary of globalisation and embraces it more than anyone else.

China, in the Russo-Ukrainian war, like most Global South countries, has adopted a position of studied neutrality. Likewise, in the ever intensifying China-US competition, the response of the middle and small powers in BRICS is not to pick sides.

Some others have compared an expanding BRICS to the Non Aligned Movement (NAM). Such a parallel is also not accurate. The strength of NAM is its moral high ground, not its economic clout.

Even before the expansion, the BRICS that comprised Brazil, Russia, India, China and South Africa accounted for 40 per cent of the world's population and a quarter of global gross domestic product. In 2020, it surpassed the Group of Seven nations in terms of purchasing power parity. The six carefully chosen newcomers, which represent the most important countries in different regions in the Global South, will add to the grouping's heft and global standing.

There is, however, one similarity with NAM, which stood out for its neutrality in the days when the two superpowers, the US and the Soviet Union, were at loggerheads. Fast forward to current times, BRICS members would not want to pick sides in any disagreement between the US and China—even though China considers itself a Global South nation and a developing country.

That said, China looms large in BRICS' future. China's share of the BRICS economic output in 2022 was 70 per cent. It is also the largest shareholder of BRICS' New Development Bank (NDB). Therefore, Beijing can contribute more than any other BRICS member with its market, investments and financial support, not to mention invaluable developmental lessons in lifting 800 million people out of poverty in the past four decades.

The addition of six new member states means the NDB will almost certainly be better positioned to push ahead with BRICS' priority programme of investing in infrastructure and sustainable development. What is more, it can provide financing for many states searching for alternatives to the World Bank and the International Monetary Fund, which notoriously stipulate political conditions—often under the guise of human rights and democracy—for their monetary support.

Looking ahead, one of BRICS' challenges is, interestingly, how to slow down expansion for the healthy development of the group, despite its own growing appeal. It is a challenge because more than 40 countries have either applied to join the bloc or have expressed an interest in doing so.

BRICS could become larger than the European Union or NATO that have 27 and 31 members respectively, if no limits are set. But the larger it becomes, the more difficult it will be in reaching consensus in a group that comprises drastically different political systems and varying economies of different sizes.

Herding cats is always a challenge for any organisation. Take Europe, for instance. Its efforts to forge a common policy on Russia's invasion of Ukraine have run into stumbling blocks. On this issue, Hungary is as much a thorn in the side of the EU as Turkey is in NATO.

One possible model to resolve this is ASEAN, which "makes haste slowly". ASEAN was established in 1967 with five members, but it was not until 1999 that it grew into today's 10 member grouping. The "ASEAN way" of arriving at consensus on issues at a pace comfortable to all is not perfect, but it has allowed a group of small nations to iron out many internal difficulties and problems. Miraculously, it has also gained the support of all major and middle powers in the Asia Pacific over its role of "centrality" in regional affairs.

One can hardly resist the temptation of comparing an expanded BRICS with the Group of 20. Like BRICS, the G20 is primarily a forum focusing on international economic cooperation, although its agenda is very much dictated by the West.

The G20 already includes five BRICS members, namely Brazil, Russia, India, China and South Africa. Could BRICS also become open to Western countries, inviting them as observers first and having bilateral dialogues one day? The Shanghai Cooperation Organisation, for example, has been open-minded enough to have Turkey, a NATO country, as a dialogue partner.

Neither BRICS nor the G20 can address common global challenges singlehandedly. It will be sad if the two groups, working towards similar objectives, are bent on fighting with each other.

CAN AN OPEN, INCLUSIVE SCO PROVE THAT A LESS-WESTERN WORLD IS BETTER THAN NATO'S VISION?

First published in *South China Morning Post*, 13 April 2023

If there is one shining example of "the West vs the Rest", it is probably the contrast between Nato and the Shanghai Cooperation Organisation (SCO). With 31 allies banded together, Nato is the largest military bloc in the world. Established in 2001, the SCO sits astride the Eurasian continent and accounts for almost 44 per cent of the world's population, with trillions of dollars of exports every year.

At first glance, both organisations are growing in popularity. This can be seen in Finland's entry into Nato on April 4 and Saudi Arabia's cabinet approving a move to join the SCO as a dialogue partner on March 28. However, appearances can be deceiving.

The challenge for Nato in the months—and years—to come is how it can continue providing sufficient military support to Ukraine without getting itself involved in a direct confrontation with Russia, something it has been trying to avoid since the onset of the Cold War. No one knows how long the war in Ukraine will last.

Another concern, though, is making sure the war does not escalate into a nuclear exchange in the heartland of Europe. Putin's hints at launching a nuclear attack might be bluffs, but his announcement of deploying tactical nuclear weapons in Belarus is certainly true. If the eventual outcome of the war is an armistice that further divides Ukraine, the question is where this new Berlin Wall will be found.

Nato has come to an impasse, in part because Western democracy is in decline. Even if Nato has been looking for new threats—say, in the Indo-Pacific—to justify its survival, it will struggle to strengthen its military instruments while democracy is receding.

The fact that even Russia's "special military operation" in Ukraine has failed to dampen nations' interest in joining the SCO—an organisation led by China and Russia—is noteworthy. At the SCO summit in Samarkand, Uzbekistan, last September, the grouping not only agreed to accept Iran as a member state but also started the accession procedure for Belarus, granted dialogue partner status to Egypt, Saudi Arabia and Qatar, and agreed on admitting Bahrain, the Maldives, the United Arab Emirates, Kuwait and Myanmar as new dialogue partners at a later date.

This latest round of expansion for the SCO is the largest yet, and it is also the clearest indication that the West's role in the world is shrinking. Indian External affairs Minister Subrahmanyam Jaishankar said last year that, "Europe has to grow out of the mindset that Europe's problems are the world's problems but the world's problems are not Europe's problems." A useful paraphrasing might be to say that Europe has to grow out of the mindset that Europe's war is the world's war but the world's other wars are not Europe's wars.

Unlike Nato, the SCO is open, inclusive and non-ideological. For it to grow sustainably, however, it cannot afford to be seen as an anti-Western club. Concerns about this have lingered for much of the organisation's existence, and they could heighten at a time when Russia is at war with Ukraine.

Therefore, coordination between China and Russia is crucial. Both Beijing and Moscow talk about a multipolar world, yet their world views are not entirely the same. Beijing is the largest beneficiary of the globalisation that depends on the existing international order, but Moscow resents that order and considers itself a victim.

As its relations with Washington grow steadily worse, Beijing has at least maintained a plausible relationship with Europe, which sees China as simultaneously a partner, competitor and rival. Such a relationship with Europe appears to be impossible for Moscow now.

Nevertheless, as long as the SCO doesn't grow into an alliance which requires common values and common enemies, such differences are unlikely to matter very much. This is why India, a country that is close to the West and also part of the SCO, is useful. With the world's fifth-largest economy included in the group, critics of the SCO must think twice before describing it as a grouping of authoritarian regimes.

Security and development are said to be two wheels of the SCO cart, but what exactly affects security? When the SCO was formed more than 20 years ago, security efforts focused on counterterrorism. This is seen in the group's joint counterterrorism exercises. Although all sorts of terrorist activities are still present today, they are not strong enough to require large, cross-border military operations.

Instead, the real challenge is to prevent war between member states. India and Pakistan, two longtime foes, could come into conflict again. It is also alarming how Chinese and Indian troops engaged in a deadly brawl in the Galwan Valley in 2020. On the eve of the Samarkand summit, Tajikistan and Kyrgyzstan experienced violent border clashes. That same week, Armenia and Azerbaijan were on the verge of another war.

Economic development is the incentive that binds everyone together. The combined GDP of the SCO plus Iran accounts for about a quarter of global GDP. The entry of Iran and Saudi Arabia, two large oil exporters, will strengthen the organisation economically.

The sanctions on Russia will make non-Western countries reconsider how to make their property and investments safe. Gradually, the SCO is expected to increase local currency settlements in trading that will spearhead the transition from a unipolar financial system based on the US dollar to a more multipolar financial system.

In a divided world, the SCO stands in contrast to other US-led coalitions. Yet it has a far harder task—to prove a less-Western world is a better world.

SCO CANNOT TACKLE TERRORISM IN EURASIA WHILE AFGHANISTAN REMAINS OUTSIDE THE BLOC

First published in *South China Morning Post*, 4 February 2022

The swift and decisive response by countries of the Russia-led Collective Security Treaty Organization (CSTO) to the riots in Kazakhstan raises a question for its peer in the region, the Shanghai Cooperation Organisation (SCO): can it become equally effective in a similar situation?

Since the inauguration of the SCO in 2001, member states have held joint counterterrorism exercises almost annually, in line with the spirit of the group's charter. But which country might really ask for cross-border help from the organisation?

The answer is probably none. Russia, Kazakhstan, Kyrgyzstan and Tajikistan, all member states of the SCO, are also allies in the CSTO. If necessary, they would seek help from the alliance first, as Kazakhstan proved recently.

China, India and Pakistan, meanwhile, are strong enough to deal with any domestic unrest without external help. The only uncertainty among SCO states is Uzbekistan, which left the CSTO in 2012.

The country in the region that needs most external help in counterterrorism efforts is Afghanistan, currently an observer state of the SCO. Cynically speaking, the heft of Afghanistan seems to lie in the troubles it might bring to other countries.

At the founding ceremony of the SCO, president Nursultan Nazarbayev of Kazakhstan described Afghanistan as "the cradle of terrorism, separatism and extremism" in his opening remarks. According to the UN, Afghanistan accounted for some 85 per cent of global opium production in 2020.

The wish of the international community is for the Taliban-led Afghan government to become moderate, inclusive and resolute in fighting terrorism. There is no guarantee of that, but at least the Taliban has said the right things, promising that people's lives and property would be safeguarded and women's rights respected.

Presumably, the leaders of this government have learned some lessons from their avatars who were in power before September 11.

The international community should therefore give the Taliban a chance to honour its promise, not least because the Afghan people are suffering from the world's worst humanitarian crisis, exacerbated by the harsh winter, drought and insufficient international aid. More than half the country's 40 million residents are reportedly facing food insecurity.

How can the SCO help? First and foremost, as de facto leaders of the SCO and permanent members of the UN Security Council, China and Russia should urge the US to lift its unilateral sanctions and unfreeze the more than US$9 billion in overseas central bank reserves as soon as possible. So far, the Biden administration has offered aid without dealing directly with the Taliban-led government it abhors.

This won't work. According to The New York Times, aid groups have warned that 1 million Afghan children could die this winter. This may be alarmist, but even if 10,000 children die, it will be a crime rather than a shame. If Afghan people are dying while their money is in your hands, people can safely argue they are dying because of you.

Concurrently, the UN should lay down clear conditions that the Taliban has to meet in exchange for lifting sanctions. The Afghan people did not choose the Taliban, who took power by force, but there is no political party in sight that looks capable of replacing them any time soon. The challenge for the UN, then, is how to define such slippery words as "moderate" and "inclusive".

If these terms mean including people who are not male or Pashtun in government, allowing women to work and girls to go to school, the Taliban would most probably agree since this is what they have already promised. At least on paper, these conditions are much easier to meet than those found in the Iranian or North Korean nuclear deals.

Although the SCO doesn't necessarily need to recognise the legitimacy of the Taliban-led government now, it should use the SCO-Afghanistan Contact Group that was established in 2005 to liaise with the Taliban. Crucially, the Taliban must break away from all terrorist groups, even if they are bound by historical friendship, ideological similarity and even intermarriage.

Looking beyond the horizon, Afghanistan needs to become an SCO member state if it is to avoid looking like an enclave that leads to nowhere. The question is when. Afghanistan applied for full membership in 2015 and has been waiting ever since.

Can Kabul only join when it is no longer a problem? Or should the SCO let it in and resolve the problem from within? Or, if the problem is one which, like the pandemic, simply won't go away, could the organisation learn to live with it?

In 2017, India and Pakistan both joined the SCO. Although the countries brought with them a seemingly irreconcilable mutual distrust, at least India's economy, now the sixth largest in the world, has added strength to the organisation.

The benefit of granting Kabul full membership is that the SCO could play a pivotal role in mitigating worst-case scenarios. As a full member, the Afghan government—no matter who is in power—would be obliged to prevent extremist movements from spilling over into neighbouring countries.

Membership would also allow Afghanistan to be woven into the political and economic fabric of the region, something which is crucial for its future prosperity. After all, more than 60 per cent of Afghanistan's trade is with SCO countries.

Afghanistan is not only landlocked, but it is almost SCO-locked as well. If it is not stable, the SCO will suffer. Striding over the Eurasian heartland is already a large undertaking. But for the SCO to become stronger, it should be brave enough to embrace a country that holds the key to regional peace and stability.

UNLIKE NATO, THE SCO NEEDS NO ENEMY
TO JUSTIFY ITS EXISTENCE

First published in *South China Morning Post*, 21 June 2017

It is hard not to compare Nato with the Shanghai Cooperation Organisation (SCO). In the same month, within four days, Montenegro joined the transatlantic security alliance as the 29th member state while India and Pakistan joined the SCO to boost the membership to eight-strong. Both organisations are attractive: on each side, a group of countries are waiting to join.

Nato is expanding faster. When Montenegro joined the alliance on June 5, it was only eight years ago when Albania and Croatia became member states. By comparison, India and Pakistan's entry into the SCO is the first such enlargement since the organisation was founded in 2001. But the SCO wins for size: it now has a quarter of the world's population and covers three-fifths of the Eurasian continent.

Nato has an intrinsic problem. As a military alliance, it needs enemies to justify its survival. What united the alliance during the Cold War was the Warsaw Pact led by the Soviet Union; now it is Russia and, most recently, Russia and Islamic State. At the

Nato summit, UK Prime Minister Theresa May placed Russia in the same category of threat to the West as IS.

How much further Nato can go remains to be seen. Nato lives on the fear of the central and eastern European countries of Russia, but it has tried its best to eschew a direct Nato-Russia confrontation, in spite of its protest at Russia's annexation of Crimea and military intervention in Ukraine. Its acceptance of Montenegro, a small country with fewer than 2,000 troops, looks more like picking a low-hanging fruit.

The SCO, by contrast, is not designed to address an external threat, so it is not directed at the West. It looks inwards to address its own problems. Its predecessor, the "Shanghai Five", succeeded in resolving border disputes among China, Kazakhstan, Kyrgyzstan, Russia and Tajikistan. Today, its security concern remains uprooting the "three evils" of terrorism, separatism and religious extremism. No one is sure when this can be achieved, but sincere efforts are being made. In 2004, an SCO counterterrorism centre was established in Tashkent, Uzbekistan. Since 2002, all military exercises within the SCO have been on counterterrorism.

Another distinctive feature of the SCO is that it is inclusive rather than exclusive. It is home to different values, religions and civilisations which, to a great extent, reflects the reality of the world today. Its missions are diverse, too. Apart from its primary focus on security, the SCO conducts exchanges in politics, economy, culture and society.

This contrasts with Nato's "common values". But do Nato members really share common values? France and Germany opposed an invasion of Iraq. The British Parliament vetoed any move to bomb Syria. Turkey, in recent years, has behaved more like a spur irritating Nato. More than once, Prime Minister Recep Tayyip Erdogan has threatened to give up its EU application in exchange for SCO membership.

The SCO is audacious. It accepted Turkey, a Nato member, as a dialogue partner.

The SCO is also credible for having no fear of trouble: it accepted both India and Pakistan as members, two countries at loggerheads. India, which enjoys robust economic growth, will add tremendously to the SCO's weight. As for Pakistan, a stronger China now looks like a godsend. The construction of the China-Pakistan Economic Corridor is in full swing. The huge investment from China might prove to be the real game changer.

So far, only five Nato members spend 2 per cent of their gross domestic product on defence, as required. Perhaps this speaks to what the majority of Nato members really think about the "threats" facing them—they are manageable and shouldn't loom large to the extent that they become more important than public spending on, say, education and public health.

When US President Donald Trump called Nato "obsolete" during his election campaign, he spoke like the child who pointed out that the emperor was not wearing any clothes. His instinct is right. Nato doesn't need to look far to find an enemy. The biggest enemy is itself.

COULD TURKEY SERVE AS A BRIDGE
BETWEEN NATO AND SCO?

First published in China-US Focus, 19 December 2016

After Turkish Prime Minister Recep Tayyip Erdogan talked again about joining the Shanghai Cooperation Organization (SCO) instead of the European Union on Nov 20, the first question is: How serious is he, this time? Since he first mentioned it during a television interview in January 2013, he has talked about it quite a few times—including making a direct request to Russian President Vladimir Putin at a press conference in Nov 2013.

To join EU or SCO, this is a zero sum game for Erdogan—he can only choose one side. For Erdogan or even all Turkish people, EU accession has been a national dream of Turkey pursued with utmost effort since 2005. Today, the prospect looks remote. Erdogan's crackdown on the coup has invited quite a few loud grumbles from Europe and the US; meanwhile, an EU plagued by nationalistic populism and economic downturn may look less attractive too. But Turkey's hope for accession is not totally shattered. In an attempt to encourage Turkey to harbor the vast number of refugees and migrants seeking asylum in Europe, countries like Germany still promise to speed up Turkey's EU bid. For Erdogan to act decisively for SCO membership, he probably needs a plebiscite in the first instance.

Even if Turkey decides to switch to SCO, there is another problem: Turkey is a NATO member state. As a NATO member for 65 years, Turkey has never flirted with the idea of leaving NATO. In fact, Turkey's ambition for EU entry comes in no small part because of its confidence as a NATO ally. On the other hand, Turkey withdrawing from NATO and joining SCO can only be a devastating blow to NATO. The primary concern of NATO today, as in the Cold War, is still Russia. The Turkish Armed Forces, with an estimated strength in 2015 of 639,551 military, civilian and paramilitary personnel, collectively rank as the second-largest standing military force in NATO. If Turkey withdraws, NATO's first line of defense against Russia will crumble.

So the real question is: Can Turkey join SCO as a NATO member state? Theoretically yes. Turkey is already a dialogue partner of SCO. It can apply to become an observer before it is finally promoted to become a SCO member state. But to become an observer, Turkey has to compete with Azerbaijan, Armenia, Cambodia, Nepal and Sri Lanka, which are also dialogue partners. If it becomes an observer one day, it will still compete with observers such as Afghanistan, Belarus, Iran and Mongolia, which have all expressed clear intentions to become SCO member states.

Turkey's bid is more than a question of procedure. The attitude of major powers in SCO is crucial. In SCO, China and Russia's de facto leadership is reflected in the working languages—only Chinese and Russian. Beijing has no spat with Ankara, although it does seek greater Turkish cooperation in curbing separatists of the East Turkestan Islamic Movement (ETIM), a terrorist organization, from launching sabotage activities in China from

Turkish territory. When a Chinese spokesman from the Ministry of Foreign Affairs commented on Erdogan's recent remarks, he said China attaches importance to Turkey's aspiration, that the Chinese side is willing to consult with other SCO members and seek consensus through close study in accordance with legal documents and regulations of the SCO. Such an expression is widely taken as a green light from Beijing.

But Moscow's attitude is less easy to read. Historically Russia and Turkey have been rivals for influence in Central Asia. Turkey is promoting the idea of the "common Turkic home" in the region. It is actively promoting the transition from the Cyrillic script to the Latin alphabet in Central Asia. If Turkey joins SCO, it is not only physically connected again with the hinterland of Central Asia, but it could also use its historic, linguistic, cultural and ethnic connections with Turkic-speaking countries to offset predominant Russian cultural, economic and geopolitical influence. For some Russians, this mirrors NATO's eastern expansion and they see Turkey as just a Trojan horse of NATO inside SCO.

By any means, Turkey's admission into SCO won't be an easy ticket. But is it impossible? SCO's goodwill to Turkey was witnessed on November 23, when Turkey was granted chairmanship of the Energy Club of SCO for the 2017 period. It's the first non-full member to become chairman of a club in the organization.

If SCO accepts Turkey as a NATO member state, it would be as bold and creative as Deng Xiaoping's "one country, two systems" defining the relationship between mainland China and Hong Kong. It could serve to improve the NATO-Russian relationship; further promote SCO economic integration; and add strength in counteracting terrorism, separatism and extremism, the primary goals of SCO.

It might also be good for a NATO that US President-elect Donald Trump described as obsolete and extremely expensive. Cooperation, for example, could start on such common interests as counter-terrorism. Should this happen, Turkey, like the Bosporus Bridge in Istanbul linking Asia and Europe, would happily find itself in a unique position to bridge the largest alliance and the largest non-alliance in the world.

SUBSTITUTE FOR A WORLD WAR OR A PRELUDE TO IT?

Remarks at Russia's Waldai Club, 18 October 2021

Thanks Mr Chairman for providing me a chance to talk at this important club. The fact that I am talking from Beijing at a conference in Sochi, Russia, shows how Covid-19 has changed the world. But we shouldn't be surprised. Throughout history, infectious disease has killed more human beings than natural disasters or wars. The plague of Justinian (541–549 AD), the first pandemic wiped out half the global population at the time. During World War I, some 50 to 100 million people died in the 1918 influenza pandemic—numbers that surpassed the death toll of the war that was being fought at the same time. Thanks to unprecedented speedy response and large-scale investment in the vaccine, the number of fatalities caused by Covid-19 has slowed down.

Pathogens know no borders. No matter how Covid should have united people around the world to fight against it, it hasn't. Instead, it sowed discord, highlighted inequality and exacerbated social divisions. In the international arena, it adds fuel to the great power competition in which the United States takes China and Russia as the primary strategic competitors. Now America's competition with China has become "extreme competition", according to Joe Biden.

I cannot speak on behalf of Russians, but I guess the reason behind China being taken by the US as primary competitor is because, according to former Vice President Mike Pence, "After the fall of the Soviet Union, we assumed that a free China was inevitable". But China hasn't become a liberal democracy. Worse still for Washington, China is getting stronger and stronger.

The thing is China has never intended to become "a free China" as Pence and his like wish. China always maintains that it is a socialist country led by the Chinese Communist Party. When the US brands China its "primary competitor", it confirms what China has long believed that all the sweet talk of the US in the past about how it wished China would be strong and prosperous are but fat lies.

And why should China become a liberal democracy like the US? According to Freedom House democracy around the globe has been declining since 2006, even in established democracies such as the US and India. I am pretty sure that liberal democracy will continue to decline in the years ahead. When an "authoritarian state" such as China overtakes the US to become the world's largest economy in terms of gross domestic product in around 2030, the influence of Western democracy will be looking at its nadir. This doesn't mean China wishes to export its model of governance and development, but it helps people to come to terms with common sense—the world, now as in the past, is always a coexistence of different civilizations, social systems, cultures and religions. There is no such myth of democracy vs autocracy.

The self-aggrandizement of the west for liberal democracy is historical myopia. Although liberal democracy traces its origins to the Age of Enlightenment, it only spread after the Industrial Revolution and the introduction of capitalism. So far the concept of western liberal democracy is less than three hundred years old, which is a shorter time span than the lengths of either the Han, Tang, Song, Ming, and Qing Dynasties of China or Russia's Romanov Dynasty. According to Freedom House, "fewer than a fifth of the world's people now live in fully Free countries". In other words, the world is never western. With full respect for the word "democracy", I wish to point out that no consensus exists on a precise definition of democracy. The late UN secretary general Kofi Annan said that "there are as many different forms of democracy as there are democratic nations in the world." Mali is ranked as "Free" by Freedom House, but is a Least Developed Country. Qatar has arguably the highest GDP per capita in the world, but has never been democratic. Which of the two countries has delivered more to its own people? And if a country fails to meet the basic needs of its own people, is such democracy still desirable?

Two years ago, the UN secretary general Antonio Guterres talked about "our 1945 moment" in which he saw the risk of "a great fracture" of the world splitting in two, with the two largest economies on earth creating two separate and competing worlds, each with their own dominant currency, trade and financial rules, their own internet and artificial intelligence capacities. In September, he further described the relationship between China and the United States as "completely dysfunctional" and warned against a new cold war "that would be different from the past one, and probably more dangerous and more difficult to manage".

I see a few more fractures. First, the West is splintering. The 2020 Munich Security Conference report is titled in one word "Westlessness". It concluded that not only was the world becoming less Western, the West itself was becoming less Western, too. Wolfgang Ischinger, Chairman of the Munich

Security Conference pointed out that "a liberal-democratic set of norms that were once taken for granted... turned out to be more fragile than most could have imagined". Worse still, the west is threatened from inside with the rise of illiberalism and the return of nationalism.

Secondly, the US as the leader of the "free world" appears more divided than ever over social issues, race, gender and the economy. America's General Social Survey in 2020 shows that Americans are the unhappiest they have been in 50 years. The fact that Capitol Hill, the supreme seat of American democracy, was taken over by insurrectionists incited by an outgoing American president tells us how deeply Americans are polarized today. CNN said Trump has left America at its most divided since the Civil War.

Finally, I believe the America-led alliance will continue to decay in spite of Biden's vow to strengthen it. In Europe, short of an apparent enemy, NATO has long lost its momentum to the extent that French President Macron called it "braindead". The ending of Afghan wars marks the end of America's global war on terrorism and the beginning of Biden's extreme competition with China in the Indo-Pacific. As a result, the US will not be back as Biden promised, it will reduce, however gradually, its attention on and support of Europe. This will of course weaken NATO and will in turn cause Europe to strengthen its "strategic autonomy" which has so far remained very much a slogan.

In Asia, the strength of America's alliance cannot be taken for granted either. Most countries including America's allies and partners in the Asia-Pacific are worried about choosing sides between the US and China, their largest trading partners. The recent AUKUS agreement between the US, Britain and Australia shows how the US could resort to desperate measures in its competition against China, even at the cost of an important ally. But if the US has succeeded in turning a once half-hearted

Australia against China, the "stab in the back" of France, as French Foreign Affairs Minister Jean-Yves Le Drian described, will have long term impacts.

Now let me come to the question raised by the organizer of the conference. Is this "Substitute for a World War or a Prelude to It"? I don't think we are sliding into a world war or even prelude to it, but there is indeed danger of conflict between Beijing and Washington in the Taiwan Strait and the South China Sea.

Biden said that US rivalry with China will take the form of "extreme competition" rather than conflict. I'd love to believe him, because neither China nor the US wants a conflict, let alone a war. But the problem is: if we are in extreme competition, are we far away from conflict? There were already quite a few accidents including a deadly collision of military aircraft in 2001 and dangerous encounters by naval ships at sea. All the accidents so far occurred on China's, not America's, periphery. Naturally enough, the US is the trouble maker.

If the 20-year war in Afghanistan is a "forever war" for the United States, then its competition with China must be "forever competition", because it will surely last longer than twenty years. In the years ahead, China-US competition will most certainly intensify in that the US will take it as the last chance to bring down a rising power, but there is no guarantee it will succeed. China's rise is from within the current international system that was to a great extent established by the west led by the US. Today China is so integrated with the system that it vows to be a guardian of the existing international order. Therefore, America's efforts to bash China will bring damage to the international system and hurt the US itself.

Although the US militarily is still much stronger than the PLA, the gap in the Western Pacific is closing in China's favor. Thanks to the progress made in the last four decades, the PLA has all the advantages of being on home turf in a conflict. As the New York times has observed, "it is far more difficult for the United States and its allies to project power thousands of miles to Taiwan than it is for China to project power 100 miles across the Taiwan Strait", "neither AUKUS submarines nor US bombers flying from northern Australia are likely to tip the balance".

China believes "the world is undergoing great changes that have not been seen in a century", but it is confident about the future. In the 21st century, no change is greater than the rise of China. The global power is shifting irreversibly from the west to the east with China playing a central role in this process. Although it is not entirely up to Beijing to choose between peace and war, China today is certainly in a better position to shape her environment and avert wars.

RULES-BASED MARITIME ORDER IN THE NEW NORM

Remarks at International Maritime Security Conference, Singapore, 28 July 2021

Chancellor Otto von Bismarck famously said, "Laws are like sausages, it is better not to see them being made". In this regard, the UN Convention on the Law of the Sea (UNCLOS) looks like the longest sausage ever made. It was negotiated for nine years by around 140 countries, making it the longest-running international law negotiation in history. Understandably, compromises are made and ambiguities that could be flexibly interpreted still found.

China, a country that ratified the UNCLOS as early as 1996 and the US, a country that so far hasn't ratified the UNCLOS have different interpretations of the Convention, say, on freedom of navigation and overflight. China believes that American military activities, such as the close-in reconnaissance and surveillance by the US Navy in China's Exclusive Economic Zone (EEZ), infringe on China's security interests and therefore cannot be simply categorized as freedom of navigation. The US maintains that its military activities fall within the freedom of navigation and other internationally lawful uses of the sea. But I wish to point out that China is not the only country that holds such a view. At least 25 other countries also have restrictions regarding foreign military activities in their exclusive economic zones or contiguous zones to varying degrees.

Such difference is understandable, but the US, based upon its own interpretations of the UNCLOS, behaves as if it is the sole guardian of maritime law. According to the Pentagon, from October 1, 2019 to September 30, 2020, U.S. forces operationally challenged "28 different excessive maritime claims made by 19 different claimants throughout the world". Therefore, a simple question arises: If the Convention is good, why don't you ratify it? And if it is not, why would you challenge others in the name of it?

China is the only country that has responded militarily to American provocations. There was a deadly aircraft collision in 2001 and a number of dangerous encounters at sea. For over two decades, the Chinese and American navies' dialogues are useful but not fruitful: the American side wanted technical discussions on how to avoid close and dangerous encounters between ships and aircraft while the Chinese side would point out that American intense surveillance and reconnaissance in China's waters were provocations to China's sovereignty that should be stopped or at least reduced; Americans asked Chinese ships monitoring American ships to keep safe distance and Chinese believe the American ships are most safe if they don't come at all. It is fair to say that neither China nor the US want an accident. But the fundamental problem exists from the very beginning: if the US doesn't want the water to boil, why keep throwing wood into the fire? After all, it is the American ships that have come regularly to China's doorstep and not the other way round.

In theory, it is only a matter of time before the next crisis occurs. Today, risk reduction for Beijing and Washington is more difficult than that between the US and the Soviet Union during the Cold War for two reasons. First, there were clearly defined spheres of influence between Washington and Moscow which allowed them to avoid direct confrontations even if proxy wars had to be fought elsewhere. But between China and the United States, there isn't even a buffer zone in the South China Sea or the Taiwan Straits where American naval vessels sail regularly.

Second, the United States and the Soviet Union were balanced by mutually assured destruction which is not found between Beijing and Washington. But in the Western Pacific, the gap in military strength is shrinking in China's favor thanks to the advances of the PLA in the past decades. A stronger PLA can only become more determined to safeguard China's sovereignty and territorial integrity. Of all the reports by American think tanks that I read in the last three years, none of them concludes that within the Western Pacific, the US military is guaranteed to win over the PLA.

If we cannot resolve the problem, we can only try our best to manage a crisis sliding into a confrontation that neither wants. Perhaps there is some light at the end of the tunnel. In October 2020, officials of the Chinese Ministry of National Defense and the US Department of Defense convened the first Crisis Communication Working Group meeting by video teleconference to discuss concepts of crisis communications, crisis prevention and crisis management. This is the first time that crisis is stressed as such because previously talks were centered on avoiding "accidents" or "incidents". The most significant part is management of crises, that is, what to do after an accident has happened, a scenario never discussed before.

For China and the US to deconflict at sea, both sides need to observe the multilaterally agreed rules and regulations of the "Code for Unplanned Encounters at Sea" (CUES) made at the Western Pacific Naval Symposium and the bilaterally agreed

"Rules of Behavior for Safety of Air and Maritime Encounters" (ROB) to avoid miscalculations. The key to avoid an accident is for ships and aircraft to keep safe distance. But what exactly is the safe distance? According to CUES, seven factors ranging from the state of visibility, the maneuverability of both vessels and understanding of the maneuvering intentions of the other vessel have to be considered in keeping safe distance. Apparently, they require not only serious discussions, but also regular training to ensure good seamanship. The two militaries conducted joint drills on CUES in 2014, 2015 and 2016. Such exercises should continue, partly because a stronger PLA Navy is bound to meet the US Navy more often in international waters in days to come.

The organizer of the conference asks us to discuss the rules-based order in the new norm. Then what is the new norm? The so-called "free and open Indo-Pacific" is not the new norm, it is a new myth. Ask yourself when the Indo-Pacific was not free and open? Oceans are interconnected. In human history, few countries have attempted to block international straits or sea lanes. The most outstanding problem in the Indo-Pacific was piracy that was rampant in the Gulf of Aden and Somali Basin from 2008 to 2013. Now it is basically eradicated thanks to the joint efforts of the international navies.

The "free and open Indo-Pacific" is in fact a thinly-veiled attack on China. It also comes at a cost to the centrality of the ASEAN. The reason is simple, geographically speaking, if ASEAN lies at the heart of the Pacific, it cannot be at the center of the Indo-Pacific at the same time.

It would be interesting to see how the Quad might evolve. If it is based upon a common resentment of China, then the glue that binds the four won't be strong enough. China is one of the top trading partners of the US and the largest trading partner of Japan, Australia and India. None of them would wish to sacrifice their own economic ties with China for the interests of the other three countries, to say the least.

In the international maritime domain, one of the new norms is that the PLA Navy is getting stronger and stronger. It already has the largest number of ships in the world. It is aiming to grow into a world-class navy by mid-century. At any given time, there are Chinese naval vessels sailing somewhere in the rest of the world.

The question is what this means for the world. Of course, a stronger Chinese navy will play a more important role in safeguarding China's sovereignty and territorial integrity, but the PLA Navy doesn't need so many ships for the Taiwan issue or the South China Sea issue. It is China's tremendous and ever-growing overseas interests and international obligations which are incumbent upon a major power that call for China to build a world-class navy. In the defense white paper, safeguarding China's overseas interests and participating in regional and international security cooperation to safeguard regional and world peace are described as "strategic tasks" of the PLA.

Another new norm is China is a new type of sea power different from all others in history. China has no intentions to police the world. Therefore, it won't attempt to control the chokepoints in the international straits. It won't establish the so-called "string of pearls". Instead, China will safeguard its overseas interests and shoulder its international obligations through international cooperation. Countering piracy in the Indian Ocean is a brilliant example of how the Chinese navy might achieve that. Half of all the 7,000 or so ships escorted by the Chinese naval flotillas are foreign ships. The significance of the Chinese navy joining the international navies in counter-piracy in the Gulf of Aden is three-fold: it is counter-piracy; it is maintenance of sea lines of communication, and it is also preservation of freedom of navigation. Such a practice might be a useful way to mitigate the ambiguity of the UNCLOS.

WHY THE INTERNATIONAL ORDER IS NOT FALLING APART

First published in China-US Focus, 19 May 2019

If you happened to attend the Munich Security Conference 2019 in February, you might think the world was already shattered to pieces when you walked out. The overarching question of the conference is "The great puzzle: who will pick up the pieces?" and according to the MSC report, "a new era of great power competition is unfolding between the United States, China, and Russia, accompanied by a certain leadership vacuum in what has become known as liberal international order".

Should one scrutinize the trilateral relationship among China, the United States and Russia, such an euro-centric conclusion looks exaggerated, if not sensational. No matter how Russia might be nostalgic of its heyday in the Soviet Union and despite its hawkish remarks sometimes, Russia should have no intention to compete with the US globally. Today Russia's ambitions are very much reduced to maintain its influence in the former Soviet Union and stop NATO's further expansion towards it. Moscow's military maneuvers have so far rarely extended beyond Europe and parts of the Middle East. Although Russia and the US point fingers at each other for violation of the INF treaty, it is the US that has unilaterally withdrawn from the treaty, as it did from the ABM treaty in 2001.

If China and Russia become allies, indeed it would realize the worst nightmare of the west and will certainly add to the competitiveness of the major power rivalry, but there is no such straw in the wind yet. China and Russia's rapprochement is in part a response to the common pressure from the United States, and in part because of their similar views on multi-polarity. The two countries, however close, are more like two lines in parallel. This explains why they always maintained that their annual exercises were not directed against any third parties.

The "best evidence" of the competitiveness between China and the United States is that China was labeled as "competitor" in both America's National Security Strategy and National Defense Strategy documents. The relationship between the two largest economies in the world is admittedly complicated, especially given that China is widely assumed to be able to overtake the US economically in around 2030–2035. Besides, a less confident Washington is now paranoid that Beijing wants to drive her out of the Indo-Pacific. But so long as China continues to engage the US wherever possible, the US can hardly turn China into an enemy in spite of its tradition of looking for enemies. In a most antagonistic speech against China delivered by Vice President Pence in October 2018, he still pointed out, "Competition does not always mean hostility".

Then, is "the entire liberal international order... falling apart"? The answer is: is there really something called "the liberal international order"? Such a catchphrase, generalizing the last seven decades after the Second World War with an apparent air of western triumphalism, is at least simplistic if not biased. It misses major events during the Cold War rivalry between the US and the Soviet Union, the independence of a few dozen countries, the spread of non-alignment movement, and the huge influence of China over countries in the third world. It also neglects the roles of new institutions that have cropped up after the Cold War such as the Shanghai Cooperation Organization, G20 and the Asia Infrastructure Investment Bank.

Perhaps the best way to pacify Europe is to tell her that nobody is trying to establish a new world order at her cost. And rather than dividing the world order into "liberal" or "illiberal" camps, won't it make better sense to take the world order as a hybrid featuring different but coexisting social systems, security architectures and above all, civilizations? Compared with ever-changing orders, civilizations last much longer and are much more stable. In a globalized village, a different civilization is no longer something at a distant horizon for one to salute. It is right next to you. Rudyard Kipling, said "East is East, and West is West, and never the twain shall meet", but today one in every three people in London is foreign-born and London and Rotterdam are both run by Muslim mayors.

It is no coincidence that both German Chancellor Angela Merkel and Chinese State Councilor (also a member of the Politburo) Yang Jiechi stressed multilateralism. In what was described as the best ever speech by Merkel, she said that multilateralism is often "difficult, slow and complicated", but "it's better than staying at home alone". Who can disagree with that? If we don't cherish the Iranian nuclear deal and the Paris climate accord - both being examples of "difficult, slow and complicated" negotiations that are hard-won, what is the realistic Plan B?

Europe's self-confidence has reached its nadir because of Brexit, nationalism further fueled by populism and an American president who once called the EU an "enemy". And the Munich Security Conference is but the best mirror of that. But the world is not falling apart into pieces because of a famous conference.

Rather, the world is like a glass half filled with water. Whether you see half is water or half is empty says more about you rather than the glass.

CHINA'S GROWING GLOBAL LINKS SHOW THERE IS NO SUCH THING AS A US-LED INTERNATIONAL ORDER

First published in *South China Morning Post*, 8 November 2022

Are China and the US on an inevitable collision course? One may wonder this when comparing the national security strategy issued by American President Joe Biden on October 12 with the report of the 20th National Congress of the Chinese Communist Party delivered by President Xi Jinping four days later.

President Biden asserted that China harbours the intention and, increasingly, the capacity to reshape the international order and vowed to "outcompete" China. Without naming the US, President Xi Jinping warned of "high winds, choppy waters and even dangerous storms" on the journey ahead and made it clear that China has the courage and ability to carry on its fight.

With the US hell-bent on competition on all fronts, Washington's offer to cooperate with Beijing on issues such as climate change appears as a tiny isle in a vast ocean. Biden is right about one thing: the next 10 years will be the decisive decade.

But even if all signs point to competition between Beijing and Washington becoming fiercer down the road, the outcome is very much known already. China's gross domestic product in purchasing power parity terms overtook that of the US in 2013.

Although slow growth has dampened expectations that the Chinese economy will be the largest by the end of the decade, the high probability is that the gap between the US and China will continue to shrink until a kind of balance is achieved, with each leading in different areas.

Competition is more about mentality. When Biden talks about the international order, he is actually talking about what he has previously referred to as the "liberal world order", in which America's leadership is taken for granted. There is no such order in the world.

True, many rules, regimes and even institutions such as the IMF and the World Bank were tailor-made by the West after World War II, but these alone do not define a system shaped by major events such as the independence movements in Africa, the Cold War, the fall of the Soviet Union and the rise of China, to name just a few.

Intrinsically, the international order comprises different religions, cultures, customs, national identities and social systems. Some of them may have survived over a millennium. It is also affected by globalisation, climate change, pandemics and nuclear proliferation.

In fact, the period that looks at best like a liberal international order is the 15 years or so after the dissolution of the Soviet Union, when China had yet to rise fully. This is but a blink of an eye in human history.

If there is no liberal international order, there can be no simplistic dichotomy of "democracy vs autocracy". According to The Economist Intelligence Unit's Democracy Index 2021, just 21 territories out of a total of 167 were deemed to be full democracies, representing 6.4 per cent of the world's population. If the liberal democratic model stands on a moral high ground, this does not explain why there is a global decline in democracy.

It does not explain why a democracy like India is considered increasingly authoritarian. It does not explain why the Shanghai Cooperation Organisation led by China and Russia—two "authoritarian states"—is growing and has even attracted Turkey, a Nato country. It does not explain why former American president Donald Trump instigated mobs to take over Capitol Hill, the highest seat of American democracy. It does not explain why China, while preserving its own social system, has become integrated with the rest of the world.

The real competition between Beijing and Washington is not how to outperform each other at home, but to win the hearts and minds of people elsewhere. In the Indo-Pacific, where the US is rallying forces, Japan and Australia look like diehard American allies at first glance.

But it is premature to conclude they will follow the US willy-nilly in going against their largest trading partner. In Southeast Asia, countries fear having to take sides between the two giants. Although Sino-Indian relations are still frosty following a border clash two years ago, bilateral trade hit a record high of US$125.6 billion in 2021.

In Africa and Latin America, China's fast-paced development makes it an inspiration. Public sentiment towards China's regional economic and political influence is largely positive, in part because China has some unique lessons to teach on how it lifted 800 million people out of poverty in 40 years. These lessons should be more useful than hollow Western moralising.

What remains uncertain is China's relationship with Europe. But even if the EU makes China a "systemic rival", it seems likely that, so long as China and Russia don't form an alliance and there is no conflict in the Taiwan Strait, the China-European relationship will by and large remain stable. Moreover, the conflict in Ukraine will expedite the shift of the global centre of gravity to the Asia-Pacific. As a result, Europe will look increasingly more to the East.

A good lesson from the Cold War is that even enemies can cooperate sometimes. China and the US are not enemies yet. And for competitors to not become enemies, they just need the common sense to know that however different we are, we must coexist. One only needs to look at a garden to know the beauty of the world lies in diversity.

IS CHINA'S PRIMACY OVER THE WESTERN PACIFIC ALREADY A REALITY?

First published in UK National Committee on China's Guest Contributor Programme, July 2021

In 1999, Gerald Segal, then Director of Research at the International Institute of Strategic Studies, made a considerable splash with his essay "Does China matter?" in *Foreign Affairs*. Touching upon the economic, political and strategic issue of China, his overall conclusion was that China's importance had been greatly exaggerated. For Mr Segal, China is but a small market 'that matters little to the world, especially outside Asia'.

Two decades later, Mr Segal must be turning in his grave to see how his argument has made him a laughing stock. Rather than "a small market", China is now the largest retail market, consumer market, e-commerce market, luxury goods market and even new car market in the world. It is also the largest trading nation, industrial nation and the largest exporter in the world and the largest trading partner to around 130 countries.

In the last four decades, no challenges have seemed able to stop China's advance by leaps and bounds, be it the Asian financial crisis or Trump's trade war with China, for instance. Amid the ravaging pandemic, China looks like the eye of global storm, the safest haven on earth. It was the first to suffer from the pandemic, but also the first to recover from it, being the only country to have registered economic growth in 2020. It is helping others, too. By the end of June, China has provided 450 million doses of its vaccines to nearly 100 countries. However impressive these facts might be, it is wrong to conclude that the 21st century will be Pax Sinica.

In fact, even in East Asia, China's home ground, China's primacy is not fully evident. By contrast with Europe that is bound together by a common culture and religion, Asia has been diversified and pluralistic from day one with distinctive geographies, diversified cultures and religions. No matter how in centuries past, the Chinese thought China was the cultural, political or economic centre of the world and their sovereign had a right to rule "all under Heaven," China never attempted to control the whole of East Asia. Deference to the Middle Kingdom and exotic gifts from tributary states were all that the Ming and Qing emperors wanted.

There is no doubt about China's economic primacy in East Asia. In August 2010, China overtook Japan as the world's second largest economy. According to the UK-based Centre for Economics and Business Research (CEBR), China will overtake the US to become the world's largest economy by 2028. With the US absent from RCEP—Regional Comprehensive Economic Partnership, the biggest trade bloc in history that accounts for about 30% of the world's population and 30% of global GDP—and with China's expressed interest in joining the Comprehensive Progressive Trans-Pacific Partnership (CPTPP) just days after RCEP's conclusion, Beijing looks a firm leader in multilateralism.

East Asia won't be Sino-centric. Even if there is talk of a "Greater China" that encompasses mainland China, Hong Kong, Macau, Taiwan and sometimes Singapore, there are no signs that the Chinese wish to export their ideological or development model. If a sphere of influence means that a state has a level of cultural, economic, military, or political exclusivity in a region in which other states show deference to that state, then East Asia won't look like China's sphere of influence under scrutiny. DPRK has developed nuclear weapons anyway despite China's disapproval. Japan, Republic of Korea and Thailand are American allies. Some ASEAN countries such as Vietnam, the Philippines, Malaysia and Brunei have territorial disputes with China in the South China Sea.

Would an ever-rising China make the world a better place? This is the ultimate question for the 21st century. Even those most critical of China cannot deny that China's rise in the last four decades is peaceful—a rare phenomenon for any rising power. China has had no war since its reform and opening up in 1979.Therefore, the brawl resulting in the deaths of 20 Indian soldiers and four Chinese servicemen in the Galwan Valley in the border areas between the two countries in June 2020 was most unusual and unfortunate, to the extent that Indian External Affairs Minister Subrahmanyam Jaishankar said that bilateral trust was "profoundly disturbed". But the fact that the troops chose to use fists and wooden clubs to fight in a stone-age manner showed they knew they should not shoot at each other under any circumstances to violate a tacit agreement. In this regard, a kind of maturity and rationality still prevailed.

Since the Chinese and Indian troops have withdrawn from the border areas that each claimed to be its own and a de facto buffer zone has been established, the situation has de-escalated. Hopefully, the deadly brawl will provide useful lessons for the two governments in finding new ways to enhance confidence-building, such as setting up a hotline between the border troops.

The real challenge in East Asia is not how China will deal with its neighbours and vice versa—they know how to deal with each other through thousands of years of historical engagement. It is how China might coexist with the US, a non-Western Pacific nation but a self-proclaimed guardian of the "free and open Indo-Pacific".

China suspects the US wants to confine Chinese influence within the Western Pacific while the United States suspects a stronger China is trying to drive it out of the region. Looking down the road, the great power competition initiated by the Trump administration will only become more fierce in days to come. The question is whether competition will slide into a confrontation that neither wants. Risk reduction for Beijing and Washington is difficult for two reasons if one looks into the history of the Cold War. First, during the Cold War, there were clearly separate spheres of influence dominated by Washington and Moscow that allowed them to avoid direct confrontations. But between China and the United States, there isn't even a buffer zone. Nowadays American naval vessels regularly sail through the waters off Chinese islands and rocks in the South China Sea and the Taiwan Strait.

Second, the United States and the Soviet Union were balanced by mutually assured destruction. This is not found between Beijing and Washington. But in the Western Pacific, the gap in military strength is shrinking in China's favour thanks to the advances of the PLA in the past decades. As a result, Washington is investing more militarily in the region and calling on its global allies and partners to gang up on China. This in turn would irk Beijing and make the situation more volatile.

There is no guarantee the US would win in a military conflict with China in the first island chain that stretches from Japan to the Philippines and the South China Sea. But should it lose, the consequence would be a domino effect: The US would lose prestige and credibility among its allies and partners in the region; The alliance would fall apart and it would have to pack and go home. Short of global military presence though, China's influence is already felt worldwide, especially through such mega-projects as the Belt & Road Initiative which is the largest project on infrastructure in human history.

A global China doesn't need to seek dominance anywhere. Instead, it needs to think globally and act responsibly in line with the great responsibility that is intrinsically associated with great powers.

WHY THE US AND EUROPE NEED TO DRAW CLOSER TO CHINA AND DROP THE HUBRIS

First published in *South China Morning Post*, 24 April 2020

The West is not in decay. It is falling apart. The novel coronavirus is a further blow to a West already at the nadir of its self-confidence since the 18th century. There is no leadership. The self-proclaimed "wartime president" of the United States has neither the interest nor the ability to lead. "American first" means Europe alone.

In Europe, each country is fighting for its own survival. Beggar-thy-neighbour policies are common. When Italy tried to invoke a European Union mechanism to share medical supplies, no member state helped. Only China sent equipment. It remains to be seen how European solidarity could return after the pandemic, even superficially. Last year, *The Guardian* reported that more than half of Europeans surveyed expect an end to the EU within 20 years.

In the East, Beijing's way of taming Covid-19 looked like the largest performance art in history: locking down a city of 10 million people, building two hospitals that could accommodate 2,000 people in 10 days, and pressing pause on the second-largest economy in the world. It worked, but at an astronomical cost. Now, it is being emulated to varying degrees around the world.

Beijing's success does not bode well for Washington, which has declared a major power competition and taken China and Russia as its main competitors. Two rounds are already being fought, the first a trading tug of war for nearly two years, where Washington does not appear to have gained the upper hand.

In the ongoing second round against the pathogen, although neither side prevailed in the war of words at the outset, the outcome is already determined, like a one-horse race. The US has become a recipient of desperately needed medical supplies from China, either through Chinese donations or its own procurement.

Besides, the US depends heavily on China for vital drugs. According to *The New York Times*, Chinese pharmaceutical companies have supplied more than 90 per cent of US antibiotics, vitamin C, ibuprofen and hydrocortisone, as well as 70 per cent of the pain reliever paracetamol and 40–45 per cent of the blood thinner heparin in recent years.

China and Europe will inevitably get closer. A divided Europe, further dismayed by the worsening transatlantic relationship, will naturally look east, while China, in competition with the US, has to enhance ties with Europe, too.

What pulls the two together is primarily their consensus on multilateralism, be it on global trade, climate change or the role of international institutions. The pandemic can only further highlight the importance of international cooperation.

This does not mean there is no competition between China and Europe. In its strategic review of relations last year, the EU described China simultaneously as a cooperation partner, negotiating partner, economic competitor and a systemic rival.

But this partner-first, rival-last sequence also highlights the priority the EU places on its relationship with China.

The creation of the EU was meant, in part, to avoid great power competition. This is also why it is difficult for the US to hijack Nato into viewing China as the enemy—most members of the transatlantic security alliance are also EU members.

Should China and the US decouple in trade and technology, Europe stands to reap benefits in a greater flow of goods, capital, personnel and technology from China.

The pandemic raises two questions, one for China and one for the West. The question for China is whether the coronavirus outbreak can become a turning point for the country to provide more public goods to the world. Beijing's antivirus help to more than 120 countries is the largest since the founding of the People's Republic.

It speaks volumes of its capacity as the world's largest industrial nation and exporter. Yes, China will remain a developing country for a long time but it is already the second-largest economy. Even if Beijing has no appetite to become a world policeman, it can still be a Good Samaritan and provide more international humanitarian aid.

China is the world's largest producer of surgical masks, ventilators, protective suits and test kits. It produces the vast majority of active pharmaceutical ingredients necessary to make antibiotics. According to *The Wall Street Journal*, China has already asserted its claim to global leadership "mask by mask".

For the West, it remains to be seen if it will discard its hubris and see the world as it is. This year's Munich Security Report is titled impressively "Westlessness". Still, one hears the lament of a narcissist. If the West looks beyond its reflection, it will see that the world, composed of 195 sovereign states with the vast majority being developing countries, has long been essentially non-Western.

The dichotomy of democracy vs autocracy is simplistic, if not misleading. As Francis Fukuyama wrote: "The major dividing line in effective crisis response will not place autocracies on one side and democracies on the other ... The crucial determinant in performance will not be the type of regime, but the state's capacity and, above all, trust in government".

For believers in limited government and open markets, China's whole-of-government and whole-of society efforts against Covid-19 pose a problem. But similar approaches by the Japanese, South Korean and Singaporean governments also show that only the state can deal with such crises and that the state has to be strong and decisive.

During the 1985 Geneva summit, then US president Ronald Reagan suddenly asked Soviet Union leader Mikhail Gorbachev if they could set aside their differences in case the world was invaded by aliens. Gorbachev said: "No doubt about it", and Reagan said: "We too."

Given the devastating pandemic, we do not need to wait for an alien invasion for the world to unite.

CHINA'S CORONAVIRUS AID IS NOT MOTIVATED BY A DESIRE FOR GLOBAL LEADERSHIP

First published in *South China Morning Post*, 13 May 2020

In fighting the novel coronavirus, China looks like anything but a developing country. It has reportedly provided all kinds of medical supplies to over 140 countries and international organisations and sent 14 medical expert teams to 12 countries. According to Cui Tiankai, the Chinese ambassador to the United States, by April 29, China had provided 14 masks for every American on average.

Since no one knows when the pandemic might end, such assistance is poised to continue. As a result, Beijing's visibility will only rise.

But make no mistake: this is not a sign of China wresting control of global leadership. Contrary to various allegations, China has not cast itself as a "global saviour" nor portrayed itself as an emerging superpower at a time that countries in the West are struggling to control domestic Covid-19 outbreaks. China has said it was only paying back the support it received when it was hit hard by the virus.

China does not harbour ambitions of global leadership in the first place. Its real ambition, as stated in its constitution, is to realise the "great rejuvenation of the Chinese nation". China has pledged a 30-year long march to achieve this by mid-century, with clearly defined goals at different stages.

The most telling example of its resolve is that even the pandemic has not dented the government's commitment to eliminate extreme poverty by the end of this year.

Besides, Beijing's influence is already ubiquitous. Today, it appears more comfortable than Washington with the international regimes and institutions that are designed by the West. While Americans have withdrawn from international treaties and institutions one after another, the Chinese have stepped in.

Chinese nationals now head four of the 15 specialised United Nations agencies that deal with economic activity, namely the Food and Agriculture Organisation, the International Telecommunications Union, the UN Industrial Development Organisation, and the International Civil Aviation Organisation.

The incorrect assumption about China's "leadership" role has been made partly because of the natural instinct to look for leadership in a crisis. In 2008, major powers worked together to restore the global economy in the wake of the financial crisis, convening the inaugural G20 leaders' summit for this purpose. Not this time.

UN Secretary General Antonio Guterres fretted this month that there was a lack of leadership in the fight against Covid-19. Donald Trump appears to be the first American president who has neither the wish nor the ability to lead. Needless to say, his decision to halt funding for the World Health Organisation has sparked a global outcry.

The best way China can help the rest of the world is not to "lead", but to provide public goods as a responsible power. The question is: how much can China provide? Citing its lower per capita GDP than that of developed nations and substantial regional differences in development, the Chinese government maintains that China is still a developing country.

But many in the West argue that the world's second-largest economy, top manufacturer, holder of the world's largest foreign exchange reserves and the biggest buyer of luxury goods cannot be a developing country. In 2019, China's per capita GDP reached US$10,276, not that far from the US$12,376 of a "high-income economy" as defined by the World Bank.

There is a grain of truth in both statements. Whatever its status, the Chinese government has repeatedly said it would offer the world assistance in line with its actual strength. Indeed, its external aid has increased substantially in recent years.

In 2019, China overtook Japan to become the second-largest monetary contributor to the UN. After Trump withdrew US support for the WHO, China announced it would provide another US$30 million to fund the agency's Covid-19 work, on top of the US$20 million it gave earlier.

The best public goods China can provide is humanitarian aid. Such support is the least controversial and, more importantly, almost tailor-made for China, whose foreign policy is anchored on non-interference. China has no appetite to replace the US as the "world's cop" nor displace it in the Indo-Pacific region.

Notably, Chinese military operations overseas have been invariably humanitarian in nature, be it peacekeeping, counter-piracy or disaster relief. The PLA Navy's hospital ship *Peace Ark*, for example, has provided medical services to over 230,000 people in 43 countries and regions in its 10 years of service.

And China is in a good position to provide humanitarian assistance. As the "world's factory", its industrial manufacturing capability is next to none. Before the coronavirus outbreak, very few Chinese—including me—realised how heavily the world depends on China for most basic medical supplies such as protective masks.

One can imagine that rich countries will do their utmost to improve their readiness for another virus attack, but what about poor nations? The need is massive. As *The New York Times* puts it, South Sudan has five vice-presidents and four ventilators, and 10 African countries have no ventilators at all.

The rising global death toll reminds us that an invisible pathogen can be far more lethal than a financial crisis or major power competition. It pushes us to rethink what is most important in life, not only for oneself, but also for families and societies.

This pandemic won't be the last. If China's assistance signals how it could again step in, come the next disaster, it is the best news for the world at the worst time.

THE TRUE BATTLEGROUND IN THE US-CHINA COLD WAR WILL BE IN EUROPE

First published in *South China Morning Post*, 2 May 2023

French president Charles de Gaulle once said: "It will not be any European statesman who will unite Europe: Europe will be united by the Chinese." He must be turning in his grave to see how Europe has been divided, rather than united, by the Chinese.

On a recent joint visit to China to show European solidarity, President of the European Commission Ursula von der Leyen and French President Emmanuel Macron, however, seemed poles apart. Von der Leyen criticised China's friendship with Russia and spoke of a need to "de-risk". Macron said Europe must avoid being drawn into any US-China conflict over Taiwan, and has maintained that Europe should not become a "vassal".

Europe's strategic autonomy lies in how it deals with major powers such as the United States, Russia and China independently, but it won't happen any time soon. With war raging in Ukraine, Europe is more reliant than ever on America. In reaction to Macron's comments, US Senator Marco Rubio said if Europe would not pick a side between the US and China over Taiwan, then maybe the US should focus on Taiwan and let the Europeans handle Ukraine themselves.

However long the Ukraine war lasts, the likely outcome is an armistice. Last year, Russia declared the incorporation of Luhansk, Donetsk, Kherson and Zaporizhzhia. Although Russia can hardly have full control of the four provinces, it must have some gains to justify its war. That leaves Ukraine with a nightmare scenario: no Nato membership and the loss of further territory after Crimea.

Europe cannot possibly grow its strategic autonomy while in the shadow of Nato, the transatlantic security alliance. Macron famously said Nato was "brain-dead". Supporters can point to Finland's entry to say Nato is becoming more popular, but Macron is still right. The war brilliantly illustrates Nato's Catch-22: no matter how strong, Nato does not dare launch an attack on the world's largest nuclear-armed state, but neither can it claim defence—31 countries ganging up on one looks ludicrous.

Nato may survive and even celebrate its centenary, but so what if it merely becomes irrelevant? The Anglo-Portuguese Alliance is the world's oldest, at over 600 years, but how many people know, and who really cares?

Much has been said about the advent of another cold war. If the only consensus between Beijing and Washington is to avoid a hot war, then we probably are in a new cold war. What makes this one different, though, is that this is a competition between two giants, rather than two blocs.

The competition, then, is first to see who makes fewer mistakes and, then, who can win over the third parties. The battleground won't be in the Global South, where the US has very much lost to China, especially in Africa and Latin America. It won't be in the Indo-Pacific either, where few countries want to take sides. It will be in Europe, where the US has most of its allies and where China is the largest trading partner.

Gradually, the transatlantic alliance will relax. Even if America's decline is gradual, it cannot afford a global military presence. It will have to retreat from around the world, including from the Middle East and Europe, to focus on the Indo-Pacific, where the US sees China as a long-term threat. Successive US presidents, Republican and Democrat alike, have asked Europeans to take greater ownership of their security. In other words, Europe has to have strategic autonomy, even if it doesn't want to.

That Europe takes China as a partner, competitor and systemic rival at the same time says more about Europe's confusion about China, than what China really is. This year has seen a blitz of visits to Beijing by European leaders. The reason is simple: Europe cannot afford to have sour relations with Beijing and Moscow at the same time. The longer the war, the more Europe will look to China for mediation.

Presumably, Europe will deal with China and the US with pragmatism, that is, making choices on issues case by case, rather than picking sides.

There is only one scenario that could change Europe-China relations fundamentally—a war in the Taiwan Strait. But there is no evidence that Taiwan is bound to become the next Ukraine.

Although most Taiwanese wish to maintain the status quo, the process of cross-strait integration has begun. An estimated 1.2 million Taiwanese, or 5 per cent of Taiwan's population, lived and worked on the mainland in 2020. So long as mainland China continues to open up, this process won't stop.

Beijing's strategic patience is also reflected in China's second military exercise around the island. Even if Beijing clearly took Tsai Ing-wen's meeting with US House Speaker Kevin McCarthy in California as a provocation, its response was much more measured than when his predecessor, Nancy Pelosi, visited Taiwan, in that it simulated attacks without the live firing of weapons.

Beijing knows more than anyone that peaceful reunification is in its best interests, and more importantly, that it is still possible.

The potent legacy of de Gaulle is that every French politician after him seems to be a Gaullist. But if de Gaulle was speaking for France, Macron was trying to speak on behalf of Europe. Time will prove that he is more prescient than von der Leyen. In a 21st-century multipolar world, a Europe that stands as a pole would look its strongest.

CAN JOE BIDEN ENSURE AMERICA'S INEVITABLE DECLINE WILL BE PEACEFUL?

First published in *South China Morning Post*, 22 January 2021

Joe Biden has been elected 46th president of the United States. Donald Trump, his predecessor, has been impeached for a second time. Both events are good news.

Looking back at the four years of the Trump administration, one might wonder why a man who made an average of 20 false and misleading claims a day and eventually incited a mob to storm the Capitol could have been elected as president of the most powerful country on Earth. Why was he supported by 74 million American voters in November's presidential election?

Two years ago, I argued that the greatest challenge we face in the 21st century is not China's rise, but America's decline. China's rise so far has been peaceful, but can the United States' decline be equally peaceful?

If the Pentagon's unabated military interventions after the Cold War have reduced the US's national strength—a point few seem to disagree with now—they also show that the US's decline, however gradual, is far from stable.

Then US Senate minority leader Chuck Schumer declared that January 6, 2021, could be added "to that very short list of dates in American history that will live forever in infamy". It is more than that. The siege of the Capitol shows that when a democracy is in decline, it may become vitriolic and violent.

The bad news is Trumpism will not easily go away. Impeachment, without putting Trump on trial, does not prohibit him from running for president again in 2024. As the headline of an article in *Time* warned in November, "Even if Biden won, he would govern in Trump's America".

With the second-highest number of votes in US history going to Trump, the US seems bitterly and almost evenly split down the middle.

"History never repeats itself, but it rhymes," as Mark Twain is often reputed to have said. Biden might now find himself in a situation echoing that faced by Abraham Lincoln, American's 16th president, after the Civil War when the nation awaited healing.

But while Lincoln's America needed nothing more than national reconciliation, which the US today needs too, Biden has to fight domestic enemies as well as take on challenges ranging from curbing the spread of the pandemic and saving the battered economy to restoring racial justice and faith in institutions all at once.

How long will that take? And how much can this 78-year-old "good man", as former US president George W. Bush called him, accomplish? Even if he has a mission, as he should have, he can hardly be Moses who led the Israelites out of Egypt.

He is more likely be the man who will lead Americans as they descend, however unwillingly, from the "city upon a hill".

This is what he probably instinctively sensed when he said, "American history isn't a fairy tale with a guaranteed happy ending. But we have the power to write the future we want for this nation."

Overseas, his job seems easier, in part because the American people are weary of the endless wars their soldiers have been fighting and their duty as the world's policeman in faraway places. The pandemic, coupled with the violence triggered by George Floyd's death and the riot at the Capitol, will increase Americans' worries about the future.

According to a national survey conducted by the Upshot and Siena College last year, Americans aren't so much fretting about themselves as they are anxious about the country. A retreat to isolationism looks inevitable.

Biden has already announced the US's re-entry into the Paris climate accord and World Health Organization, which he had promised to do "on day one".

But rejoining the nuclear deal with Iran will be tougher. Iran is expected to demand a high price to return to the deal. According to *The New York Times*, the "breakout" time for Iran to possibly make a nuclear weapon—an ambition it denies—is now shorter than a year.

Unlike Trump, who called the European Union a "foe", Biden will embrace the US's allies. But, despite the rhetoric, the enthusiasm that characterised the relationship in the past has dimmed.

Much has been said about European "strategic autonomy", a concept which has triggered more alarm, disagreement and mockery than appreciation. But the core issue is that Europe regards itself as a world power, and the US looks increasingly unreliable to Europeans. It remains to be seen how Biden will convene the much-touted summit of democracies.

It is a bit of a stretch to imagine how he might deliver a speech that doesn't look like a joke against the backdrop of the US's tarnished image.

Then, there is competition with China. In the era of great power competition, as defined by the US, if the two nations can only cooperate on a couple of things, such as climate change and crisis management, then we are effectively in a new cold war since America and the Soviet Union also managed sporadic cooperation on things such as eradicating smallpox and space exploration.

Sadly, the two largest economies in the world cannot even agree on working together to address the Covid-19 pandemic.

Competition with China is one of Trump's main foreign policy legacies and is backed by bipartisan consensus. Biden can hardly thwart it, but he can save China-US relations from going into free fall.

Precisely because the relationship has already deteriorated significantly, Biden could return it to normality by moving in the opposite direction from Trump.

A good example is the investment agreement that China and Europe signed after seven years of negotiations. Wouldn't a similar China-US trade deal be better than Trump's unsuccessful trade war with China?

When he announced his presidential campaign in 2019, Biden said, "History will treat this administration's time as an aberration". Now he has a chance to change the country's course.

PRIDE BEFORE A FALL

TIME FOR ARROGANT US TO REALISE IT'S JUST ANOTHER MEMBER OF THE INTERNATIONAL COMMUNITY

First published in *South China Morning Post*, 27 October 2018

The US believes it is exceptional. This dates back to 1630 when English Puritan lawyer John Winthrop, one of the founders of the Massachusetts Bay Colony, addressed his fellow colonists in a sermon titled "A Model of Christian Charity". Quoting directly from Jesus' Sermon on the Mount, he told them that their new community would be "as a city upon a hill", watched by the world.

Such pride goes in tandem with the unrivalled strength of the United States. It makes the US a self-styled saviour looking down upon others. The latest example is American Vice-President Mike Pence's speech, at the Washington-based Hudson Institute on October 4, on the Trump administration's policy towards China.

Chinese jaws dropped when Pence—echoing US President Donald Trump—claimed that the US "rebuilt China over the last 25 years", then accused China of initiating "an unprecedented effort to influence American public opinion and the 2018 elections".

The first statement sounded like—to use Pence's own words—a "wholesale theft" of the collective efforts of the Chinese people in the past four decades. Moreover, it should be pointed out that the US$375 billion trade deficit in China's favour could be much reduced if the US had lifted its ban on hi-tech exports to China.

As for his accusation of election meddling, just two days before Pence's speech, Homeland Security Secretary Kirstjen Nielson had said there was no sign China was trying to hack the US midterm vote.

Pence is right on one point: America's hope that "freedom in China would expand in all forms" has gone unfulfilled. The rise of new economies represented by the rise of the G20 and the decline of the G7, a grouping of the world's most industrialised economies, tells us that countries can develop and prosper through ways other than by following the Western democracy model.

And a "democracy" like Haiti, created through military intervention by Washington's "Operation Uphold Democracy" in 1994, remains the poorest country in the western hemisphere. Not too long ago, the world was stunned to hear Trump describe it as a "s* * *hole" country.

It is interesting to note how China is being further integrated into the international system while the US is withdrawing from the very system it led in creating. While Beijing now calls for multilateralism and free trade, Washington proudly proclaims its unilateralism and protectionism.

If Brexit is costing Europe in no small way, then America's withdrawal from the international system and its undisguised contempt for the United Nations are far more consequential. In terms of morale and credibility, the US has fallen off the hill.

On Trump's decision to end the Iran nuclear deal and impose trade tariffs on Europe, president of the European Council

Donald Tusk put it this way: "With friends like that, who needs enemies?"

The West does not need to fear a rising but open China. China's rise is peaceful, and it is in China's own interests to continue to rise peacefully.

As a responsible member of the global community, China is stepping up in more ways than one. Over the past decade, the Chinese military has drastically increased its efforts in peacekeeping, counter-piracy and disaster relief overseas to shoulder more international obligations. And in 2017 alone, more than 600,000 Chinese studied abroad.

In the years to come, China's Belt and Road Initiative will tie it up even more closely with the rest of the world.

Thus, US suspicions are largely unfounded. Even if Pence's speech was aimed at a domestic audience, rather than at China, it further aggravated the Chinese, who were already rankled by the US national defence strategy that named China and Russia as the country's two strategic competitors. The question is: is Pence's speech a manifesto of America's stance in a new cold war?

Unlike the Soviet Union during the Cold War, there is no evidence that China is trying to export its ideology or social system to other countries or aligning itself with others to form a bloc.

Non-alliance gives China the moral high ground. If China could maintain its stance of non-alignment decades ago when it was one of the least developed countries in the world, why should it give in now when it is the second-largest economy in the world?

And it is highly unlikely that the US could gather its allies and partners together for a showdown with China. All of its allies and partners have deep economic relations with China, to say the least.

At the Shangri-La Dialogue in Singapore this year, Indian Prime Minister Narendra Modi avoided mentioning the "Quad", the grouping of the US, India, Japan and Australia that is widely perceived to be a counterbalance against China's presence in the Indo-Pacific. Instead, he described the Indo-Pacific as a "natural region" and lauded India's "multi-layer relations with China".

The future of China-US relations is most probably a kind of "corpetition", a mix of cooperation and competition. The question is how to make sure cooperation prevails over competition, or, in the worst-case scenario, competition doesn't spill over into conflict.

This won't be easy for the US. China is widely expected to overtake it within the next two decades to become the world's largest economy. For most Americans, this will be the first time that they will see an America that is no longer "first" in the world. This is a sea change.

If ignorance is the father of arrogance, then "a city upon a hill" looks more like pride inflated into prejudice. After all, the US is no more than a member of the international community, like the rest of us. When it admits that, it is the start of its walk down the hill towards the plain, where the weather is certainly less chilly than on a hill.

AMID GREAT POWER RIVALRY, THE UN IS A VITAL SECURITY SHELTER. IT CANNOT FAIL

First published in *South China Morning Post*, 19 September 2020

The UN is 75 years old. When the UN General Assembly celebrates the anniversary on September 21, the question for the septuagenarian is not how to survive, but thrive.

The importance of the UN is, first of all, psychological. It is older than most people; therefore most people would take it for granted. For the first time in history, the largest intergovernmental organization born out of the ashes of World War II looks like a big family where things are discussed peacefully among 193 family members on equal footing. This gives people a feeling of assurance and protection.

The best way of understanding the UN is to think for a moment of the world without the UN: who is going to take care of our common education, health and humanitarian needs and social, economic and cultural development? According to the UN, 690 million people still go to bed on an empty stomach each night. This is why the UN World Food Program plays an indispensible role in helping those in need.

Second, the UN has by and large fulfilled its primary role of saving people from "the scourge of war". As a result, we have enjoyed "long peace"—an absence of major wars between the great powers from the end of World War II in 1945 to the present day. Such a period of relative peace has not been documented in human history since the Roman Empire.

The fact that we are seriously discussing second-tier threats ranging from terrorism, spread of small arms to human trafficking and non-traditional issues like climate change is because we know subconsciously that major wars are less likely today.

A test of the UN around the corner is who will be elected as American president in November. If Donald Trump is reelected, he won't be an "aberration of history" any more as Joe Biden has described. For a man who has ordered a pull out of the Iran nuclear deal, the Paris climate deal and the World Health Organization, to name just a few, the question is what other damage he will inflict on the organization in the next four years.

If Joe Biden is elected, America First is more likely to become America-led. He has pledged to demolish some Trump policies on day one including restoring U.S. funding and membership to the WHO and rejoining the Paris climate agreement. What he can hardly change, however, is the growing weariness of the American public about the current international system that doesn't always deliver for US interests.

The efficiency and effectiveness of the UN depends primarily on how the five permanent members of the UN Security Council compromise on their divergent national interests. China and Russia have joined hands ten times to veto on Syrian issues. But it would be naïve to conclude the Security Council is already divided into two camps with China and Russia on one side and the US, Britain and France on the other side. In August, America's two strongest allies in the Security Council joined China and Russia to reject Washington's attempt to reimpose

UN sanctions on Iran. Trump is a proud nationalist. But French President Emmanuel Macron said almost in his face during the 100th anniversary of the end of World War I that "nationalism is a betrayal of patriotism".

As major power competition unfolds, the UN has unsurprisingly loomed as a main battle ground for China and the US. Beijing's support for and Washington's withdrawal from the WHO is a typical example. This is a huge risk for the UN in that the world's two largest economies are also the two largest financial contributors to both the UN general budget and the UN peacekeeping budget. At the 74th session of the UN General Assembly last year, UN Secretary-General Antonio Guterres talked about his fear of a Great Fracture—the world splitting in two with the two largest economies on earth creating two separate and competing worlds.

But even if Washington looks like a determined wife filing for divorce, the UN is still useful for the estranged couple to get along. During the 1948 Berlin blockade, it was in the UN that US and Soviet diplomats still exchanged messages and ideas. Even those most hostile to China in Washington have yet to describe China as an enemy while Beijing still calls for cooperation. Today, Washington still needs Beijing to strike compromises, say, on sanctions on the DPRK.

It is obvious China's influence in the UN has risen significantly. Unlike the US which complains about the UN regularly in the domestic mainstream media, China consistently calls for enhancing the UN. China is now a cheerleader of multilateralism. Recent years have found Chinese nationals taking more posts including senior posts in different agencies of the UN. The numbers of Chinese nationals have at least doubled in the past decade.

The UN, too, has all reasons to see a stronger Chinese role. China's call for multilateralism cannot be sweeter for the largest multilateral institution on planet. In fact, the theme of the meeting of the UN General Assembly on 21 September 2020 is "Reaffirming our Collective Commitment to Multilateralism'. Unlike the US which owes the UN more than $1billion in unpaid dues, China always pays its due financial share to the UN on time and in full. It has been doling out voluntary funds to different UN bodies. For UN's 2030 Sustainable development goals, China's efforts to reduce extreme poverty among its 1.4 billion people by the end of this year can only be a shining example for other developing countries to follow.

It is ironic to see how China is integrating herself with the international system while the US is withdrawing from the very system it led to create. China has joined almost all the international treaties and conventions, therefore even in theory, Beijing should have no intention to challenge the rules-based order as the US has asserted.

Nor is Beijing seeking abdication of America's global leadership as Washington suspects. This is most clear in the UN. The US is the largest provider of financial contributions to the UN, providing 22 percent of the entire UN budget in 2020 while China as the second largest contributor contributes 12 percent. The gap is too huge for China to close even if it wants. And precisely because China is the second largest financial contributor, it is in Beijing's own interests to work with the US to make the UN more effective and efficient.

At a recent symposium in Beijing to mark the 75th anniversary of the UN, renowned Singaporean scholar Kishore Mahbubani asked if the United Nation is a sunrise or sunset organization. Well, an organization that is already 75 years old can hardly be described as a sunrise organization, but it certainly doesn't look like a sunset organization. It looks more like a vast shelter that, if properly maintained, could provide security for us all. It is too important to fall.

A STRONGER CHINA HAS NO REASON TO SEEK A SPHERE OF INFLUENCE EVEN AS US POWER WANES

First published in *South China Morning Post*, 6 November 2020

Does a stronger China need spheres of influence? I asked myself when I came across "The New Spheres of Influence", an essay written by Harvard professor Graham Allison in *Foreign Affairs*. Allison argues that after the Cold War, the entire world had become a de facto American sphere. But now the unipolarity is over. The United States must share spheres of influence with other great powers such as China and Russia.

I imagine for a moment where a Chinese "sphere of influence" might be. Not in Central Asia where Russia's influence is dominant. Not in South Asia where India's influence is paramount. Only East Asia looks the likeliest, given its historical and cultural ties with China.

But if a sphere of influence means a state has a level of cultural, economic, military, or political exclusivity in a region in which other states show deference to that power, East Asia can hardly be described as China's sphere of influence. DPRK has developed nuclear weapons anyway despite China's disapproval. Japan, Republic of Korea and Thailand are American allies. Some ASEAN countries such as Vietnam, the Philippines, Malaysia and Brunei have territorial disputes with China in the South China Sea.

With Chinese and Russian as the only official languages, the Shanghai Cooperation Organization short of any western countries might look like a co-sphere of influence of China and Russia. But it has proven more inclusive than anticipated. Turkey, a NATO member, is a dialogue partner of SCO. President Erdogan even asked to join the organization as a full member. India and Pakistan became member states in 2017. Presumably the two long-time archrivals would bring in problems, but their membership also increases the influence of the organization that geographically strides across the Eurasian continent and brings in strength to curb the so-called "three evils" of terrorism, separatism and extremism that have plagued the region.

Perhaps nowhere looks more like China's sphere of influence than the South China Sea. Much has been said how China is turning the region into a "Chinese lake", especially given China's land reclamation that has enhanced China's physical presence there. But no international laws prohibit land reclamation, and some other claimants did exactly the same before. China maintains that around 100,000 ships transit through the South China Sea without problems of freedom of navigation. What China opposes is military activities against the interests of the littoral states in the name of freedom of navigation.

All the governments of PRC have declared that China won't seek hegemonism even if it becomes developed. Although this might sound rhetorical, it has a trace in history. For two millennia, much of East Asia was part of the Chinese sphere of influence, but the influence was primarily cultural. Admiral Zheng He's seven voyages in the Indian Ocean showed the sweeping power of the Celestial Empire during the Ming dynasty, but he didn't bother to establish a single military base there. Only the PLA established a logistic base almost 600 years later in support of counter-piracy in the Indian Ocean.

Influence and sphere of influence are two different things. Today, China's influence almost overlaps with that of the United States. Such influence will grow further since China is widely expected to surpass the United States to become the largest economy in terms of GDP in 10–15 years. In other words, a global China is already influential enough to demand any spheres of influence.

This then invites two most important questions for the 21st century: How will the world accommodate China's rise? And what can China bring to the world? China's Belt & Road initiative might provide an answer to the second question. No ambition is greater than this initiative in human history, but it is not a gilded instrument of a new Chinese order, as *The Economist* asserted. It is not charity—China invests for mutual benefit. It is not a "debt trap"—who will spend trillions of dollars to lay such a mega-trap? It might take generations to finish. But it will surely change the economic landscape of the developing countries along the belt and road for the better.

Contrary to Allison's suggestions, the last thing the US wants is to cede any sphere of influence to China—its primary competitor in "a new era of great-power competition". In East Asia, the challenge is how Beijing and Washington with overlapping influence could coexist. The United States suspects China is trying to drive it out of the region. It has stepped up its much-hyped provocations in the Taiwan Straits and in the South China Sea.

These provocations are like dangerous games testing the patience of the ever-stronger PLA. Winston Churchill once famously quipped, "there is only one thing worse than fighting with allies, and that is fighting without them." Not really. In East Asia, America's allies have already tightened their nerves and are tiptoeing between their ally and top trading partner. So far, none of them have joined the US Navy in FONOPs in the 12 nautical mile waters off Chinese rocks and islands in the South China Sea.

There is no guarantee the US could win in a military conflict with China in the first chain of islands stretching from Japan to the Philippines and the South China Sea. But should it loose, the consequence is not moot: It will lose prestige and credibility among its allies and partners in the region; The alliance will fall apart and it may have to go home. In that sense, only the United States can displace the United States in the Western Pacific.

Allison is right to conclude that the illusion that other nations will simply take their assigned place in a US-led international order is over. But even if that means there are indeed spheres of influence in the world today, China should beware and stay away from them. They look more like perilous traps than power vacuums awaiting China to fill.

TRUMP'S AMERICA NEEDS TO DO MORE, NOT LESS, TO SUPPORT THE UN

First published in *South China Morning Post*, 28 March 2017

John Bolton, former US ambassador to the UN, once (in) famously stated: "The [UN] Secretariat Building in New York has 38 storeys. If you lost 10 storeys today, it wouldn't make a bit of difference." Now it looks like there's a real danger it may lose 10 floors. According to *Foreign Policy*, the Trump White House is seeking to cut US$1 billion in funding for UN peacekeeping operations and hundreds of millions of dollars for other UN programmes that care for needy children and the world's poorest.

Such a cut would make the UN stumble immediately. The US is by far the UN's biggest funder, providing 22 per cent of its operating budget and 28 per cent for peacekeeping missions. There are currently 16 peacekeeping missions around the globe, the highest ever in history, with operations far more complicated than just observing ceasefires. In the Central African Republic, peacekeeping involves up to 10 tasks, from protecting civilians and supporting the transition process, to protection of human rights, and support for justice and the rule of law. In Mali's hostile environment, where peacekeepers are often attacked and killed, there's a dire need for helicopters, intelligence surveillance and reconnaissance, counter-explosive ordnance devices and armoured personnel carriers.

Expectations for peacekeeping are at an all-time high. A UN report last October found more than 65 million people forcibly displaced and armed conflict impacting the lives of record numbers. At the 2015 Leaders' Summit on UN Peacekeeping, more than 50 countries pledged more than 40,000 troops and police, 40 helicopters, 15 engineering companies and 10 field hospitals. The UN, which has never had a standing army of its own, announced the setting up of a 4,000-strong rapid deployment force composed of member-state troops. But without adequate funding, it is hard to see how it can afford operational and staff costs, and reimburse uniformed personnel and member states.

America's lukewarm attitude towards the UN is well-known. As of February, it only had 68 people working on peacekeeping, compared with 8,321 from Ethiopia, the top troop contributor, and 2,567 from China, a fellow permanent member of the Security Council. But the US is credited as the largest financial contributor to peacekeeping. If the US cuts funding, the UN's image and credibility will be hit hard, and invite negative consequences for the international system and the people it claims to help.

Cutting costs on diplomacy and the environment is a strange strategy for President Donald Trump to "rebuild the depleted military" of the US. The irony is, this "depleted" military is the strongest in the world, and the US defence budget is still more than the combined total of the eight countries behind it. Trump has called for a 10 per cent increase in the defence budget, as if a big threat is imminent. But if indeed his main strategic target is fighting Islamic State, as he declared, does that require an increase from 276 to 350 ships and submarines? After the Cold War, the US has been involved in wars almost non-stop. Why can't its first-class military do more peacekeeping that would put it on higher moral ground and be welcomed by all?

The UN is left with two options: either downsize its missions or ask other member states to increase their financial contributions to fill the gap. If it is the latter, the UN might first turn to China, the world's second-largest economy and a firm supporter of the UN. China is now the third-largest financial contributor to the UN and second-largest financial contributor to peacekeeping. But the question is: why should China pay for an American "default"?

The UN is a tree grown out of the ashes of two world wars. The seed, planted by the founding members in 1942, is simply a wish that such wars never happen again. Yes, one could easily hear a litany of complaints against the UN, such as oversizing, low efficiency and bureaucracy, but it is still universally recognised as indispensable. Rather than weakening it, all member states, including the US, need to make it stronger.

Remember, it was a US president, Franklin D. Roosevelt, who coined the term "United Nations". And, today, the UN headquarters stands on American soil.

WHY JOE BIDEN WILL STRUGGLE TO REBUILD THE DECAYING TRANSATLANTIC ALLIANCE TO COUNTER CHINA

First published in *South China Morning Post*, 22 January 2021

The first countries which could not wait to congratulate Joe Biden's presidency are America's allies. This is no surprise. In the last four years, Trump's America First and threat to leave Nato have unnerved them all. They could only rejoice and embrace a man who said "We are going to be back in the game. It is not America alone".

According to *Financial Times*, the EU has recently drafted a plan calling on the US to seize a "once-in-a-generation" opportunity to forge a new global alliance to bury the tensions of the Trump era and meet the "strategic challenge" posed by China.

This is probably easier said than done. The damages to the transatlantic ties are not some hairlines and chips on a vase that can be easily restored. Trump is the only American president who called Nato "obsolete", but he is certainly not the first one who frets that America has been free-ridden by Europe for too long. The only difference is that his relentless bashing on allies, however unbecoming of a president, has worked. Now eight European allies, compared to four by the end of the Obama administration, have met Nato target of spending 2 percent of gross domestic product on defense. It remains to see how "good man" Joe Biden—as George W. Bush would call him, could do the same.

To some extent, the success of trans-Atlantic bonds rests on American willingness to be free-ridden by allies. When the Soviet threat is gone, western solidarity starts to fray. Although the United States and Europe still share some common goals, they are of a different order of urgency and seriousness. Europe is no longer the priority of America in retrenchment. The more the allies pay their dues, the quicker the United States might shake its responsibilities and withdraw from Europe.

There are only two scenarios in which the American-led alliance could be strengthened. The first is American allies joining the United States in confronting China—America's primary competitor. But China is the largest trading partner to almost all America's European and Asian allies. Brussels and Washington can hardly bury the hatchet both between the transatlantic powers and within the European bloc when it comes to how to deal with China. For Washington's allies in the Indo-Pacific, it is one thing to chant, say, freedom of navigation, in America's tone, it is another if they have to confront the second largest economy in the world. Take Australia for instance. About a third of its total exports are destined for Chinese shores.

The second scenario is China and Russia come into alliance to trigger a new cold war. Beijing and Moscow are getting ever closer, partly because they are both taken by Washington as primary competitors. Therefore, any pressure from Washington on Moscow will only drive Moscow closer towards Beijing and vice versa. Not only do China and Russia conduct joint exercises on annual basis, but recent years have found them conducting more sophisticated anti-missile war games and "joint air strategic patrol".

Asked in October whether a union between Moscow and Beijing was likely, President Putin replied that "we don't want it, but, theoretically, it's quite possible to imagine it."

The value of the America-led alliance is more political than military. The primary objective of Nato, as indicated on its website, is to "promote democratic values". But China has shown no intention to challenge any western values. China has made it clear that it won't export its ideology or development model. Although China's influence is already global, it is felt primarily in the economic sector. The People's Liberation Army has increased its activities overseas, but these activities are so far restricted to humanitarian areas.

China's challenge to the west is not ideological, rather, it is psychological: how can an "authoritarian" state develop so quickly and could even become the largest economy one day? A short answer is: Because China's rise is from within. As the largest beneficiary of globalization and the market economy, China has no need to challenge the current international system. Beijing only proves that not all roads necessarily lead to Rome; and people having different development models and values could still succeed.

The problem with the west is that it has narcissistically equated the seven decades after World War II with "the liberal international order" and wishes the order could continue. There is no such order, even if most of the institutions and regimes were indeed designed and built by the west after World War II. Since 1945, such major events as the independence of more than 50 African countries, the rivalry between the United States and the former Soviet Union, and the rise of China, to name just a few, have reshaped the international order as well. China and

Russia's veto power in the UN Security Council also matter in no small way to international security. What appears like a liberal international order at best is but a short period of 15 years or so after the dissolution of the Soviet Union when the influence of the West was overwhelming and China's rise was still not in full swing.

When small nations band together against a big external threat, it is understandable. But when the strongest nation on earth calls for strengthening alliances, it is questionable. James Buchanan, the 15th American president, once said, "to avoid entangling alliances has been a maxim of our policy ever since the days of Washington". Not today. It is ironic to see how far America has gone in the opposite direction.

THE US IS RIGHT THAT CHINA HAS NO ALLIES—BECAUSE IT DOESN'T NEED THEM

First published in *South China Morning Post*, 13 June 2016

The latest round of attacks from the US on China— following American criticism over "freedom of navigation" and "militarisation"—is on China's image. In January, Admiral Harry Harris, commander of the United States Pacific Command, said at a Washington think tank that "we have allies, friends and partners where China does not". And, earlier this month, US Secretary for Defence Ash Carter asserted at the Shangri-La Dialogue that Beijing is "erecting a great wall of self-isolation".

Such remarks can be brushed aside almost effortlessly. China has no friends? China is one of the top tourist destinations in the world. A hundred million people visit the Chinese mainland each year. China has no partners? China is the largest trading nation in the world and the top destination for foreign investment. By 2015, 124 countries, including the United States, have China as their largest trading partner.

Nevertheless, Admiral Harris is right to say China has no allies.

The thing is: China doesn't need allies. States engage in military alliances to protect themselves against threats from other states. However, China doesn't need alliances for survival. During the stand-off during the Cold War between Nato and the Warsaw pact, China's non-alliance and non-interference policies won it many friends, particularly from the Third World.

Today, China is the second-largest economy in the world and a nuclear weapon state. China has become, as Deng Xiaoping said, a pole itself. An invasion into the Chinese mainland by any country is next to impossible. As the late Germany chancellor Helmut Schmidt said: "You [China] are big enough and you will be able to stand alone."

More importantly, China is not a hegemonic power with an ambition to police the world with a Pax Sinica. However different China might be in its social system and ways of development, it has no intention to overthrow the existing world order from which it has benefited enormously. A stronger China today is happy to promote its culture abroad through its Confucius Institutes and so on, but the offer is voluntary rather than missionary. China's military presence abroad is restricted to humanitarian operations such as peacekeeping, anti-piracy missions, disaster relief and evacuation of non-combatants during a crisis.

If China develops alliances, particularly with Russia, the American hostility towards China will only heighten. The China-US relationship will certainly become more volatile. True, the US is rebalancing towards the Asia-Pacific and beefing up its alliances against China in the South China Sea, but it is irresponsible to conclude that the US wants a conflict with China.

Even the worst pessimists have yet to describe China and the US as foes. Joseph Nye has famously warned that if you treat China as an enemy, you are certain to have an enemy. But the same is true the other way, too. In the South China Sea, China needs to rightfully react but not overreact against American provocation.

No matter how China and Russia have supported each other's agendas, they can hardly become allies. Neither nation wants the

US as the enemy, albeit for different reasons. It is as difficult for China to take sides with Russia in the Ukraine spat as it is for Russia to take sides with China in the South China Sea issue. Another thing is that allies are hardly equal. In a "China-Russia alliance" scenario, who would have the final say—an economically stronger China or a militarily stronger Russia? In the Shanghai Cooperation Organisation, which is not a military alliance, China and Russia don't have to compete for leadership.

America's alliances and partnerships with some 60 countries need not be envied. It is maintained at huge political and economic cost. None of these allies and partners are blind followers. Israel demands almost unconditional support from the US in any Israeli-Palestinian conflict. Japan wants an American security commitment in any potential Diaoyu Islands conflict. Germany and Britain ruled out carrying out air strikes on Islamic State militants in Syria, a day after President Barack Obama authorised the start of US air strikes there.

The recent invitation to Montenegro as the 29th Nato member may be hailed as a fresh proof of the continuing popularity of the alliance, but only five members meet the standard of spending at least 2 per cent of their GDP on defence, in spite of the "Russian threat". The US vows to continue to sail and fly in the South China Sea, in part for its credibility among allies. But the USS *John Stennis* carrier strike group costs US$6.5 million a day.

Having no allies won't diminish China's appeal. It attracts even Nato, the largest alliance in the world. Since 2002, China–Nato security dialogues have helped to foster mutual understanding between the largest military alliance in the world and a country that believes in no military alliance. Beijing is assured that Nato doesn't have a policy towards Taiwan or in the South China Sea; Nato will not take sides with Japan over Diaoyu Islands disputes. Both sides also cooperate to counter piracy in the Gulf of Aden.

Rather than a "great wall of self-isolation", the non-alliance is one of China's highest moral grounds. It has not only served China's national interests for decades, but has also helped to reduce hostility and confrontation in a dangerous world.

WHY US-LED, ANTI-CHINA QUAD IS EITHER MEANINGLESS OR DOOMED TO FAILURE

First published in *South China Morning Post*, 2 April 2021

The largest question hovering over the Quadrilateral Security Dialogue, or Quad, grouping of the United States, Japan, Australia and India is what exactly it is.

Initiated in 2007 by Japanese Prime Minister Shinzo Abe, the forum did little to coordinate policy in the Indo-Pacific. This shows why when US President Joe Biden hosted the first virtual Quad summit on March 12 with Japanese Prime Minister Yoshihide Suga, Indian Prime Minister Narendra Modi and Australian Prime Minister Scott Morrison, it caught the world's attention, especially the announcement of a "Quad Vaccine Partnership" that committed to provide 1 billion doses of vaccine to Southeast Asia.

However, this summit is not necessarily a springboard to success. As if to indicate this is a concert of democracy, the catchphrase of the Quad is a "free and open Indo-Pacific". When has the Indo-Pacific not been open and free? Security challenges including piracy, terrorism, territorial claims, illegal fishing and criminal trafficking are not new, and they are not exclusive to the Indo-Pacific.

Since 2008, the most outstanding problem affecting the security of the international sea lanes in the region is piracy in the waters off the Horn of Africa. This problem has been resolved thanks to the joint efforts of some 25 international navies in line with the UN Security Council mandates.

The Quad is really about China, even if China was not explicitly mentioned in the summit. The problem is that if the Quad is against China, the glue that binds the group is not strong enough. If it is not, then there is no need to establish the Quad at all.

Let us start with the worst possible scenario. Should a conflict arise between China and the US in the South China Sea or the Taiwan Strait, Japan and Australia would struggle to figure out how to fulfil their obligations as American allies without burning their own hands.

India would not give a damn about taking America's side at all. The likelihood of India getting involved militarily in a China-US conflict in China's periphery is as remote as America's military involvement in a China-India conflict along the Sino-Indian border.

Admittedly, the brawl resulting in the deaths of 20 Indian soldiers and four Chinese soldiers in the Galwan Valley last June was shocking, to the extent that Indian External Affairs Minister Subrahmanyam Jaishankar said the tie was "profoundly disturbed". But the fact the troops chose to use fists and wooden clubs to fight in a stone-age manner showed they knew they should not shoot at each other under any circumstances.

Since the Chinese and Indian troops have withdrawn and a de facto buffer zone was established, the situation has de-escalated. Hopefully, the deadly brawl will provide useful lessons for the two governments in finding new ways to enhance confidence-building, such as setting up hotlines.

India is central to the Quad as the other three countries are already allies. Although India is not happy with the presence of the PLA Navy in the Indian Ocean, which it considers its own backyard, there is no evidence of conflicting interests. The Chinese navy only has a logistical supply station in Djibouti, and Chinese flotillas only conduct counter-piracy operations. In May 2011, the Chinese and Indian Navies cooperated with Nato in rescuing a Chinese merchant ship *Full City* that was hijacked by Somalian pirates.

If India chooses to embrace the United States, it will invite two consequences it cannot afford. First, it risks India's strategic autonomy and manoeuvrability among major powers. This matters as India is one of the founders of the non-aligned movement.

Second, it risks a decline in India-Russia relations. India is the world's biggest arms importer with Russia as its top supplier, garnering 70 per cent of the Indian market. Any move by New Delhi towards Washington will only alert Moscow, one of Washington's strategic competitors alongside Beijing.

However the Quad might evolve, it is unlikely to become an "Asian Nato" targeting China. This is not because all parties have disclaimed any defence role for the grouping at one point or another, but rather that each Quad member has a strong economic relationship with China.

China is one of the top trading partners of the US and the largest trading partner of Japan, Australia and India. None of them would wish to sacrifice their own economic ties with China, let alone for the sake of the other three countries.

Likewise, it is doubtful that "Quad-Plus" countries such as South Korea, Vietnam and New Zealand would wish to join the Quad as full members for fear of Beijing seeing them as members of an "anti-China club". They might still participate in a few multilateral naval exercises such as the Malabar Exercises in the future, though.

What holds Quad members together will not be the much-touted partnership on climate change and the Covid-19 pandemic. These are global challenges that can only be addressed through collective global response. If the Quad's future is maritime security cooperation, as most people would agree, there is also a limit as to what it can achieve.

The Indian and Pacific Oceans are too vast for four policemen. Besides, cooperation on addressing maritime issues such as terrorism, human trafficking, humanitarian aid and disaster relief is the purview of regional institutions such as the Asean Regional Forum and Asean Defence Ministers Meeting (ADMM) Plus. Those groupings already include major regional players such as China, the US, Japan, Australia and India.

Unless the Quad takes common strategic issues in the region as driving forces and proves itself to be inclusive rather than exclusive, the future of the small group is not bright. It can survive, but it will not thrive.

ONLY A CHINA-RUSSIA ALLIANCE COULD REVIVE A 'BRAIN-DEAD' NATO. BUT WITH THAT UNLIKELY, THE TRANSATLANTIC ALLIANCE MAY BE ON ITS LAST LEGS

First published in *South China Morning Post*, 1 January 2020

If the Nato summit held in London in early December is remembered at all, it will not be because it marked the 70th anniversary of the North Atlantic Treaty Organisation, but because it confirmed French President Emmanuel Macron's comment that the transatlantic alliance was "brain-dead".

Rather than a show of unity, the summit was marked by public spats, open divisions on policy and dramatic effect. United States President Donald Trump called Canadian Prime Minister Justin Trudeau "two-faced" after a video appeared to show him and other world leaders mocking Trump.

Since the Berlin Wall fell in 1989, Nato has been trying to kill two birds with one stone: portraying Russia as a threat to ensure Nato's survival and the alliance's solidarity. Trump is not the first American president to fret about Europe's "free riders"—as Barack Obama termed them—but he is more successful in bashing them about their obligation to spend 2 per cent of gross domestic product on defence, with his erratic and offensive behaviour.

While Nato's European members might wish Trump away, their fear is that a US that decidedly pivots towards the Indo-Pacific will gradually reduce its lion's share of Nato's spending, leaving Europe's security to Europeans. To hedge against this, the Europe Union started the Permanent Structured Cooperation (Pesco) in 2017 with a vision of building a European army one day.

Nato's real problem is not its budget, Russia or terrorism. It is that it does not have an agreed enemy. At the most tense points of the Cold War, the defence spending of Britain and France were above 5 per cent of GDP. Faced with genuine threats, no Nato country would hesitate to spend more than 2 per cent of its GDP on defence.

Russia continues to top the list of threats in the London Declaration, but Nato's European members spend three to four times more than Russia does on defence every year. Citing terrorism as a threat second only to Russia proves precisely that Nato has no major threats.

Terrorists can hardly attack all 29 Nato member states at once. In any case, faced with modern warfare such as the drone attack that halved Saudi Arabia's oil output overnight, Nato is incapable of responding quickly.

It is interesting to note that the "opportunities and challenges" presented by China were recognised at the Nato summit. The US, having identified China as its top strategic competitor, almost certainly wants Nato to follow its lead in meeting the "challenges" posed by China.

But first, there is the "tyranny of geology"—China and Nato members are geographically disconnected. Second, most Nato members are also EU members and the Sino-Europe relationship is warming. This is not only because of a shift in the centre of gravity towards the east, but also because there is mutual agreement on a multilateral approach to address issues ranging from climate change and Iran's nuclear policy to World Trade Organisation reform.

For China, the more its relationship with the US sours, the sweeter will be its ties with Europe. China's Belt and Road Initiative has been well received in Central, Eastern and Southern Europe. Should China and the US decouple, Europe stands to reap the benefits of a greater flow of goods, capital, personnel and technology from China.

This is why it is difficult for the US to hijack Nato into seeing China as the enemy. On the contrary, a Europe alternating between its EU and Nato hats may play a unique role. According to *The Economist*, Macron thinks Europe can best establish its global influence as a power that mediates between the gorillas of China and the US.

There's only one scenario where it's possible to imagine the revival of a Nato in decline—if China and Russia become allies. China and Russia have repeatedly stressed their non-alliance but, interestingly, this non-alliance appears much stronger than Nato's twisted alliance.

The latest example is President Vladimir Putin's announcement that Russia is helping China to build an anti-missile defence system, of which Beijing has said nothing. But, if China must have allies, then no nation is more important than Russia, and vice versa.

But how likely is such an alliance? Neither Beijing nor Moscow wants another cold war. But it goes beyond that. Russia, which is under Western sanctions, resents the international order while China, as the largest beneficiary of globalisation, has vowed to guard the order. In other words, even if Beijing and Washington are at loggerheads, they compete within the same system.

This was certainly not the case during the Cold War when the US and Russian superpowers fought from conflicting systems. If the last thing Washington wants is the nightmare of a China-Russia alliance, then the Pentagon has made a strategic blunder by pronouncing both as strategic competitors.

Back in 2011, former US defence secretary Robert Gates talked about Nato's "dim if not dismal future". The future looks more dismal now. Allowing a few more countries, such as North Macedonia, to join will not change the situation.

Nato will not die tomorrow, but neither will it be effective for another 70 years, as US Secretary of State Mike Pompeo hopes. When all that awaits a brain-dead man is death, does it matter how long he can survive?

NATO'S LATEST EXPANSION PLAN COULD BE BEGINNING OF THE END AS WANING WEST TARGETS 'RUSSIA THREAT'

First published in *South China Morning Post*, 27 July 2022

When the audience at a concert hears a singer hitting the highest note, they know the song is probably coming to an end. And Nato's future will be much the same: when Sweden and Finland join—a sure thing in the near future—the 32-member transatlantic alliance may well have reached the end of its expansion.

Of the other three candidates on the waiting list for Nato membership, Georgia and Ukraine's requests appear doomed by Russia's warring response. It remains to be seen whether Moscow would react as it has warned if Bosnia and Herzegovina takes steps towards joining Nato, but the alliance might also think twice after seeing what has occurred in Ukraine.

The Cold War in Europe never really ended with the fall of the Soviet Union. The battlefield in Ukraine is a stage of continued rivalry for spheres of influence between Nato and Russia.

Does Russia have a legitimate sphere of influence? If Moscow believes there is one, and would fight for it, then it does. This is easy to understand if one thinks of how the United States reacted when the Soviet Union placed missiles at its doorstep in 1962. The Cuban missile crisis brought the world close to the brink of an all-out nuclear war.

Military alliances survive on "threats". If they fail to find one, they will create one. But for a juggernaut such as Nato to survive, it needs to constantly expand.

Examples of Nato seeking out threats can be seen in the 78-day bombing of Belgrade in 1999 during the war in Kosovo. It can also be seen in the 2011 operation by a Nato-led coalition against Libya and its ruler Muammar Gaddafi. The operation led to Gaddafi's ousting and the country was plunged into the depths of civil war.

But no threat is bigger and more useful than a "Russia threat". Yes, Russia is not the Soviet Union, but who looks most like the Soviet Union? Only Russia. Both Mikhail Gorbachev and Boris Yeltsin expressed interest in Nato membership for Russia, but unsurprisingly they were rejected. Russia's membership in Nato would render the alliance meaningless and dissolve it from the inside.

The war in Ukraine has strengthened the solidarity of Nato, but only for a while. Instead, it might well become a turning point in the eventual disintegration of the alliance. Out of fear of Russia, more European countries in Nato will most certainly increase their defence spending. This will add to Europe's strategic autonomy from Washington.

A typical example is Germany. Before the war in Ukraine, the richest country in Europe had consistently spent less than 2 per cent of its GDP on defence, which is an obligation for Nato members. But in February, Chancellor Olaf Scholz announced that Germany would spend more than 2 per cent of GDP on defence every year. Like a magician who suddenly pulls a rabbit out of his hat, he announced a €100 billion (US$102.1 billion) fund for the armed forces.

Europe's strategic autonomy would allow the US to leave Europe to the Europeans so it can focus on China, which it perceives to be a greater long-term threat than Russia. For Washington, an ideal situation is one where Nato stays focused mainly on collective defence in Europe while at the same time European allies support the US in containing China in the Indo-Pacific.

This is a daydream. So far, Britain, France and Germany have not done much beyond a few symbolic sailings through the South China Sea in the name of freedom of navigation. Although China was identified as a "systemic challenge" for the first time at the Nato summit in June, Nato has yet to explicitly describe China as a "threat".

For European allies of the US, too much focus on China risks diverting the alliance from the real threat: Russia. China and Nato are too far away from each other. It's inconceivable that China would one day send troops to fight against a European country. Likewise, it's hard to imagine that Nato would get directly involved in a potential conflict in the Taiwan Strait.

Even though Nato invited leaders from non-allied partners Japan, Korea, Australia and New Zealand to attend this year's summit for the first time, an "Asian Nato" is unlikely to take shape. In the Indo-Pacific, even the closest ally of the US might not wish to be seen as a member of the anti-China club.

An Asian Nato has already been tried once in the form of the Southeast Asia Treaty Organization. Founded in 1954 and described by Sir James Cable as "a fig leaf for the nakedness of American policy", it was primarily created to block further communist gains in Southeast Asia, but it was only in existence for about two decades. Today, Asean is China's largest trading partner.

Only if China and Russia become allies can Nato thrive in a new cold war. But there is no evidence of a Sino-Russian alliance if one watches through the prism of the conflict in Ukraine.

Beijing has managed, however painstakingly, to strike a balance between its strategic partner Russia and Ukraine, which has China as one of its largest trading partners.

China's carefully calibrated neutrality might not be what Europe wants, but it should be acceptable to Europeans who are nervous about a potential Sino-Russian alliance. The fact that China hasn't provided military assistance to Russia should be a relief.

If small nations get together for self-defence, it is understandable. But if the largest alliance on Earth wishes to expand, it is not about defence but enforcing its own values on others with a big stick. No alliance will last forever. As long as the West continues to decline though, Nato will be on the wane. French President Emmanuel Macron called Nato "brain dead", but perhaps it looks more like a zombie that is still walking.

IS CHINA THE NEW ENEMY FOR NATO?

First published in *South China Morning Post*, 18 April 2019

China has never before been a key conversation topic for NATO. Therefore it is interesting to see how at the 70th anniversary celebration of NATO in Washington in early April, China's rise was reportedly discussed as an issue for the first time by the foreign ministers of NATO member states. American Vice-President Mike Pence was quoted as saying "perhaps the greatest challenge NATO will face in the coming decades is how we must all adjust to the rise of the people's republic of China," he said, "and adjust we must".

The question is how. Thanks to the "tyranny of geography", China and NATO member states are geographically disconnected, although Turkey, a NATO member state, is currently a dialogue partner of the Shanghai Cooperation Organization. China's security concern is primarily in her periphery while NATO remains very much focused on security concerns originating from its immediate neighborhood, namely, Russia, the Middle East and Northern Africa. NATO has no specific policies towards Taiwan, Diaoyu Islands and the South China Sea.

The "greatest challenge NATO will face" is how NATO member states, most of whom are also EU countries, might "adjust" to avoid being hijacked by the US. China is already taken as primary competitor by the US, but China is the second largest trading partner of the EU. China's huge investment in Europe includes generous financing for infrastructure improvements in Eastern and Southern Europe as part of its One Belt & One Road initiative. If an accident between a Chinese and an American ship triggers a conflict, say, in the South China Sea, would NATO consider this as a Chinese "attack against them all" according to Article V of NATO's founding treaty? Or would NATO just provide a kind of political support to the US?

NATO's secretary general Jens Stoltenberg recently said in an interview with *Der Spiegel*, a German news magazine, that Chinese naval drills in the Baltic and Mediterranean seas had brought the Chinese military closer to NATO member countries, and that joint exercises with the Russian Navy in 2017 and 2018 had been of particular concern to the outside world. If these joint military exercises really raised concern because they were in NATO's "backyard", what about NATO's partnership with Afghanistan, Japan, ROK and Pakistan in China's periphery? Can't China equally argue that because warships of Britain and France, two NATO member states, have sailed in the South China Sea, therefore NATO has come to the South China Sea?

Should NATO decide to stand on the American side against China, it has to consider a potential consequence of China and Russia getting ever closer. So far the two countries are like two lines that are close but paralleled. Although two lines in parallel will never meet in theory, what if they keep moving towards each other? Pressure from the west on any one of them will drive the one further tilting towards the other. The last thing NATO wants to see is "a grand coalition of China and Russia"—which was described by Zbigniew Brzezinski as the "most dangerous scenario".

The real threat to the security of Europe comes from nowhere than from its very core, the US. First, if President Trump's remarks of NATO being "obsolete" and EU a "foe" could be brushed away as badmouthing, America's unilateral withdrawal from the Intermediate-Range Nuclear Forces Treaty (INF) will expose Europe to the nightmare of Russia retargeting its nuclear weapons at continental Europe. Second, since the US now takes China as primary competitor, its focus will gradually but almost certainly shift from Europe to the Indo-Pacific region. Therefore America's lion's share of two-thirds of the defense spending in NATO will simply reduce in the long run. In other words, NATO members have to increase their own defense spending.

Here is the rub: if all European allies meet the standard of spending no less than 2% of national GDP on defense, why should they need an American umbrella anyway? A military alliance lives on "threats" if not "enemies" for self-justification. If it cannot find one, it will create one. Even if Russia is taken as a threat today, Russia's economy is smaller than that of Italy. The total GDP of NATO's European members is more than ten times that of Russia. And Britain and France are nuclear weapon states.

Ironically, the sustainability of trans-Atlantic military alliance depends largely on whether America is willing to be free-ridden by its allies. An integrated and independent European defense will make NATO redundant and create what French President Emmanuel Macron called "a true European army" that can only irritate Americans. This is why, short of major threats, most NATO member countries are using a delaying tactic against America on their promises of spending no less than 2% of national GDP on defense. At the tensest points of the Cold War, the defense spending of the UK and France were at above 5%.

China-NATO relations don't have to be hostile, even if NATO "accidentally" bombarded China's embassy in Belgrade in 1999. The fact that China and NATO already have four policy dialogues and have joined hands in counter-piracy shows that the relationship can at least be business-like if not mature. The "lesser" but more rampant "evils" in the post-Cold War era have provided opportunities for cooperation. As pointed out by former NATO secretary general Anders Fogh Rasmussen, China and NATO have common security concerns regarding "transnational terrorism, nuclear proliferation, cyber threats, regional stability, energy security and maritime piracy".

In spite of media hype, in his 40-minute address to American Congress, Stoltenberg made not one mention of China. This doesn't look like a coincidence. If NATO's challenge is how to survive without obvious enemies, the art of survival for this septuagenarian is: don't make a new enemy.

ACKNOWLEDGEMENTS

This book is a selection of my writings from the past eleven years.

Although the views expressed in the book are completely mine, I am deeply grateful to the Office for International Military Cooperation of the Ministry of National Defense, where I worked for nearly three decades in different positions, handling the PLA's external relations with foreign armed forces.

I also wish to express my heartfelt thanks to the Center for International Security and Strategy at Tsinghua University and its China Forum, where I have been working as a senior fellow since 2020, following my retirement from the military. Working in academia, in spite of its own challenges, has been a pleasant change for someone like me, who has spent a long and disciplined time in the military. I have hugely benefited from the interactions I have had with my colleagues. I received a lot of useful advice and tremendous support from Ambassador Fu Ying, former Vice Minister of Foreign Affairs and founding director of the center; Professor Da Wei, director of the center; Xiao Qian and Chen Qi, deputy directors of the center. I also had support wherever possible from Xu Zhengrong, Wang Jie, Han Hua, Guo Jia, Xu Xinyun, Wu Yiqi, Zheng Lefeng, Shen

Qingqing, Chen Xi, Qian Jiatong, Shi Chang, and Liu Jiawen. Some of them have since left the center. I understand this is how life goes, but I am glad they are thriving elsewhere.

Finally, I wish to thank my parents, my wife and my daughter. They have provided love and support every day, and have been patient listeners and readers of my writings for the past eleven years.

INDEX

INDEX

INDEX